# River Time

## Racing the Ghosts of the Klondike Rush

## John Firth

NEWEST PRESS

**National Library of Canada Cataloguing in Publication**
Firth, John, 1953–
River time : racing the ghosts of the Klondike rush / John Firth.

ISBN 1-896300-66-9

1. Firth, John, 1953- —Travel. 2. Klondike River Valley (Yukon)—Gold discoveries—History. 3. Yukon River (Yukon and Alaska)—Description and travel.
4. Historical reenactments—Yukon Territory.
5. Yukon Territory—Description and travel. 6. Alaska—Description and travel. I. Title.

FC4017.3.F57 2004    917.19'1043    C2004-900767-X

Editor for the press: Don Kerr
Cover photos: The two contemporary photos on the front cover and the photo on the back cover are from John Firth; the two archival photos are from the Yukon Archives.
Cover and interior design: Ruth Linka
Author photo: Wilson Photo Studios
Maps: Johnson Cartographics

NeWest Press acknowledges the support of the Canada Council for the Arts, the Alberta Foundation for the Arts, and the Edmonton Arts Council for our publishing program. We also acknowledge the financial support of the Government of Canada through the Book Publishing Industry Development Program (BPIDP) for our publishing activities.

NeWest Press
201-8540-109 Street
Edmonton, Alberta
T6G 1E6
(780) 432-9427
www.newestpress.com

1  2  3  4  5  08  07  06  05  04

PRINTED AND BOUND IN CANADA ON ANCIENT-FOREST-FRIENDLY PAPER

*For Dawn, Erin, Delia, T. A., John, Fred,*
*the spirits who dwell along the river,*
*the volunteers, sponsors and participants*
*of the 1997 and 1998 Dyea to Dawson Races.*

*The Chilkoot Trail*

PHOTO COURTESY OF: SKAGWAY CENTENNIAL COMMITTEE

# TABLE OF CONTENTS

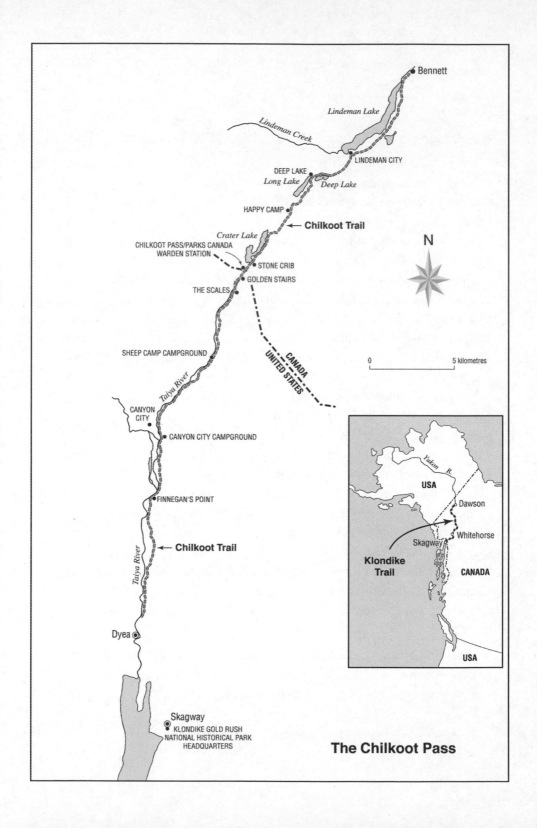

Bennett

*Lindeman Lake*

*Lindeman Creek*

LINDEMAN CITY

DEEP LAKE
*Long Lake*     *Deep Lake*

HAPPY CAMP

← **Chilkoot Trail**

*Crater Lake*

CHILKOOT PASS/PARKS CANADA
WARDEN STATION
STONE CRIB
GOLDEN STAIRS

THE SCALES

N

CANADA
UNITED STATES

0          5 kilometres

SHEEP CAMP CAMPGROUND

*Taiya River*

CANYON
CITY

CANYON CITY CAMPGROUND

*Yukon R.*

USA

Dawson

FINNEGAN'S POINT

Whitehorse

Skagway

CANADA

**Klondike
Trail**

← **Chilkoot Trail**

*Taiya River*

USA

Dyea

Skagway
KLONDIKE GOLD RUSH
NATIONAL HISTORICAL PARK
HEADQUARTERS

**The Chilkoot Pass**

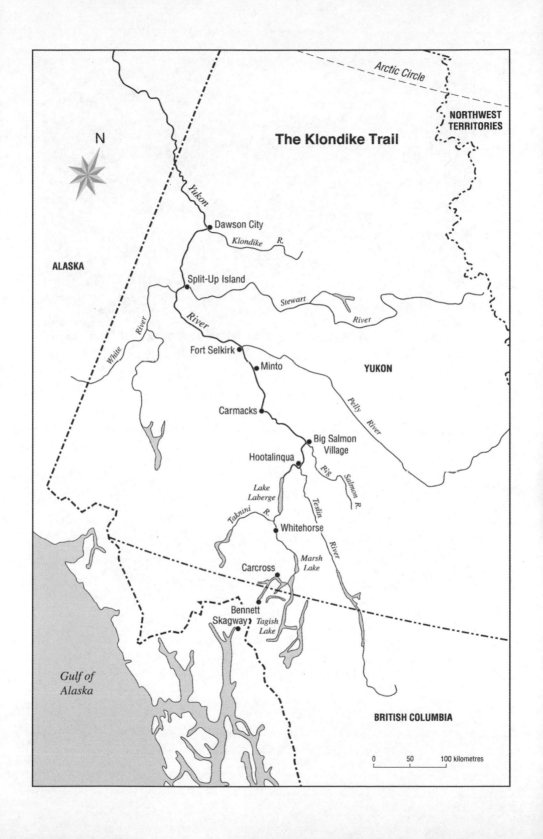

*H.W. Firth*

# INTRODUCTION

I never knew Mrs. Hunter was black. To me she was grey, like dust. Just like her kitchen with its two-burner electric tabletop stove, airtight wood stove, one chair covered by a blanket, painted gold pans, and wooden crates that filled the rest of the space from floor to ceiling. A lifetime crammed into one room and illuminated by dim light barely filtering through the single, unwashed windowpane in front of her house. There were no lights or candles. She had no need for illumination since she couldn't see.

My mother sent my sister Nancy and me up the street with a basket of food. Mrs. Hunter sat there silently, with her sunglasses on, her hair braided and tied up on top of her head and a grey shawl across her shoulders. She never said much more than "Thank you" to us, but always with the hint of a crooked smile. Then, as we left, she leaned forward onto her cane, chuckled, and tilted her head as if sharing an intimate joke with her right shoulder.

The only time she appeared black was at night when my friends and I tried to see how close we could creep to her house. At first glance the front porch looked empty, but there was the crimson glow at the end of her cigarette moving slowly, back and forth, back and forth, as she worked her rocking-chair. We usually couldn't get very close. The blind have good hearing. She must have been exceptionally blind since her hearing was exceptionally acute.

"You boys go away and play somewhere else." Even her voice sounded dusty. It wasn't until years later that I discovered Lucille Hunter wasn't grey. One of the few African Americans who came for the gold rush, she gave birth to a daughter in the wilderness and was possibly the first black person ever seen by the northern Indians. She operated gold claims and businesses in Dawson City, Mayo, and finally in Whitehorse after her husband died in the 1930s and her daughter Teslin left the North. Few took notice when the last surviving woman to have climbed the Chilkoot Pass during the Klondike Gold Rush died in 1972 at the age of ninety-four.

Or there was my father: the last man to be elected mayor of Whitehorse by "coin toss" politics, and it made him the only person in Canadian political history to be the mayor of two capital cities (Dawson City, 1951–52, and Whitehorse, 1966–67). The businessmen of Whitehorse gathered a couple of months before municipal elections and tossed coins to determine who would fill what seat on the city council.

The reward for winning the coin flip in the first round was being exempted from having to stand for office. The losers kept flipping. They were committed to running for alderman, but the biggest losers of all would campaign for mayor. When Dad lost the last toss, the outgoing mayor Ed Jacobs, our across-the-street neighbour, congratulated him. "We've had one from my side of the street," he said. "Now it's your turn."

Dad never liked politics and refused to campaign. He made no promises. Gave no speeches. Never kissed a baby. Never knocked on a door. Just let his name stand and left it at that. "If they want me," he shrugged, "they'll vote for me. If they don't, they won't." They did. Howard Firth served his term and stepped down quietly. Not until his funeral in 1977 was there any acknowledgement of his unique place in Canadian history.

There were others I met but never really learned very much about—like the elderly, semi-shaven fellow with the tooth-gapped grin and floppy hat who sat in front of the KeeBird Store on Main Street on bright summer days. (The KeeBird is a rarely seen northern species that is most often recognized by its distinctive winter call—"Kee-Kee-Kee Rist it's cold!"). He handed out candies to every kid who came by.

He sat there in the sun for years, then one day was gone. A few years later, when I asked about him, no one remembered him at all. I never knew his name nor listened to any of his stories. Maybe I should have, but what kid doesn't expect things to be the same tomorrow as they are today? I often heard my father lament that he hadn't asked his father more about his experiences during the Klondike Gold Rush: "There were so many like him around me that his stories weren't much different from anyone else's. It was just something they all did. It didn't seem to me exceptional or unusual, so I didn't pay much attention when they talked about it. It wasn't until I left the Yukon that I realized who they were and what they had accomplished, but by then it was too late."

When you grow up surrounded by history and the people who make it, you tend not to recognize it as such. It's only as the old men and women, who spend their time rocking and reminiscing on the front porches of the hotels and nursing homes, start to die—their experiences unrecorded—that we begin to realize their stories are being lost beyond the edge of living memory. Sneaking up on Mrs. Hunter, and singing along with Polly the Parrot (about whom you will learn more later in the book), was as close as I ever got to the gold rush era until I competed in the 1997 and 1998 Dyea-to-Dawson races, which now have their own place in history.

This story is about the Klondike Gold Rush, the same one *Fabulous*

*Fortunes* magazine referred to in August 2000, when it called Microsoft a "modern-day Klondike" and its founder, Bill Gates, "Swiftwater," after one of the more flamboyant promoters of that time. The same one to which Scrooge McDuck rode a love-sick moose and discovered a fortune in gold for the Walt Disney studios in 1947. That inspired an advertising executive in Chicago, Illinois, in 1954, to dream up what is still the greatest promotion in advertising history—The Klondike Big Inch Land Co.—for the Quaker Oats Company. That led *Canoe and Kayak* magazine, in its 1998 *Canoe Journal* edition, to list the Yukon River as its first choice for "Paddling into the Past—Canoeing North America's Historic Waterways"—ahead of the mighty Mississippi and the rivers that Lewis and Clark used to open the American West.

This story is about, and for, those who lament the time they are born in, who envision the past as romantic and exciting when compared to their pedantic present. They are the individuals who believe it is important enough to reach back into time to try to recapture some of that dream. To bring new vitality to legendary times and places with events such as the Dyea-to-Dawson Races, the 1973 Klondyke Canoe Pageant, or the River of Gold Tour in 1998— or with schemes like the building of a modern-day sternwheeler, or the preservation of an old one. Or by living along the banks of the river and surviving the same challenges of the wilderness that humans have encountered since they first walked here fifteen thousand years ago—the earliest record of people on the North American continent.

For a moment we find ourselves in a time warp, beyond what we have, until now, considered our normal measure of the world. It is a place you can't see. You feel it. Here there is a wider sense of place—planted in our intellect by people we never met or knew and by events we never witnessed. On the Yukon River it takes hold of you as you drift around each corner and discover some new remnant of time. A fish trap. An abandoned village. Familiar tales of Indians struggling for survival in a merciless environment. An old dredge. A boat wreck. A derelict wood camp. Testimonials of men and women loaded with tools, booze, and attitude, played out against a golden backdrop of false purpose.

No tour book, no tour guide's fantastic tale can compare with how the dead feel for those who strive to bring them back to life. Museums and historical sites are no longer enough. They are hosts to the dead. It is the ghosts with whom we walk among the ruins, whom we fall in with as we paddle down the river, who are alive.

*Steve Cash on top of the first false summit. Shadows of competitors*
*behind him can be seen on the snow.*
PHOTO COURTESY OF: YUKON NEWS

# The Chilkoot Pass

*T. A. Firth*

# CHAPTER ONE

## Seattle, Washington
Saturday, 17 July 1897

R u m o u r s   a r e   t h e  pieces with which the game is played. The player manipulates the facts, throws in a dash of fantasy, tones down the negatives, tunes up the positives, creates illusions of great riches to be achieved, and, adding a pinch of pizzazz, sells it to speculators who have money just burning holes in their pockets. It is not a con. It is a business of high-stakes gambling based, to a certain extent, on the spin of the tale. Millions of dollars are gained or lost in speculation about which rumour or insider tip to believe, and which to ignore, in the mining promotion game. The Forty Mile gold discovery in 1887, in a vague northern Canadian location, was one of those tales that persistently turned up among the mining promoters peddling their wares in Seattle, San Francisco, and New York. Players constantly exploited it, refueling old truths with new angles to make it palatable to a stock market hungry for any semblance of good news in the lean days of the 1890s. For the wealthy, or those who lived outside of the United States, it was the "gay nineties." For the poor and the middle-class unfortunate enough to live in the US at that time, it was a time of hardship, hopelessness, and despair.

America had plunged into an economic "panic" in 1893 from which it appeared destined never to emerge. The reasons given for the panic ranged from Free Silver politicians, who sought to abandon the gold monetary standard, to public concern over corporate debt. The truth was that the world economy had changed, and the protectionist United States hadn't changed with it.

There was a run on the banks, forcing over six hundred of them to forever close their doors. Millions of bank customers watched helplessly as their savings simply vanished. Then a massive sell-off of shares, crippling the stock markets. Of the twenty-two industrial issues that constituted the New York Stock Exchange index in 1893, only one, General Electric, survived into the next century. And, finally, watching the US economy self-destruct, foreign investors decided it was time to pull out. Small companies went into bankruptcy and large corporations laid off their work forces in an effort to stay afloat.

Hungry people will do what they must to survive. Four million men left their homes and families to roam the continent in search of employment. Entire towns were emptied of their young and not-so-young able-bodied men. They fled the overcrowded East Coast cities or headed west, only to find it was no better out there. Whatever work they could find paid poorly, and lasted only as long as the employer could or would pay.

Shantytowns sprang up across the nation, populated by desperate men starving for food and faith. Violence and paranoia ran rampant as the refugees lost their sense of purpose; random beatings and motiveless murders became commonplace in the economic prison camps.

Those that these men left behind were forced to cope with a poverty of hope, and a life that had no place for pride or dignity. Wives and children survived as best they could, relying on whatever meager pittances they could earn in the sweatshops, and praying their husbands and fathers would return with news of a better life.

Thomas Andrew Firth, Tommy to his friends, was already in the West when the panic of '93 struck. Since leaving his parents' home in Meaford, Ontario, at the age thirteen in 1880, he had worked at odd jobs across the United States, moving on whenever the urge struck him to do so.

It was the kind of freedom every boy dreamed of when reading picture book stories of the Wild West. The carefree adventurer, taking risks and meeting new challenges, sampling the banquet of experiences life had to serve— this was hardly a lifestyle that could be endorsed by either his father, John, ordained as a Baptist minister in 1878, or his mother, Ruth, a direct descendant of United Empire Loyalists. From a cloistered existence in small-town Ontario, Tommy fled to limitless horizons, developing a sense of value in a world less earthbound—like a bird pushed from the nest discovering it can fly. But, like a bird taking to wing, he learned freedom is no more than the exchange of one set of restrictions for another.

Life on the road meant constantly being on guard, surrendering your right to privacy, disguising your intimate feelings, avoiding personal questions, and speaking prudently. Possessions and relationships became as transitory as life. You developed a skill for making short-term friends of long-term strangers.

Tommy taught himself to read and write while riding freight railcars, or bouncing along in the back of wooden buckboards. Like many of the men he encountered on the road, Tommy became a bit of an expert on the Bible.

When isolated from home and family, and cut off from the securities of civilization, the wanderer seeks solace in the Holy Book. While not a Sunday-go-to-meeting type of Christian, Tommy lived by moral and ethical ideals that he believed kept him close to God.

He loved being the centre of attention—developing a hawker's command of the spoken word and becoming the master of ceremonies for many shanty-town functions. But his flamboyant public image existed in sharp contrast with his private self. A man little given to intimate physical expression, he found it difficult to reveal his innermost feelings—even to those who mattered most to him. It was safer to keep a reasonable distance in relationships, and thus reduce the possibilities of personal pain and heartache. Yet, when he set pen to paper and composed verse, much of his road-imposed censorship was swept aside, and it was in his writings that those closest to him were able to see the hidden Tommy.

While home visiting his family in Meaford in 1892, Tommy travelled down the road to Owen Sound where he met Phedelia Warrilow. The slender, curly-haired brunette with the shy smile and striking eyes captured his heart. From the moment he first saw "Delia" on the veranda of her home, Tommy knew he would marry her.

The short, powerfully built Tommy had a slightly less immediate impact on Delia. Hesitant at first, because there were few physical indications of Tommy's affection, Delia at last set her cap for the handsome bard who wooed her when she read his poetry. But there were a few elements of married life and domestic partnership that simply didn't agree with a young drifter still smitten with wanderlust. It was the fellow's role to provide housing and an income to support his new bride. Delia came from a comfortable middle-class family and lived in a stylish three-story house surrounded by manicured lawns and fruit trees. Wiring money from wherever he happened to be, and whatever he happened to be doing, just wouldn't do; nor was the bohemian lifestyle of the road any place for a lady.

Tommy rode the rails once again and continued courting Delia through the US Mail. In his letters he bared his soul to her, declaring over and over the depth of his love and his conviction that they would one day be together, forever. His affirmations were enough to convince her that her time as part of Tommy's life would come. So Delia waited, and confronted a challenge of faith that tested her resolve for most of the next two decades.

In previous panics, the unemployed had remained in their hometowns—most either couldn't or wouldn't venture too far from their homes and families. The panic of 1893 was different. The railroads provided a fast, convenient means of mass transportation and the unemployed could, for the first time, go in search of employment elsewhere. And they did so, in unprecedented numbers. When competition for jobs, not to mention space in the freight cars, started to heat up, Tommy recognized the time had finally come to move on.

Tommy understood that economic turmoil inevitably resulted in the poor getting poorer, while the rich were preoccupied with becoming richer. Even in dire times such as these, however, there seemed to be dreamers with money to invest—and there had to be someone to provide them a vehicle for their dreams. And what better place to find such a vehicle than a stock market brought to its knees? Tommy got into the mining promotion game, and he played it in San Francisco, and Seattle, and on the occasional jaunt to New York (with side trips to visit Delia in Owen Sound, or in Warren, Pennsylvania, where her sister lived). By night, he studied Andrew Carnegie's philosophy of business. By day, he practiced it.

Tommy learned how to hold his cards close to this chest, how to negotiate without volunteering much information—an invaluable asset for a player of the game. He read that knowledge was power, so he studied accounting practices, legal affairs (such as land titles, wills, and affidavits), and natural resources (geology, minerals, claims, and the like). He mastered the three "ups" of public speaking: Stand up. Speak up. Shut up. The transformation was complete when Tommy departed from the frugal ways of the vagabond and adopted one of Carnegie's favourite adages—spend money like you'll always have it, then you'll never be without it. Tommy's dashing new profession demanded a stylish wardrobe, so he bought one: a Prince Albert suit and a Derby hat—the trappings of the successful businessman that were to become his life-long trademark. For four years he prospered in a game characterized by high attrition. He liked the risk inherent in the play. In reality, it wasn't much different from the day-to-day gamble of life on the road. It seemed that Tommy had finally found his niche.

Then, one Sunday morning, before the city had fully awakened, Tommy went to breakfast and picked up the early-morning edition of the *Seattle Post-Intelligencer*. The front page riveted him on his seat.

When he first heard the stories of the arrival of the steamship *Excelsior* two days ago, from colleagues in San Francisco, they reminded him of the

Forty Mile promotions he had occasionally dabbled in. But the Forty Mile, while it had similar qualities, couldn't hold a candle to what he was reading that morning. A remote northern location. A gold discovery. Unwashed men and women sailing into Seattle, dressed in threadbare rags and demanding to be driven directly to a smelter to have their gold assayed and sold before bathing or buying new clothes. And speculation that untold mountains of wealth were still to be uncovered.

The headline—"Gold! Gold! Gold! Gold!"—screamed out at him.

The steamer *Portland* was due to dock in Seattle later that morning. On board were sixty-eight prospectors bringing a ton of gold with them in boxes, carpetbags, and gunnysacks; it was wrapped in bedrolls and whatever else they could cram it into. There were indications that a massive migration of gold seekers would head north in the wake of the ship's arrival. Already, the paper's advertisers were calling themselves "Suppliers to the Klondike." Gold diggers would just be aching to profit without making the physical journey. The market was ripe for a fleck of glittering gold to grow in the imagination into a nugget, into a fabulous strike. In Tommy's professional world this mythical land of gold had not yet been discovered. For the right promoter, it could turn into a stock market bonanza.

Tommy considered the alternatives. There was the ever-patient Delia, steadfastly loyal in her love for him for five years now. He almost had enough money to marry her and bring her out to the coast. With the potential income he could generate by promoting the Klondike, he could afford a small house and keep her in the manner into which she had been born. Approaching thirty years of age, Tommy wasn't as youthful as he once was, and the road, as he well knew, was a young man's place. There was definitely an upside to this stationary lifestyle with its creature comforts—Delia being the most important one.

Then there was the itch in his foot, which, since reading the paper, was starting to get unbearable. It was an intriguing thought—that all you really needed in life was a pick and shovel to strike it rich and change your social status. It was no wonder that it appealed to the homeless masses. No wonder that it appealed to Tommy. Not only an opportunity to possibly make his fortune in the mining game, but also to be a participant in what could be man's last great trek for gold! Just one final grand adventure, then he would come back to Delia.

Checking his pocket watch, he noted there were a couple of hours before the *Portland* arrived. He also noted that, even though it was Sunday, he had just a short time before his first business meeting of the day, where he could, potentially, pitch the Klondike to a prospective investor. Either way, Tommy's ship was coming in. He stood up, tucked the newspaper under his arm, and started to stroll towards the docks.

Tommy could not have anticipated that the Klondike was just the first in a series of events that would heal the ailing US economy. The gold itself was insignificant. It was the gold rush that caught the imagination. It was hope reborn for the desperate and destitute. Six months later, the Spanish-American War did what the grim reality of armed conflict frequently does— it awoke an industrial giant. By 1900, the United States was poised to become the dominant economic power of the next century. The spiritual vacuum that had dominated the nation for most of the 1890s was part of its vanquished past.

# CHAPTER TWO

## Skagway, Alaska
Sunday, 15 June 1997

He should have known better.

The last time I called my nephew, John Small, and asked if he wanted to take part in a race, we started by heading towards a marathon in Victoria, British Columbia. We ended up running one in Chicago, Illinois, instead. A good experience, just not the one we had originally planned for.

So when I called him last September and asked, "Hey, John, I need a partner in a race. You interested?" you might have thought that he would have been a tad more suspicious.

"Yeah! Sure!" he responded, with the trusting nature of a wide-eyed innocent. "When?"

"Next June. And it shouldn't cost you anything other than time off. I already have a sponsor."

"A sponsor! This sounds like it's more than just another marathon." Apparently he did remember Chicago.

To be honest, I had some idea of what the proposed Dyea-to-Dawson event entailed, but no first-hand experience. I had organized one-thousand mile professional races through the northern wilderness, but I had never run one. I had been on five hundred mile river trips by canoe, and backcountry hikes in the thirty to forty mile range—but never in combination with each other—and never as a competition. To travel . . . no, not travel . . . to sprint through six hundred and ten miles of wilderness, using only my feet and arms, was wholly beyond my seasoning.

When T. A. Firth made the decision to head north in search of gold, it was a challenge beyond even his worldly knowledge. Only by following his lead can I start to learn about the man to whom my entire life has been connected. His accomplishments, and those of my father, had always been dangled before me as an exemplar.

"Think about what you do," my mother used to tell me, "remember who you are. Don't do anything to embarrass the family name."

It didn't take much convincing. The more I told John, the more he liked

*Chris Guenther, Buckwheat, Wendy Cairns, Jeff Brady*

the idea. Of all the members of our family, John is possibly the one who can relate best to T. A.'s early years. "There's a lot of parallels with him and myself," he says; "just the times are different. He broke away from his family at a young age. He travelled, trying various things and doing a hundred jobs. Just like me."

John spent much of his youth travelling around the world, partying in Central America, working on a kibbutz in Israel. In the last few years, he decided to make his home in the Yukon. Now he has two young sons with his partner, Sharon Denton, and a publishing company to run.

೧೦೧

It wasn't hard to determine that we had similar goals—to do the best we could competitively and to be as social as possible, with the second objective actually taking a slightly higher priority. "I've got ten or twelve days to enjoy myself," mutters John, "and I'm not going to waste it by being number one. But I don't want to be last, because it is a race and you do your personal best. Who cares if you're in the top five or bottom ten. As long as you push yourself."

I expect it will be an interesting ten or twelve days. While John and I have known each other all of his life, we've never really done anything together. Not on this scale anyway. We will either get to know each other, or discover we have nothing at all in common. The key to survival in an event like this is the ability to compromise—but that's not always as simple as it sounds. Both of us can be pretty stubborn at times. We like each other well enough now; maybe that will change under the kind of pressures I expect we will encounter. I have visions of us parked on a gravel bar in the middle of the Yukon River, cutting bags of dried fruit and power bars in half, not talking, our own little Civil War pitting uncle against nephew.

೧೦೧

So here we are, nine months later, with ninety-six other participants at the mandatory pre-race meeting at the United States National Parks Service Headquarters in Skagway, Alaska.

Skagway is called Alaska's "Garden City." It's a halfway honest claim. Residents do tend gardens and planter boxes resplendent with flowers of amazing colours, shapes, sizes, and varieties. The valley hillsides are lush with ferns, trees, berries, and undergrowth which have crept down to lay claim to portions of the downtown core. A monster rhubarb plant dominates one street corner, while a small sign proclaims it is the oldest and largest of its type in the state. But this small town bears no resemblance to a city, even though a hundred years ago it was the most populous metropolis in Alaska.

While the gardeners are the beneficiaries of the warm and wet summer climate, it is the icy winds, which blast out of the interior in winter, that gave Skagway its name—"home of the north wind." It refers to a mythical old woman from a Tlingit legend who keeps the triangular valley free of snow by blowing it away with her frigid breath. She inhabits the mountains north of the valley, and her breath is chilled as it passes over the glaciers that stream down between the peaks.

In 1976, the town sites of both Skagway and Dyea, along with the Chilkoot Pass and White Pass trails, became the Klondike Gold Rush National Historical Park—an idea first suggested in 1933, then set aside, then revived when Alaska became the forty-ninth state in 1959. The park is unique because one of its interpretive centres is located two thousand miles outside the park boundaries, in Seattle, Washington.

Skagway is a living monument to its role as the "Gateway to the Gold Fields." In summer, the streets are packed daily with thousands of tourists from cruise ships, hungry for a taste of what it must have been like during the gold rush. This throng is, itself, a recreation of that era when twenty-five thousand gold seekers temporarily over-loaded this place. In their own way, simply by virtue of their numbers, the tourists themselves become a part of what they seek.

They frequent the stores located in restored 1890s and early twentieth-century structures along the main street, Broadway, and on the side avenues, called "off-Broadway." They visit the museum, the first building to lodge the Arctic Brotherhood—a fraternal order formed by Alaska and Yukon gold stampeders. Built in 1899, a geometric façade was added in 1900, constructed with twenty thousand pieces of driftwood found on the beaches. And they wander in a small park where they can walk through the first log cabin ever built here by the town's prophetic founder, steamship captain William Moore.

Moore, who landed here on 21 October 1887, and homesteaded the area, firmly believed that one day there would be a mineral find of significance in the interior, and that this valley would be the jumping-off point for the stampeders when they came. He even envisioned a railroad snaking its way up through the Coastal Mountains, via the White Pass, before there was ever reason for such a thing to exist. He was right on both counts. Most tourists take a ride on the White Pass and Yukon Route, built in 1899 and 1900 as the railway to the gold fields. Considered one of the seven wonders of the modern world because of the engineering that enables trains to climb through the most beautiful, and challenging, mountain range in North America, it is one of only fifteen sites on earth currently declared an International Historic Civil Engineering Landmark—a list that includes the Statue of Liberty and the Eiffel Tower.

Plastic prostitutes peer suggestively from behind parted curtains above the Red Onion Saloon, hinting at the unwholesome reputation Skagway earned in 1897 and 1898 under the domination of con man and crime boss Jefferson "Soapy" Smith. Smith ran a sink-hole of iniquity populated by faro dealers, pawnbrokers, blackjack boosters, shills, bartenders, and prostitutes who worked out of establishments like The Mangy Dog, The Grotto, The Home of Hootch, The Pack Train, and Palace of Delight. His thugs terrorized the streets—beating and killing with impunity—and stole what money and belongings couldn't be conned out of the stampeders' pockets. He died in a gunfight with vigilante Frank Reid on the Skagway docks on 8 July 1898. Like any town with a turbulent past, it is the infamous that are best remembered. Smith still lives and dies today for multitudes of visitors to "The Days of '98 Show," and through the restoration of his central place of business, Jeff Smith's Parlour. At the exhausted end of a long, hot day of touristing, you can take a refreshing shower with "Soapy on a Rope."

It was here that my first attempt to cross the Chilkoot Pass came to naught in August 1968. My friend Doug Springer and I planned all summer long for the hike while we worked as baggage handlers in Whitehorse for the White Pass and Yukon Route. But when we arrived in Skagway, we did what any fifteen-year-old boys suddenly free of parental guidance would do—we acquired a bootlegged bottle of Captain Morgan's Rum. Doug never did make it back into the tent. He spent the night under a picnic table about twenty feet away. I got the top half of my body into the tent, but that was it. In the morning we were soaked and cold from the dew, and our enthusiasm for the Chilkoot was a hazy memory. We climbed onto the next train back home—an experience, just not the one we planned for.

Competing in the Dyea-to-Dawson is an experience that was limited to only 206 people over the course of two years. Current restrictions on the number of hikers permitted over the Chilkoot Pass each day guarantee that this event, or one similar to it, will never take place again. To convince the US

National Parks Service and Parks Canada to agree to the 1997 and 1998 races had taken organizers Jeff Brady and Carlin "Buckwheat" Donahue over four years of negotiation.

Jeff thought about the project for quite a while before the work actually began: "This idea has been around for a long time . . . the idea for a race to commemorate the gold rush. It probably started the year after the gold rush. I'm sure somebody out there thought, 'Wow. Would this be a great race or what!!'"

Other than the gold rush itself, there has been only one other race over this route. Thirty-five competitors, in seven-man teams that represented the Yukon, Alaska, Washington, British Columbia, and the Northwest Territories, gathered in Dyea in 1973 to start the Klondyke Canoe Pageant—a reenactment of the gold rush to celebrate its seventy-fifth anniversary, but without most of the rush or any of the gold.

When Jeff Brady became aware of the 1973 pageant, it started to shape his concept of just how such a race could be run. However, he wanted something that more closely paralleled the gold rush itself. There had to be a prize of gold waiting for the first people in, and those that followed had to be content with the experience of just being there. Jeff reflects, "It [the Klondike Gold Rush] has always been described as one of the last grand adventures. Right from the beginning, we intended this to be not just a race, but a re-enactment of something that actually happened. We wanted to recreate, as closely as we could, the rush to Dawson City. We expected everything from ultramarathoners to people just out to experience the entire gold rush over again."

Even the ability to enter the race mirrors the gold rush. In 1997, only people from Alaska and the Yukon could enter. In 1998, entries were accepted from around the world. In 1897, those who were already in the North had the first chance to stake their claims in the Klondike. Then word finally reached the "outside," and the stampeders arrived from around the globe in 1898.

The Dyea-to-Dawson was not to be contrived reality. It was to involve real people in real situations. The group dynamic versus nature. The individual versus nature. A combination of adventure, history, and psychology.

Hands-on history is not just a passing interest for Jeff. Re-enacting history, rather than reading about or studying it, is his life. Originally from North Carolina, he arrived in Skagway in 1974 on a camping trip and met wilderness tour guide Skip Burns. Burns promptly hired him to work for the

*John Small*

summer as a guide for his company, Klondike Safaris, to take people over the
Chilkoot Pass. Jeff returned each summer until 1978, when he finally made
the move to Alaska permanent.

A writer by trade, Jeff took over publication of a monthly newspaper
called *The North Wind* in Haines, just around the corner from Skagway on the
Lynn Canal. The building that housed his press burned down in 1981. He
headed to Skagway in 1982 to re-start the long defunct *Skaguay News* and
eventually re-open the Skagway News Depot—a bookstore that hadn't been in
operation since the early part of the century. Jeff, his wife Dorothy—one of
those rare individuals who was actually born and raised in Alaska (most residents seem to have come from somewhere else)—and their children inhabit
an historical home. Jeff admits, "I definitely have a nostalgic bent. It's kind of
neat that we can have a '100-Years Ago Today' column in the newspaper."

Carlin "Buckwheat" Donahue came north for a holiday in 1982. A petro-
leum land man in Denver, Colorado, he needed a break from the stress of
negotiating with other oil companies, governments, and individuals to
acquire exploration rights for junior oil companies. He was travelling with a
friend who was leaving Denver in search of a new life in Alaska.

It was one of those trips that defy logic. Buckwheat's friend never found his "new life," and eventually he left the North, never to return. Buckwheat, in contrast, fell asleep on the ferry, missed his stop in Juneau, Alaska, and woke up in time to disembark in Skagway. The first person he met on the dock was a woman named Dianne Upper, who talked him into staying in Skagway rather than turning around and heading back to Juneau. "Within four or five hours, she had introduced me to Jeff [Brady], the mayor, and city council. The next thing I know, I spent my entire two-week vacation in Skagway."

One of the things Buckwheat did in 1982 was to take a short trip on the Yukon River with Brady. The world it opened up to him was one he had never suspected existed:

> I went further north (from Skagway) and it just got better and better. Wilder and wilder. All of a sudden, I was living in a dream . . . except it wasn't a dream. It was real. There's something about the Yukon River that just gets ahold of you and you can't let it go. . . . The people up here seem to me to be more vibrant, more self-confident than you would find down south. To be around people who are so bold. To be in this country that seems so bold. If you are from somewhere else and all of a sudden you have an opportunity to live in that kind of world, the only option—the only choice—would be to move there and live there. That's what I was faced with and that's what I did.

Buckwheat makes his living by guiding hiking and canoe tours during the day, and reciting Robert Service's poetry to tourists in the evening. His trademark is the world-class, multi-task Buckwheat howl, with which he tends to greet people, start conversations, or terminate them. Occasionally, he'll throw one in the middle of a poem, just to make sure his listeners are still awake.

Buckwheat first heard of the Dyea-to-Dawson idea in 1986. He was putting together a long-distance cross-country ski race in the mountains between Skagway and Whitehorse when someone asked him, "Why are you doing that? What you should do is have a race from Dyea to Dawson."

By 1992, he was a seasoned veteran organizer of races and a member, along with Jeff, of the Skagway Centennial Committee, a group set up to make plans for the one hundredth anniversary of the Klondike Gold Rush. One of the ideas being kicked around by the committee members was a race from Dyea to Dawson. Jeff was the first to offer his services, "but only if Buckwheat was interested." Buckwheat wasn't interested. Since the gold rush was in Canada, maybe someone from the Yukon should organize the race. The committee threw hints at centennial organizers in the Yukon. There were no takers.

Jeff continued to suggest that Buckwheat should get involved. Buckwheat continued to resist. The breakthrough came during a meeting in the Skagway Public Library in 1993. Jeff was at it again, pushing, pushing, pushing. Buckwheat tried in vain to listen to the speaker at the front of the room, but Jeff, the persistent bastard, just wouldn't go away. Buckwheat glared at him. "Yeah. We'll do it," he growled. Jeff broke into his "gotcha" grin.

"We needed to do this," Buckwheat admits. "It was a chance to get a glimpse of what those guys did. Just a glimpse—that's all we get because we can't recreate exactly what was going on. It opened everybody's eyes. The participants. The volunteers. The reporters. It made everyone think more about where we're living. What it means to live here. What the history means to us."

They make an interesting pair. Jeff, a stocky man of average height, with black hair and a beard, is quick on his feet verbally and possesses a relaxed intensity contagious to anyone he talks to. Buckwheat, who sports long, flowing grey-white hair and a beard, appears larger than life. A broad man in any case, he carries his stage persona with him and seems to fill completely any space he is in.

ဢ

This morning they supervised the loading of canoes and gear onto the train that would take them ahead to Bennett—the northern terminus of the Chilkoot Pass and the entry point for navigation on the Yukon River. For two hundred yards alongside the flatcars, canoes were lined up three and four deep—a cacophony of colour and activity. Every brand name you can think of was represented: brown Wenonahs, yellow Clippers, green Old Towns, red Rat Rivers. And every material a canoe can be made of: plastic, kevlar, fiberglass, canvas. There was even a home-built Cedar-strip canoe—wooden boats are a rare sight since the advent of lighter, faster synthetic materials.

Traditional canoe paddles are a common sight, but so are bent shaft paddles—allegedly modified to maximize the efficiency of the paddling stroke.

Not even the paddles are made exclusively from wood any more. Graphite composites have made them stronger than iron and lighter than your toothbrush. Few canoes have wooden or woven seats in them—too heavy. Now the seats are molded plastics mounted on lightweight aluminum tubing. The competitors were doubled over, heads buried in the bowels of the canoes, crouching or kneeling beside their boats, fitting spray skirts—a cover to prevent waves or rain from filling the boat—and duct-taping cylindrical plastic containers, dry bags, or paddles to the struts.

Duct Tape—a.k.a. "Hundred-mile-an-hour tape," because of the days when it was used to repair aircraft wings—is invaluable to the modern adventurer. One team secured their spray skirt with it. Another used it to make their canoe meet the requirements for the race: they duct-taped pieces of plastic to the top of their gunwales to raise the sides to the legal limits. A competitor tore the seat of his pants and patched it with duct tape. Still others would wrap the tape around their fingers to prevent chafing and blistering in the days of paddling to come.

Once packed and passed by race officials (the canoes were measured and the mandatory gear was checked), the boats were lifted overhead to wooden cradles built on the flatcars. This wasn't as easy as it might sound. The bottoms had been waxed to help them glide more rapidly through the water, and thus they were slippery and awkward to lift.

In the afternoon, Jeff and Buckwheat preside over the mandatory meeting. As we sit in the theatre, listening to the officials and parks people talk to us about the rules and regulations, beaver ponds and bears, I don't think I'm alone in having my mind wander. I review our preparations over the past few weeks and the final choices I'll have to make tonight about exactly what to carry tomorrow. I don't know why, but it always seems that there's something that you overlook. Then, when the breakdown occurs, you can't figure out how you missed the obvious.

No race is fun until it's finished. This one has so many potential obstacles beyond our full control: the weather, equipment breakdowns, our ability to perform when sleep-deprived, the demands of our bodies contained by the physical limitations of the canoe and the psychological burden of being isolated in a restrictive space for days with one other person. You can't know in advance how a race will end. There is a long way to go, both mentally and physically, and you're as likely to fail as to succeed.

Hope for the best. Prepare for the worst. Travel light. Freeze at night.

Tonight, John and I must select exactly what we are going to carry in our packs over the next two or three days. The mandatory gear, split evenly by weight, is already allocated. We both carry a light sleeping bag. I have the food and stove. John gets the tent. We want to keep our packs as close to the minimum fifty-pound weight restriction as possible, so we must be selective in our choice of clothes.

Will it rain? Will it sun? Will it blow? How much snow will there be near the summit and what condition will it be in? Why am I worrying? Clean underwear and power bars will get you through anything. We'll make our final decisions, then I know I'll spend the night dozing fitfully, mostly lying awake going over lists mentally, and fretting. Tomorrow, once we begin, my doubts will melt away, leaving me to concentrate solely on the challenge of the formidable distance yet to be travelled.

All of us—organizers, participants, volunteers, and officials—are preparing, hoping, and praying for a good experience. That's the one we plan for.

*Yukon and BC teams, 1973*

PHOTO COURTESY OF: WHITEHORSE STAR

# CHAPTER THREE

## The Klondyke Canoe Pageant
August 1973

The Yukon's Voyageur canoe still lies, badly weathered and slightly rotten, in the back yard of Duncan's Sheet Metal in Whitehorse. A trophy, topped by a miner packing a Trapper Nelson and carrying a rifle, gathers dust in Howard Firth's office; in the basement of his office building is a paddle, signed by all thirty-five competitors and race marshal G.I. Cameron. The paddle he prizes above all else, for it is a one-of-a-kind memento that contains something of each individual involved in the event, and it stirs up memories of that experience.

 споі

The trophy is a source of ironic pride for my brother Howard, who was the hometown team captain. The Yukon team finished well back in the over-all competition, but it won the very first portion of the race—a sprint over the last seven miles of the Chilkoot Pass. That was the only segment of the entire race for which any hardware was presented to the winners. Teams from the five regions impacted most directly by the Klondike Gold Rush— the states of Washington and Alaska, the province of British Columbia, the Northwest Territories, and the Yukon—were invited to participate in the seventy-fifth anniversary event. They started in Dyea on 1 August with instructions no more detailed than to be at Lake Lindeman by the night of 2 August. On the morning of 3 August, a rifle fired into the air started them on a seven-mile sprint to Bennett. Six of the top ten positions, and the trophy, went to Yukon runners.

Once in Bennett, the teams of seven (six paddlers and one spare) climbed into their twenty-five-foot Voyageur canoes and started paddling. There were no competitive races during the day. Each team was given a deadline by which they were to be at a designated spot each evening. Whether it was first to arrive or last didn't matter, but once all the teams arrived a mass start of canoes in an all-out sprint was held. The race distances ranged from two to four miles in length and were usually run on a circular course identified by large orange buoys floating in the water. Points were awarded to each team based upon the order in which they finished the sprint.

It was obvious from the first race in Carcross on 4 August that British Columbia—led by an experienced canoeing professional, "Baldy" Jackson, and his son Bob—was the team to beat. They won again in the Six Mile River the next day. The race reached Whitehorse on 7 August—a day of embarrassing disaster for the Yukon team.

For the official arrival in Whitehorse, Howard decided that the Yukon flag needed a taller standard than those of the other teams. Half of the population of the city lined the banks of the Yukon River or hung off Robert Service Bridge, under which the canoes had to pass. The home team led the procession into town, the flag pole jammed behind the stern man's seat. "It wasn't until we were almost under the bridge," Howard reflects, "that it dawned on me that our flag was too high to get under the bridge."

The flagpole hit the bridge and tore the back seat right out of the canoe as it almost catapulted Howard into the river. Picking himself off the bottom of the boat, he squatted down in the rear and steered the canoe to the landing spot. They managed temporary repairs to the seat for the sprint race, but it was two inches lower on one side than the other and it threw the canoe off balance. They missed the up-river buoy in the sprint and finished a distant last. The Northwest Territories team, captained by Phil Blake, finally broke the BC win streak.

Support for the pageant was provided by the Canadian Army and the Yukon Government. Every night, the Canadian Army set up camp and prepared hot meals for the paddlers. Every morning, they cooked breakfast, broke camp, and, using large support boats, leapfrogged ahead to set it up again. It was very comfortable. Other than having to pack their own personal gear, the paddlers didn't have to do a thing except paddle.

For some reason, the Yukon Government decided that every team should get two cases of beer for personal consumption every night. But not everyone wanted to drink beer every night, and most didn't drink at all. Each morning, the military collected the unconsumed beer and packed it to the next campsite. And every afternoon the Yukon Government added two more cases of beer per team. Eventually, the volume of beer exceeded the capacity of the escort boats to carry it. A helicopter was brought in to sling the beer along with the tenting supplies. A few days later, the beer needed its own sling load and was the first item moved by the helicopter each morning.

At Minto, the Army cooks were the second morning load to land. They started to drink the beer. In the late afternoon, one cook staggered down to the river to get a bucket of water. Leaning over the back of a boat, he dipped the bucket into the water. The river current caught the bucket and pulled it downstream—along with the cook who was too inebriated to release the handle. A short distance down the river, a fisherman was almost pulled into the river when something very heavy, drifting just under the surface of the water, snagged his gear. Tangled up in the fishing net—still breathing and still hanging desperately to the bucket—was the cook. After that, they made sure the cooks went in first and the beer last.

When the teams arrived in Fort Selkirk on 12 August, they became part of a ceremony to honour the history of the Yukon Field Force's role in the gold rush in 1898. The Canadian Army members were dressed in the nineteenth-century military uniform and regalia of the Field Force. They put on a marching display, accompanied by a full brass band, and politicians gave speeches. At the ceremony's conclusion, cannons, flown in for the occasion, fired off a final volley. The booms of the great guns echoed off the Palisades, a massive rock face across the Yukon River from Fort Selkirk.

The Yukon team, by this time so far back in the standings that little could make any difference, decided a little strategic planning was in order. They drew the inside position on the start line, in shallow water right alongside the riverbank. When the starting gun went off, the team, instead of paddling hard against the current like its competitors, jumped out of the canoe. They ran in the shallow water—towing their canoe for a couple hundred yards before jumping back on board with a substantial lead. It helped, but BC still won the sprint, just barely edging the Yukon team at the finish line.

The plan worked so well the first time that the Yukoners decided to try it again in Dawson City, on 14 August. But instead of gravel, the Dawson riverbank was composed of silt, and the team bogged down. Trailing badly because of the miscalculation, they changed tactics: on the final leg, when the other teams turned to cross the river for the downstream sprint to the finish line, the Yukon team continued heading upstream for another five hundred yards or so before making their turn. As the current kept pushing the other teams downstream away from the finish line, the same force was pushing the Yukon canoe towards the finish line. The ploy almost worked, but "Baldy" Jackson didn't like to be beaten by superior strategy. He drove his team hard and their paddling skills once again nosed out the Yukon team.

"The whole story is down there on the paddle: BC won most of the races because they were the best athletes there, and they got the prize money. But," Howard gloats, "we got the trophy."

23 August 1897
Dyea, Alaska

My Dearest Delia,

What have I gotten myself into!?

I am exhausted. I am covered from head to foot with salt water and mud. I am hungry. And I begrudge every minute of this time, being forced to stay so long separated from you. I had completely given up hope of ever sitting again quietly at a desk and writing you the pen-and-ink letter I have had in my mind for the past two weeks. It is almost impossible to compose these words this night, sitting on one box, using another as a writing table, under the open sky—my only light a sputtering hurricane lamp.

The night here has a chill swept down by a gentle breeze from the mountains. I am wearing a heavy coat purchased in Seattle. I now understand why the merchants at Johnston and Kerfoot did not think it strange that I demanded their winter wares in the midst of their summer season.

When we boarded the ship in Seattle to begin our journey here to Dyea, I was as restless as the ship rocking from side to side in the waves, hissing steam from its stacks, and straining at the lines that tied it to the solid footings of the dock. The decks were heavy with boxes towered upon boxes and bags upon bags. I have never seen so many cases of tinned foods (mostly baked beans, but also cheese, puddings, fruit salads), dried goods and makes of crackers outside of a grocery store.

The journey up the coast, which was completed mostly in thick, white coastal fog through which we slipped like a phantom without mishap or adventure, is (according to my maps) the longest part of our mad quest for gold, but I am beginning to suspect that a more terrible plight is yet to beset us. This day I saw grown men break down and weep like infants.

Dyea is in a marsh, surrounded on three sides by mountains piled

*Dyea 1897*

upon mountains wearing a glorious mantle of white snow and blue ice. When we arrived early this morning, it was low tide and one could barely see the town, five miles from the steamer's anchorage, across the most dismal mud flat you can possibly imagine.

"We have to unload you here," our captain told us, "but you'd better start lightering your outfit to above the high tide line right away. You let the salt water get into your food, and you better be able to afford a passage home."

There were scows, rafts, and rowboats to take us to the muddy shoreline—for a price.

The confusion is indescribable. The very air is vibrant with the noise of a vast and uncontrollable multitude disembarking from ships of every size and origin. We were constantly wrangling and arguing with other arrivals, Franklin even coming to profanity and almost blows on one occasion. I stepped between he and the other man. No circumstances justify one man laying violent hands upon another.

There are those who, having horses, dogs, or oxen, are out on the glistening mud offering to ferry your outfit to the town for exorbitant prices. We could afford to hire one with two swayback horses for, in my thinking, we couldn't afford not to hire him. When I budgeted for our journey to the gold fields, I had not included a return trip for all four of us to Seattle.

All day long, we loaded the sorry beasts, tramped the distance to dry shore, then unloaded and returned to repeat the same chore over and over, and over again.

But there were others who either couldn't or wouldn't pay the asking price. As we travelled through the outfits stacked on the mud flats, we saw those poor souls as they pushed, pulled, or packed their goods, one box or one bag at a time. For them, the worst was yet to come. As the evening crept forward, so did the tide. Even we, who were relatively nimble in moving our outfit, weren't untouched. Our final boxes were finally loaded as we stood ankle deep in the rising waters. My shoes, I believe, are probably ruined.

Those men who valiantly attempted to save their outfits struggled tragically, rolling boxes or wallowing through the mud with bags on both shoulders, barely keeping ahead of the surging tide. Looking back, we could see boxes and barrels being swept away by the currents. Bags of flour, sugar, oatmeal, baking powder, soda, salt, yeast, dried potatoes, and dried fruit being overwhelmed by the oncoming waves. Men, witnessing the drowning of their life's earnings and their dreams, sat on the shore and wept.

Already we have heard stories of those who have turned back. Selling their outfits, or what was left of them, for the price of steerage to Seattle. Yet, for every man who has turned back, there seems to be another who purchased those goods and again has enough to continue. There are mountains of supplies piled willy-nilly on the beach and throughout the shantytown. Every new freighter dumps scores of gold seekers and more supplies onto the mud flats. With each tide, there are different men to sit and weep. And there are more men who have a second chance.

My shoes are ruined. Just looked them over, drying by the fire. The rest of the supplies that got wet seem to be in fine shape. Tomorrow we must go into the town to buy a pair of boots for myself and determine the best means of transporting our outfit up the valley towards the Chilkoot Pass. We can delay not a moment. I asked one man this evening how far we had to go.

"Two months," he said to me, "you have two months to go to the bottom of the Chilkoot." He has been here for three weeks, carrying his equipment further up the trail. He's not sure how far he has moved his outfit. The first day he loaded his pack as heavy as he could carry, walked as far as he could, and has spent every day since packing back and forth to that same spot, which he calls Canyon City. Tomorrow will be his final load, just as it will probably be our first. Then, he tells us, he will start again ferrying his gear for another three or four weeks and that should get him to an area called The Scales, right at the bottom of the final ascent to the top of the pass. Then he expects it will take him another month to get everything to the summit.

He hasn't seen the final ascent, but has been told that it goes straight up, seemingly forever, and is a hard climb even in summer. Unless we hurry, he warned me before departing our fire this evening, it will be winter before we get there.

Franklin, Paul, and Robert sleep. I am the first watch tonight. We have been told that while the greatest thievery is in Skagway, another place like this just a few miles south, there are also men here who will pilfer your outfit. I haven't had time to tell you of Paul and Robert yet. We joined up with them just before leaving Seattle. Robert is much like Franklin. A rugged, stubborn pioneer made from high-grade material—like old oak or finely tempered metal, lean and creased as a walnut.

If today's effort is any indication, Robert is fearless, but not reckless. He has the woodman's economy of movement and, once committed, he shoulders ahead with an indifference to obstacles. He and Franklin are both builders by trade and spent much of their time on the ship discussing what we shall require to complete our journey to the gold fields (while I, having now seen what others are carrying, spent most of my time fretting over whether I had acquired sufficient supplies).

Paul is a remittance man. A polished man of mint-julep and oyster-stew tastes, with a delicate twist of scholarly humour and a baked-bean diet. Indiscretions, but discreet. Rough, but cultured. Cordial. Interesting, with a marked New York accent. He never talks of his past and I wonder what sordid and sorrowful details of his life he seeks to forget by coming to this place. Imagine not wanting to know where you came from. Where are all your yesterdays? Your lives? Your loves?

Like waking up and not knowing where you were last night—only worse. He is the one in whom we must place our faith once we get onto the northern waterways since he apparently has sailing experience off the New York/Maryland coast.

Dyea is bedlam, with a nocturnal life unlike any I have ever encountered in my travels. Fires and lanterns cast an orange, flickering glow over everything. Men who move are spectres of black, rippling shadows against the uneven light. Hundreds of men and beasts stamping in and out constantly as the movement inland never seems to cease. I can hear the creak of leather straps being tightened over bags loaded on pack boards. The banging of spoons against cooking ware and cups on coffee pots. Dogs bark. Horses neigh. Men whisper.

Within my sight, men are sitting and sleeping in every possible position. In tents, using blankets as a mattress, lying on the bare earth with no shelter, propped up against their outfits—their eyes closed and their mouths open. Oh Delia, ahead of me lies a land that is unknown to the rest of the world—only vaguely known to those who have been there. What is the truth? Most of us here can only guess and imagine. A newspaper man by the name of Wells told me to discount the newspaper reports and books. Many of those "eyewitness" reports, he informed me, were written by men who are not here and have no knowledge of the North.

Wells has been here before. It is very tough, very hard, and very beautiful, he says. A strange mixture of stark and grim mountains, abundant forests, and great rivers. Seasons teeming with life; seasons without life.

Our future appears so undefined. Will we find the wondrous riches we seek? Or will we find a place of small hopes and small successes, buried like inconsequential treasure just beyond most men's reach? We must not be discouraged, keeping in our minds that those who shall succeed must expect disappointments, persecutions, and tribulations.

As I sit here this night, I begin to believe that it is the saying of "good-bye" that is so hard. I felt more distant from you at that moment than at any other since. Strange that I should feel closer to you now than when we were last together at our farewell. Distance is mental, not physical. What matters is that we are apart—not how

great that distance might be.
Oh! Tell ere the night has passed
That I have still thy heart
Oh! Tell me, fairest love of mine,
Our lives must never part.
The smiles that wreath thy lips, so pure,
Haunt me by day and night;
Thy brilliant eyes do pierce my soul,
And guide me like a light.
Yes, guide me from inconstancy,
And bring me to thy side,
So tell me, dearest heart of mine
That thou will be my bride.
Tommy

*The start*

PHOTO COURTESY OF: SKAGWAY NEWS

# CHAPTER FOUR

## Dyea, Alaska
Monday, 16 June 1997

T h e  m u d  f l a t s , over which the tides rolled in 1897, are high and dry. They rise marginally each year, pushed up by the bottom of the Pacific Ocean as it slips ever so slowly under the North American continent. Along the flats are barely-visible parallel rows of rotted pilings covered with green moss—all that remains of a dock, built in early 1898, that ran for almost two miles from the shoreline. The old shoreline, the one that T. A. would have aimed for after being dumped out in the mud, is still visible, its edge identified by clumps of alders, young spruce, hemlock, willow, ferns, and berry bushes. Once there was a town, but it's gone now, overgrown with grass, trees, and flowers.

Walking through the old streets you find depressions in the ground, once used as cellars and basements. Occasionally a lantern, a stovetop, or a piece of metal whose purpose can only be surmised emerges from the thick under-brush. Rarely does any greying lumber or rubble identify where there were buildings; only one false front remains standing at the east end of what is called "the Avenue of Trees." Several buildings were lost as the Taiya River, which flows down from the Chilkoot Pass, gradually altered its course over the years. The Dyea Cemetery is in danger of eroding away.

When the Chilkoot opened as a recreational hiking trail in 1961, Dyea was still recognizable. Old cabins and discarded goods littered the valley floor. Buildings, grey and shrunken, continued to defy gravity. A dory, turned upside down almost seventy years earlier to protect it from the weather, remained untouched. Gaining access to the area, other than by boat, was to be had via a hand-operated cable car across the Taiya River. Visitors stood on a platform suspended from a pulley riding on a cable strung high above the river; they pulled themselves across, hand over hand, along a rope stretched just below the cable. In the mid-1970s, the Taiya River was bridged, which enabled automobile access and the scavengers inevitably followed—pillaging whatever usable lumber they could find, burning in campfires what they couldn't use, and packing off the artifacts. It wasn't so much an effort to deface history as it was an attitude prevalent in that decade: there was just so much lying around that surely nobody would miss one or two little items. The concept of leaving artifacts in context to preserve their historical integrity simply hadn't occurred to most people. With the creation of the Klondike Gold Rush National Historical Park in 1976, the US Parks Service imposed restrictions on camping and the removal of artifacts.

There are no human occupants on the town site any more, just a variety of birds, small rodents, an occasional mountain goat, and the odd bear. The last human inhabitant of the town site was the self-acclaimed "Mayor of Dyea," Emil Hanousek, who built a cabin in 1949 and lived here alone until his death in the late 1960s. Coincidentally, his brother Ed was the bona fide mayor of Skagway in 1965.

The Chilkat Indians were the first to live here, and used the area as a seasonal hunting and fishing camp long before white men appeared in the 1820s. They used the valley to access Vlekuk, the name by which they knew the Chilkoot Pass, which served as a trading route to the interior; they protected this monopoly by suppressing knowledge of the pass when dealing with white men. The name Dyea is believed to be from a Chilkat word, meaning "to pack" or "to load," and probably referred to the beginning of the trading journey over the pass.

The Chilkoot was kept free of white people until 1876, when a prospector named George Holt succeeded in crossing it. Others followed him. Recognizing that their trade monopoly along this route was coming to an end, the Chilkats showed good entrepreneurial sense by going into business as packers and guides.

In 1886, John Jerome Healy, already known to the law on both sides of the border for his management of "Fort Whoop-Up"—a notorious whiskey trading post near the Montana–Canada border—opened a trading post. It was a sad affair of shacks and small cabins, but was still the first permanent sign of modern civilization in the valley. There were white men in the valley prior to Healy's arrival but they were transient and worked as packers and guides, staying only as long as it took to build up a grubstake so they could move on.

In the village, during the winter of 1886–87, was a Tagish Indian from the interior known to prospectors as Skookum Jim because of his amazing size and strength. He was rumoured to have once carried a load of two hundred and fifty pounds over the Chilkoot Pass. Another character was George Carmack, a Californian who shunned the company of other white men and simply wanted to live the trapping and fishing lifestyle of the Indians. He was married to Jim's sister Kate, who also worked as a packer. Jim's nephew, Tagish Charlie, was there also. Together, the four of them were a decade away from becoming household names around the world.

One night in March 1887, an Indian appeared at Healy's trading post pulling a sled containing an unconscious white man named Tom Williams. They had been crossing the Chilkoot Pass from the interior side, he said, when a storm had blown in. When Williams later collapsed, the Indian carried him as far as he could, then ran into some prospectors camped below the summit from whom he had then borrowed the sled. A few hours after reaching Dyea, Williams died without waking.

"Why did he try crossing the pass in winter?" the men at Healy's Trading Post asked the Indian. He took a small bag from his belt and dumped its contents on the counter. "Gold," he replied; "all same like this." In this way, word of the first major gold strike in the Yukon River Valley, at the confluence of the Yukon and a river called the Forty-Mile, finally made its way to the "outside." The Klondike Gold Rush, ten years later, changed the face of the valley forever.

It is estimated that over one million people around the world made plans to head for the Klondike in 1897 and '98; approximately one in ten of those actually set out, and just over forty thousand completed the journey. The population of Dyea during that period was about three thousand—but it was a different three thousand each day as gold seekers passed through. There were surveyed streets, lined with first-class restaurants, saloons, brothels, barbershops, stores, laundries, homes, wooden sidewalks, and power poles. Dyea had a hospital, a 112-room hotel called the Olympic, and Alaska's largest brewery. Passing through were people who had either made their mark or were destined to do so.

A struggling, young writer named Jack London. Seattle mayor W. T. Wood. Duff Pattullo, who would eventually be elected premier of British Columbia. Boxing promoter Tex Rickard, who would later turn New York's Madison Square Gardens into the world's greatest sporting venue. Playwright Wilson Mizner, future owner of Hollywood's Brown Derby restaurant. Writer Joaquin Miller, known as the "Poet of the Sierras" and the "Byron of the Rockies." Martha Louise Purdy, only the second woman to be elected to a seat in the Canadian Parliament. General Evangeline Booth, co-founder of the Salvation Army. The man who would later manage Jack Dempsey to the World Heavyweight Boxing title, Jack Kearns. World Wrestling Champion

Frank Gotch. Alex Pantages, the Greek waiter who would start the Famous Players Theater chain and gain international media infamy in the 1930s as the man who jilted "Klondike Kate" Rockwell—the most famous of the Klondike music hall entertainers—who also passed through Dyea. A legendary figure from the Wild West, Martha Jane Canary, better known as "Calamity Jane." Sid Grauman, builder of the Chinese Theatre in Hollywood. The inventor of the not-yet conceived Mack Truck, Augustus Mack. "The Poet Scout," Captain Jack Crawford. Inventor-turned-filmmaker Thomas Edison.

And, of course, there was T. A. Firth. As I look across the Dyea flats this morning, I wonder if he could even have imagined that a grandson (though not of his blood) and a great-grandson would walk in his footprints—part of another grand adventure a century later.

Dyea's heyday lasted but two years. When the White Pass and Yukon Route was completed to Bennett in 1899, the Chilkoot Pass was no longer needed. By 1902, Dyea was a ghost town.

ఒం

Huge wooden signs on a dike alongside the Taiya River point out the trailhead just before it crosses the bridge to Dyea. We won't have time to warm up to the trail, since there is a steep quarter-mile climb to confront almost as soon as we start. Once up the slope, we will travel over a path beaten into the hillside by thousands of hikers over the past thirty-eight years. Then we will drop back down to the valley floor and follow old logging roads that are flat and wide for approximately three miles. Along the way, we will pass Finnegan's Point, a camping area on the banks of the Taiya River. It's hard to imagine that Finnegan's Point, now just a wider portion of the trail through the trees, once had a blacksmith's shop, a restaurant, and a saloon. There is absolutely no sign of the corduroy road and bridge across the Taiya River that was here in 1897–98. Now, the only man-made structures are an outhouse, tent platforms, and a cook tent. When I hiked this trail in 1979, it poured rain all the way from the trailhead and we finally stopped at Finnegan's Point to spend the night, waiting out the deluge. It worked. If you don't like the weather up here . . . wait twenty minutes: it'll change. Of course, it may not always change the way you want it to. A Yukon adage warns: "The one thing you can count on with the weather in this part of the world is that it's gonna get worse."

There is no fear of rain this morning. The sun has not yet climbed high enough to be seen over the mountains, but the sky is clear. We wait for our turn to weigh our packs and have our mandatory gear checked by Buckwheat, who stands guard over a set of bathroom scales that rest in the back of a pick-up.

"OOOOOH YAAAAHHHH!" he greets one competitor. "Isn't this a good day for a race!!! Welcome to Dyea, brother."

"Forty-four pounds, my friend," he says to another, as he balances his pack on the scales; "better bulk up a bit and try it again." Packs must be fifty pounds or heavier at the beginning and the end of the hike. Individuals whose packs are too light can pump up the weight by packing rocks, extra bottles of water, or borrowing gear from those who have too much. Some of the packs weigh upwards of seventy pounds. The overweight help the underweight by stripping off the excess and loaning it to them. If only it were so easy in real life.

Maybe those mannequins above the Red Onion Saloon are for real. Boa feathers, draped over bare shoulders and barely disguised cleavage, adorn several women of seemingly dubious morals who are mixed in among the spectators. They are employees of the Red Onion Saloon who feel these modern-day stampeders, dressed in their spandex, Gore-Tex, and polypropylene, need all the distraction they can get before starting this foolhardy trek.

"If you climb any mountains," invites well-endowed lady of liberty "Madame Spitfire," "they'd better be mine."

"Will ya look at some of these big, strapping fellas," flaps "Miss Molly," wrapping her scantily clad top in pink feathers. "It's enough to give a girl the chills."

They chase one pair of competitors up the trail, leaving random feathers and perfume hanging in the air, imploring them not to leave. Then, realizing the futility of their pursuit, send them on their way with one final request: "Bring me back a poke full, honey!"

"The only thing better than gold," "Madame Spitfire" gives the next duo of racers a suggestive flutter of her eyes, "is the man bringing it to me."

There is no starting gun. Just Buckwheat holding a clipboard, watching a stopwatch, and counting down the final few seconds: "Three. Two. One. YEEEEEEE HAW!!!!!! Now we're going folks!"

John McConnochie, owner of a racquet club in Juneau, Alaska, and dentist Phil Moritz are the first two competitors to head up the trail. They have their eyes fixed firmly on the gold waiting for the winner in Dawson City, six hundred miles away.

*The Beaver Pond*

"There's so much that's unknown," says Phil; "the weather alone can make a big difference."

John McConnochie, who swam for New Zealand in the 1972 and 1976 Olympics, knows what it takes to win. "Phil and I know where that fine line is between pushing too hard and going too easy. The most important thing is finding a sustainable pace."

Behind them, ninety-two more competitors are lined-up, waiting their turn. Just like the stampeders a century ago, we are an odd mixture of professions and experience: archeologists, biologists, geologists, physicians, lawyers, ministers, an art gallery owner, professional dog mushers, teachers, commercial fishermen, carpenters, engineers, prospectors, journalists, volunteer firemen, and artists. We share only one thing in common: a unity of vision inspired by phantoms who challenge us to follow them from their place in history. The youngest is seventeen-year-old Jeb Timm, an assistant canoe guide teamed up with his father Hank, both from Robertson River, Alaska. The oldest is author Yvonne Harris, sixty-one, from Whitehorse, Yukon. She is writing a book based on this event: "The race is going to give me all the experience, torture, and adventure my heroine is eventually going to face."

Third to leave are Brendan Hennigan and Anne Lynagh. They are a Canadian Broadcasting Corporation (CBC) television crew filming a documentary about the 1997 race. Rather than just being a part of the media contingent, they entered the race as competitors to gain better access to the participants. The focus of their project is "The Two Johns"—myself and John Small—and T. A. Firth. Brendan, a native of Yorkshire, England, who now lives in Whitehorse, got the idea while guzzling a Guinness with my nephew in December 1996. He liked the historical connection and called Anne, a sound technician from Yellowknife, Northwest Territories. She agreed to leave the comfort of her houseboat on Great Slave Lake and abandon her preferred lifestyle—partying and swimming naked in the freezing lake waters—to abuse her body and mind on the trail for two weeks. In addition to their fifty-plus pound packs, the two of them carry their camera and sound equipment, another sixty-or-so pounds split between them.

Right behind them are lawyer Greg Fekete and Ross Phillips, a physician with a personal motive for being here. He wants to best his little brother, Thane, who will be leaving with his partner, Joe Bishop, in twenty-fourth position. It is a rivalry the local media has fed on for the past week with headlines like "Un-brotherly love: siblings to battle in Dyea race." Greg, who has just recently become a father, and Ross Phillips, who still remembers working thirty-hour shifts while doing his residency in medical school, believe their advantage is knowing how to cope with a lack of sleep. "I think wisdom will overrule youth and eagerness," the older Phillips suggests.

"I'll never let him forget it when he loses," replies the younger Phillips. "We just want to see how far we can push ourselves and what happens to our bodies as we approach the limits."

Other teams head out, including Todd Boonstra, a three-time cross-country skiing Olympian for the United States (1984, '88, and '94), and his partner, Adam Verrier, another US Olympian (1994).

As well, the Cardiac Kids hoof it out in sixteenth position. Both Fred O'Brien—living proof that you can remove the man from Ireland but not Ireland from the man—and his partner, Karl Dittmar, had bypass heart surgery in the past two years. Karl is the solid, unflappable outdoorsman who has provided most of the equipment and all of the experience. His surgery gave him a philosophical reason to be part of this race: "You've got to enjoy life as long as you have it."

Fred is the indoorsman. He wears the type of clothes that most of the stampeders would have worn during the gold rush: dress shoes, cotton work pants, a cotton shirt, and a backpack my grandfather would have considered an antique. For him, the race is a spiritual quest and he sings in Gaelic a lament he has loved for over forty years: "What are we going to do without timber. The forests have come to an end. Our way of worshiping the creator is no longer practiced." He stops singing and sits in silence for a moment. "I think that is very close to what has happened here and I just want to see these forests. Get over that mountain and go down into those valleys and experience some of that wilderness myself. This is a personal journey."

When it is suggested that they call themselves "The Tin Men," Karl laughs: "We still have hearts—damaged, but they're there."

Eco-Challenge (1996) and X-treme Games competitor Roman Dial is paired up with Vern Tejas, the first person to successfully complete solo winter ascents of Denali, North America's highest peak (in central Alaska), and Mt. Logan, Canada's tallest mountain.

One participant looks beseechingly at Buckwheat. "What are we doing?" he asks.

"I think you're crazy," Buckwheat reassures him. "But I like your kind of crazy." Then he sends them on their way.

Dawson City Women's Shelter worker Wendy Cairns and nurse Christine Guenther decided that if this was going to be a re-creation, they were going to go all the way. The two stand at the start line dressed in hiking boots, can-can dresses, and gold-flecked false eyelashes. Christine hadn't originally wanted to enter the race, but it seemed all her friends were entering, so a month or so ago she started looking for a teammate. She climbed over the Chilkoot once before, but it rained all the time and she didn't get a glimpse of what the country looked like. This seemed like a good time to find out. Wendy never even thought about the race until Christine asked her if she was interested: "I was flattered when Chris asked me. I thought, 'Oh my God. Chris is this incredible jock, training for a marathon. I had better train!'" The two don't anticipate winning anything, so they came up with a theme based on Wendy's experience as a can-can dancer. It was her first job when she arrived in Dawson City in 1986. "I figured I could still kick my leg up to my ears. And the opportunity to wear big, false eyelashes again. . . ."

Christine adds, "It actually makes it more fun—getting up at 5:30 in the morning to put on our fake eyelashes and getting into our frillies for the hike."

John and I are not the only ones in this race sharing a connection to the gold rush. George "Geo" Ljljenskjold believes his grandfather crossed the Chilkoot as a member of the North West Mounted Police in 1899. He bolts out of the starting area carrying a shovel in one hand; a bearskin rug covers his pack, out of which protrudes a pole bearing a full-size Yukon flag, and he is followed by his partner, Steve Cash.

"Gold," hollers Geo as he starts into the first climb, "there's gold in the Klondike!" As they wait, the following competitors can hear him fade away in the distance, still shouting as he charges through the forest.

Whitehorse psychologist Bill Stewart has a journey to complete when he starts with his partner, schoolteacher Steven Jull. As a competitor in the Yukon Quest Sled Dog Race, a one-thousand-mile race between Fairbanks and Whitehorse in February each year, he has raced portions of the Yukon River when it was frozen.

> I thought it'd be interesting to tell my grandchildren that I raced all the way from Skagway to Fairbanks, either by canoe or with the dog team. It's the human spirit. Always looking for some kind of adventure. Pushing a frontier and finding new limits and new ways of experiencing ourselves. Mankind has conquered a lot of those summits . . . so we invent it now. The kind of adventure we try to simulate has some infinite appeal. It's our way of going one step beyond where we would be if we just went to work for another day—which potentially puts the human spirit to sleep.

Sandy Sippola and Marjorie Logue are in the Dyea-to-Dawson Race because they shot a moose together last fall. The moose had dropped close to the riverbank after being shot, so the two women hopped out of their boat to dress the animal out. However, they cut one hindquarter too large for the two them to easily handle. After trying to lever it into the boat with their paddles, Sandy knelt down and, putting her bum close to the ground and holding onto the gunwale with her hands, she formed a ramp with her body—up which Marjorie then pushed and rolled the massive chunk of raw meat.

When Marjorie heard of the race, she called her neighbour. "We're going to enter," she told Sandy. "If we could get that moose into the boat, we can do anything."

"You're out of your mind," responded Sandy, but here she is eight months later, standing at the start line.

"We are not doing this for the money," Gerard Cruchon explains. "We are doing it for the fun. We were thinking of taking a bottle of champagne to the summit . . . we are French you know." Gerard took a year's leave of absence from his job in Paris, France, to travel the world in 1983. He discovered Dawson City. Captivated by the abundance of empty country and the wilderness lifestyle, he now spends his summers living either on the Yukon River or in his cabin north of Dawson City. He works, in winter, as the custodian of the same school that Marjorie Logue teaches in.

Marjorie started talking to him about the Dyea-to-Dawson race and it appealed to him. Gerard went looking for a partner and found Jacques Chicoine, another expatriate from France. "Jacques," he said, after explaining the race to him, "you come with me."

Jacques just looked at him: "No. I don't want to do that."

"It's going to be a beautiful trip," Gerard replied. "Think about it."

A couple of days later, Jacques bought a canoe and the two started training.

Steve Landick travelled this route once before—by kayak, and backwards. He paddled upstream the entire length of the Yukon River, from its mouth in Norton Sound to the end of navigation at Bennett. Then he carried his kayak over the Chilkoot Pass to Dyea. His partner, Solomon Carriere from Cumberland House, Sakatchewan, is a four-time world marathon canoeing champion.

On his first day at work for the Kwanlin Dun Indian Band in Whitehorse, Mike Winstanley met his new boss, Chief Joe Jack.

"How do you feel about going in a race?" was one of the first questions Joe asked.

"A race?" Mike asked. Wanting to make a good first impression, he said, "Great! What do I have to do?"

"Ever done any paddling?"

"No, not really. Just when I was a kid."

"That's OK," replied Joe. "You're in."

Dan Morrison, from Austin, Texas, attended several lunatic—fringe athletic events in his fifteen years as a freelance photo-journalist, but he didn't compete in any until he teamed up with Cathy Tibbetts from Farmington, New Mexico, a nationally-ranked ultra-marathoner with numerous one-hundred-mile races under her belt. Through his experience as a journalist Dan had become an adventure cynic. "The word adventure," he elaborated, "has been abused to the point that it's lost all meaning. I believe a true adventure should have four components. It must be physically strenuous. It must be in an exotic location. The outcome must be in doubt. The risk of injury or death must be real." During the gold rush there was no doubt that this journey met all of his criteria. The next few days will tell us whether it still does.

I have the advantage of having a family that is used to my involvement in personal adventures. My spouse, Dawn, and I have only one child to raise, Erin—who is now in grade twelve—and my involvement in marathon racing and the organization of long-distance races has always been a part of our lives together. Dawn's been fully involved in every decision, in the preparation and the training, to the point that she has accompanyied us on six-mile hikes or four-hour paddling sessions. However, my undertakings don't always meet with unqualified acceptance. "Thank God there are only two of these things," she grumbled. "It's not knowing exactly where you are that bothers me. Once you contact me, or I see you or someone says they've seen you, then it's OK. But when I go for days without knowing. . . ."

We scramble over the hill, bolt along some old roads, and then encounter the dreaded beaver pond. Unable to go around it, we plow forward into the middle of it. The water goes on for a couple of hundred yards, mid-calf deep, and anything that looks like firm ground is pure muck. The trail here is located in a narrow right-of-way. Title to much of the property on either side of the trail was granted in 1991 to three brothers by the name of Mahle, from Skagway, who claimed it as traditional First Nations' land. Other landowners followed behind them until the trail was contained within a narrow easement between private properties. Trespassing by hikers is not tolerated.

⌒⌒

As we roll past Finnegan's Point in our soggy boots, we pass two people who aren't part of the race, sitting by the side of the trail and lost in their own world of historical fiction. Time travellers, following in the footprints of ghosts, in search of adventure and a taste of history.

*Racers take a break at Sheep Camp*

# CHAPTER FIVE

## Sheep Camp
16 June 1997

Yukoners have two natural advantages over everyone else on the Chilkoot. We have the Yukon Slouch—that is, we walk with our shoulders hunched up around our ears. Originally developed as a posture assumed to prevent cold winter air from sneaking under the collars of our parkas, it is also perfectly suited to the body position required to carry a heavy backpack. The more pragmatic Alaskans simply developed a parka with a higher collar, and they tend to walk more upright. Everyone else lives in a warmer climate.

Second, we know the best beverage with which to keep our body fluids topped up on the kind of day when being hydrated is important.

"Where's the beer?" It's a rhetorical question, but Gerard Cruchon sure looks like he could use a cold brew. His face dripping, and his shirt soaked with perspiration, he drags his feet up the last rise to the sign that marks the campsite at Sheep Camp.

It's a hot day. At first, shaded by the trees, we're comfortable. When we start to gain elevation and get into the sun, it's like hiking in a blast-furnace. Combine this with discovering which parts of the backpack are going to chafe your skin raw and expose what feels like every nerve ending in your body and then rub on it until it pains and itches abominably, which strap is going to cut mercilessly into your shoulder, and how many silver-dollar size blisters your heels and toes can accommodate. You start to get the impression that this is one of those bad things that can happen to good people.

Sitting on the ground at Sheep Camp, Yvonne Harris is tending to the remains of a blister that possessed most of her big toe before it ruptured and became a ragged, raw open sore. "I actually thought this was going to be torturous," she says, grimacing as she peels off another loose flap of flesh: "It was." She and Kevin McKague started out too fast. They set a torrid pace; then she hit the wall. Her legs went rubbery. Her lungs burned. Her head spun. "I just took a look at myself and thought I'd better stop going so fast," she said. "Start drinking. Start eating. I recovered, and by the time I came in I was fine."

Vern Tejas is happily playing away on his harmonica as he unwinds. "It's actually more competitive than I think people expected. There are some real hard-core outdoors people here," he muses. "I think, because of that, people are uplifted. We're actually performing at a higher level than I expected."

Other competitors are setting up their tents or hobbling out to the Taiya River to doze on the rocks or soak their feet in the glacial stream. Fred O'Brien strips down and immerses himself in the freezing water. When we passed Fred earlier in the afternoon, he was standing at the side of the trail, peering beneath a log, then checking behind a rock. "I've lost my other sock," he explained, waving one sweaty sock in the air. "I just stopped here to change them and it just disappeared." Anne Lynagh—she who likes to swim naked—declines the invitation to indulge her passion in the frigid river. Instead, she and Brendan Hennigan drop their backpacks and continue to film.

Kevin is preparing dinner for himself and Yvonne by cutting a salami sausage into slices with his axe, on the picnic table. John and I set up our stove to cook dinner. We have eaten only power bars so far today; even freeze-dried lasagna will taste good after that. The table is covered with propane tanks, burners, plastic containers, pots and pans, freeze-dried food wrappings, knives, forks, cups, and plastic bags. The clamour of voices still buzzing with adrenaline is constant as competitors swap first-day stories and strategies. Snippets of conversations jump out of the babble. "We got bogged down in the beaver pond." "You're Joe? I've heard about you. Glad to meet you at last." "We decided we would walk the hills and not run them . . . not very efficient." Teams are still coming in. The checker, seated in a comfortable chair beside the Sheep Camp sign, asks the same questions as each competitor drags himself up the trail.

"What's your number?"

"Team forty-two."

"Where's your partner?"

"She's right back there. Lady in the green shirt."

"Thank you. Welcome to Sheep Camp. Your site is just up the trail. Just before you get to the bridge, turn left and go in about twenty yards."

Each designated site accommodates two tents. John and I share our site with Suzanne Crocker and Gerard Parsons, two physicians from Dawson City. The bottom of my right hiking boot is separating itself from the top. The front part of the sole hangs loose, and each time it snags on a rock or root it tears away a little bit more. Out here, I don't have the luxury of simply dumping them and getting a new pair: I'll have to figure out some way to fix it or to continue with it, hoping it won't get so bad I have to go barefoot. With our packs so closely measured to meet the fifty-pound weight limit, things that might be helpful in these circumstances—such as a pair of running shoes—were left behind.

Solomon Carriere arrived in camp with a rope holding his backpack together. A strap broke just two steps into the race, forcing him to jerry-rig a repair on the spot and hobble up the trail with most of the weight pulling on one shoulder.

When Bruce Todd started to set up camp, a piece of clothing tripped the safety latch on his bear repellant canister and orange pepper spray blew straight up his right arm and onto the side of his face. His skin was burned a bright pink and felt like a severe sunburn for the next couple of days.

Realizing their traditional camping fare was too heavy, Joe Jack and Mike Winstanley spent most of their time in camp walking from competitor to competitor, offering to share their bannock and dried wild game meat—a taste treat eagerly snapped up by those of us who carried dehydrated meals and power bars.

Sheep Camp is the only stop at which all of us will be together. Once the race starts again tomorrow, on the summit, everyone will travel as long, as fast, and as far as they can before reaching the first mandatory stop in Whitehorse. After tonight, the only other competitors we will see will be those travelling at about the same speed. The terrain will also get more difficult. Old timers tell you that on the Chilkoot some miles are longer than others. So far, it has been a hiking highway. Tomorrow—about a mile above our campsites, where we emerge above the tree line—the valley starts to narrow down and the miles get longer. The climb, known as "The Long Hill," becomes steeper, and the well-trodden trail will turn into barely recognizable routes between, and over, piles of rocks and boulders—some as small as your fist, others the size of a small car.

Only a few adventurous souls dared to challenge the Chilkoot Pass before trail restoration work started in 1961. They beat their way through willows and buck brush without the benefit of a path. Occasionally, they came upon portions of old roads or decaying cabins. Often, they considered turning back after the first couple of days, but, not being sure how far they had come or how far they still had to go, they continued.

Ground was often gained at extreme risk to life and limb. Only by bal-

*Sheep Camp 1897*

PHOTO COURTESY OF: YUKON ARCHIVES, ERIC HEGG FOUNDATION

ancing their way across downed trees that bridged the larger creeks and the Taiya River could the hikers make progress. The only direction people could be sure of was up: as long as you were going up, you were probably okay. Until you crossed the summit. Then it was mostly down, with some up.

Hikers carried a photo or detailed map of the summit area so they would know where to go when they reached The Scales. There is a second pass, Pederson Trail, that looks easier, making a low, sweeping turn into the mountains just past the actual Chilkoot. Appearances can be deceiving. The Pederson Trail is an unstable route, known for its frequent rock-and-snowslides.

By the time those early adventurers reached the railroad at Bennett Lake, their clothes and equipment were in tatters. Becoming lost or injured and having to be rescued was almost as common as finishing the trek successfully.

It wasn't until 1967 that significantly increasing numbers of hikers started to cross the pass. By then, most of the trail restoration had been completed on the American side of the summit and work was well underway on the

Canadian side. On 3 August of that year, a group of fifty-four Boy Scouts and eight Scout leaders became the largest single group to tackle the climb since the actual gold rush. That remained the modern-day record until we arrive in 1997.

In 1970, over one thousand registered hikers traversed the pass. By 1997, the total number of recreational hikers to cross the Chilkoot since 1961 vastly exceeded the number of 98ers that had used the trail to reach the gold fields. As the trail was improved and developed, hikers sought their own novel ways of making the route more challenging. Whitehorse resident John Dines, a recreational hiker in August 1998, was passed near Sheep Camp by two men clad only in sunscreen, mosquito repellant, hiking boots, and backpacks.

The actual location of Sheep Camp, a half-mile or so up the trail from our campsite, was also the original camping area used by hikers and park staff. There was a rustic cabin, built in 1963, with a wood stove, some bare wooden bunks along the walls, and a picnic table. Outside, hikers pitched their tents on any flat piece of ground and cooked over open fires. A few springs ago, the Taiya River overflowed its banks and wiped out the tenting area. Although the cabin was spared, it is now closed to overnight camping. Instead, it now houses a photo and artifact display. The Parks Service moved the campground down the valley to its current spot rather than rebuild on the flood plain.

Now covered with heavy underbrush, the whole area—from the tree line above us to Pleasant Camp, a tenting location a mile below us where the media contingent has bivouacked—was once a forest of hundreds of structures that ranged from a two-storey hotel to mud wattles built by New Zealand Maoris. The "City of Tents" was, and still is, the last decent camping area before the final, tough grind across the summit, which is still four miles and 2,600 feet above us. Sheep Camp, which predates the gold rush, apparently came from the use of the area by a party of sheep hunters. Personally, I believe it simply refers to the presence of the mountain sheep, which can be seen grazing peacefully along the rock cliffs on both sides of the valley.

ᚺ

Occasionally, alongside the trail, the remains of massive cables sometimes appear, and tripods can be seen above us on the valley walls, perched on lonely rock outcrops. They are the vanishing remnants of entrepreneurial ventures that had their origins near another campsite that we passed through earlier in the day. Canyon City, three miles past Finnegan's Point, is one of the most attractive spots on the Chilkoot Trail. There, a small, bubbly stream runs down out of the mountains in a series of small waterfalls. A wooden cabin is sheltered among the trees and a short suspension bridge crosses the Taiya River. The bridge, built in 1970, links the campsite with a short side trip to the town site of Canyon City, which is home to the best collection of accessible Chilkoot Trail artifacts. Swede saw blades. Cooking utensils. Wood stoves. Metal brackets with "Majestic" written on them in raised letters. Items that look like old grader blades. A giant boiler, slightly bent, with "Carlton Iron Works, S. F. 1886" emblazoned on the front door. Massive flywheels coated in green moss. Rusting braided-wire cables as thick as your arm.

They give the modern hiker an idea of the magnitude of the effort expended to move twenty-two thousand people over this pass in just a few months.

The boiler was carried up the valley to this place as part of a project to construct a narrow-gauge railway from Dyea to connect with an aerial tramline strung from Canyon City to beyond the summit. The Dyea-Klondike Transportation Company also used it to generate electrical power for the communities at Canyon City and Sheep Camp. The project was scaled down when competing companies opened their doors for business. At its peak, Canyon City was host to two aerial tramlines. Three shorter trams were based in Sheep Camp. The simplest, operated from Sheep Camp, was a rope on two pulleys powered by a horse at the summit. The most complex, anchored in Canyon City, consisted of buckets hanging from a copper cable run by a steam plant owned by the Chilkoot Railroad and Transportation Company. It was, in 1898, the longest single-span tramline in the world.

The most innovative line was one built in 1894 and '95, before the gold rush, to assist the packers working for the traders. It wasn't an aerial tramline, but one at ground level that could only be used during the winter since it rode on top of the snow. The idea was that gear would be loaded into a sealskin sled at the snowline. The sled then travelled up one side of the tramline, pulled up by the weight of snow being loaded into sleds coming down the other side. The system didn't work very well, however, because the loads going up had to be very small in comparison to the immense volumes of snow packed into the sleds coming down.

In 1898, work allegedly started in the Canyon City area on the construction of a railway tunnel under the Chilkoot Pass. The tunnel was to be approximately three-quarters of a mile long, twelve feet high, and ten feet wide. Eventually, the idea was abandoned in favour of another that featured a train that would carry passengers to the foot of the Chilkoot Pass. The train would then be disassembled and raised one thousand feet to the top of the pass, one car at a time, by an elevator powered by a waterfall. No evidence exists today to bear testimony to either idea.

ை

As evening advances, everyone starts to settle down. Some take their sleeping bags and Thinsulates towards the riverbank and bed down under the stars. Most crawl into their tents and zip the doors shut against the ever-hungry mosquitoes.

Sleep comes a lot easier this night than it did last night. Not many decisions are left to be made about preparing for tomorrow. We have what we remembered to bring. We left behind what we forgot, and that can't be changed. This is a final opportunity to get a good night's sleep. To dream dreams in which we don't overestimate our abilities or underestimate our ignorance, and in which we become the superior competitors we want to be. My dream starts out as a nightmare. Battling our way through a storm that has brought all the other competitors to a standstill. Then the dream turns into pure fantasy: we emerge from the other end of the tempest with an insurmountable lead and paddle ourselves to fame and glory. There's nothing like a race perfectly run to bring instant relief from all the worry. Unfortunately, we all have to wake up. Reality awaits us, then, with all of its imperfections—and no storm.

*RCMP and Canada Customs check racers at the summit.*
*Racers are Frank Timmermans and his daughter Mary Louise Timmermans.*

# CHAPTER SIX

## The Chilkoot Pass
Tuesday, 17 June 1997

M a r i a h  J o h n s  c o n s i d e r e d  the Klondike Gold Rush to be "easy money" because she was paid substantially more for doing the same job she had done every day of her working life.

While the village at Dyea was predominantly Tlingit and Chilkat Indians, there were a number of Tagish Indians from the interior residing there. "The Tlingits from the coast, they just went up on top of the Chilkoot and they refused to pack any further than that," says her granddaughter, Tagish elder Ida Calmagane. "They told the people they were working for that they wouldn't pack any further than that because, they said, 'This is Tagish people's country. You have to get them to pack.' That's why the Tagish people were camped right there in Dyea."

The Tagish are, on average, shorter and stockier than Europeans, and were thus better suited to the arduous task of carrying heavy loads across the mountains. More than one vertically challenged observer in the 1890s—T. A. Firth among them—noted that taller people didn't fare as well when ferrying their outfit over the pass. The Tagish's experience in negotiating with prospectors, traders, and explorers over the years—offering knowledge of the country and strong legs in exchange for remuneration—also proved them to be astute business people. They understood fully the rule of supply and demand, and how to turn it to their advantage.

Like most of the Tagish children in Dyea, Mariah had been a packer since she turned ten years of age—working for the traders in exchange for trade goods and a little cash. It was a normal day for her to shoulder an eighty-to-one-hundred-pound load in the morning, climb over the pass, and unload it at Lake Lindeman twenty-six miles away. Then she would make the return journey home that same night. Her wage for the day: between six and nine cents per pound. At the end of each day, one of the trade items she always selected for herself was a five-cent bag of candy. It was her own personal treat for the work she had done that day. "She always used that as an example to all of us because, you know, she lost all her teeth," Ida recounts. "'That's what happened to my teeth,'" she said, 'because I ate too much candy.'"

By 1897, Mariah had grown into a young woman with four young children. With the arrival of the stampeders, the price for each pound packed became much more volatile—ranging from ten to forty cents—and depended upon the number of packers available, whether you were haggling with a trader or a stampeder, the weather conditions, and the size of the individual loads. Each morning Mariah negotiated a price, shouldered a pack, and headed off to Lindeman. Her stepmother looked after the children until she arrived back from her trip that night, with her usual bag of candy.

"Because she had babies at home," Ida explains, "she'd go over and then she'd come back the same night. She did this every day."

When the White Pass Railroad reached Lake Bennett in 1899, it signaled the end of the packing trade. The Tagish Indians returned to the interior, the Tlingit and Chilkats moved away in search of greener pastures, and the Taiya River gradually changed course, devouring the village. "There was a spirit house there," recalls Ida. "A nice, big spirit house. But when the water changed the spirit house fell down."

Ida climbed the Chilkoot herself in July 1976.

> I didn't have an eighty-pound pack. I did carry my sleeping bag and my extra clothes that I needed. . . . I'm sure if they didn't have that big rope [a wire cable from one of the aerial tramlines] there I would have had to go up on my hands and knees. I think I was, in places, on my hands and knees going over. Because it's really steep, that last little stretch. And when you get to the top and you look at that big wire rope—it went around a big rock just once. The way we were pulling at it, if it ever gave way you'd sure go for a long fall.

Once on top, Ida fell prey to another hazard that awaits many hikers. During summer, the snow sometimes melts from the ground up, a process called "undermelt." The result is a hole that is concealed under a thin layer of snow. While crossing part of the snowfield, her foot punched through the wet snow and she sank in up to her hip, wrenching her back.

That night, when Ida staggered into Happy Camp—the first camping site on the Canadian side of the summit—she was a long way behind the rest of the group and could barely walk. She was so exhausted, and her back so sore, that when she sat down she couldn't get up again. Since she couldn't get to where the tent was, the tent had to come to her. The two men accompanying her erected it right over top of her. She now has a greater appreciation of the stories her grandmother used to tell her: "It really felt good to be going up that hill because so many had gone over it. And so many of my people had gone over that trail. It was really fantastic. I'm glad I did it. I wouldn't do it again, though. Not like my grandmother—every day."

When comedian Charlie Chaplin wanted to include a defining scene in his silent film *The Gold Rush,* he not only selected a realistic re-creation of the climb up the Chilkoot Pass, he made sure his audience knew it was Chilkoot Pass. He understood that Hollywood could never write a fictional scene that could evoke the type of emotional reaction he wanted to generate in the way that an image of the real thing could. His attention to detail earned the film the cover of *Time Magazine* on 6 July 1925.

The Yukon Government adopted as their logo the scene of miners under their burdens, climbing single file, moving hand-over-hand up a line, suspended against a white background that could be the fog, snow, or cloud of the mountain winter. Alaskan vehicles have the same image on their licence plates. It is one of the most recognized scenes from Canadian and American history.

Observers at Brazil's Serra Pelada mine, in the 1980s, compared the sight of thousands of men and boys carrying bags of earth on their backs, climbing wooden ladders out of the massive crater, to the thin black line inching its way up the Chilkoot Pass.

When I was hitchhiking in New Zealand in 1977, I caught a ride with a young fellow just outside the town of Nelson.

"Where in Canada are you from?" he asked. He had spotted the flag sewn to my backpack.

"The Yukon."

"I know where that is!" he declared. "My grandfather was there, for the Klondike Gold Rush. He was in the Coromandel [a minor gold-bearing area of New Zealand's North Island], but when he heard about the Klondike he went. He used to tell me all about Dawson City, and the Yukon River, and the Chilkoot Pass. He thought that was quite something, that Chilkoot Pass."

If there was one thing that almost every stampeder remembered to their final days, it was the scene that each of them saw when they made that slight right turn in the valley that finally brought the pass into sight.

At the bottom, there's a wide, sort-of-flat area known as "The Scales," because it was there that pre-gold rush packers kept a set of scales to weigh their loads. Piles of gear were stacked as tall as houses. In winter, when snow fell fifteen or twenty feet deep, the tops of poles sticking up in front of the mounds of equipment marked the existence of other outfits buried beneath the snow. Tents and cabins, standing on top of the rocks in summer, were also buried and were accessible only by descending down ramps carved in the snow.

Above The Scales, a thin black unbroken line of humanity filed up towards a small depression in the jagged peaks. Each person in that line would spend six hours ascending the final one thousand feet. None stepped aside for a break, since to do so meant losing your spot in the line—then waiting for hours for an opening to appear. Alongside was a deep, icy furrow in the snow down which stampeders, having dropped off their loads up top, slid to the bottom to start the whole ordeal over again.

All of the stampeders talked with equal emotion about being a part of that line. They described it in simple, vivid words—their recollections as sharp as if it had all happened weeks ago and not fifty-five or sixty years in the past. The Chilkoot Pass was a geographical funnel that didn't respect social standing, financial status, or sex. Everyone lined up single file and pulled themselves up, one step at a time, just like the persons in front and the persons behind. Below them they heard the commotion of The Scales, but on "The Golden Stairs" the stampeders recalled only an unearthly silence—broken only by the crunch of boots on snow and the rushing air of their own lungs. It could take up to two months to move an outfit up this imposing quarter mile.

This was the point of no return. Many stampeders spent extra days at The Scales, debating in their minds and hearts whether or not to continue. There was no shame in retreating. Most of them were not the kind of people who had ever before encountered a mountain, or the kind of hardship that lay ahead. To proceed meant putting aside everything they knew and accepting that their lives would never again be the same.

Some people hold that you leave a little of who you are in everything you touch. T. A. walked here before me. We both step on the same stones. See the same stunted green-grey trees. Taste the pure sweetness of alpine streams. Smell the crisp winds that blow down from the glaciers. How much of him will I touch on this mountain? When we share a place or a sensation, will I feel some phantom reach forward across time, grateful for the temporary companionship?

It is this experience that Jeff Brady and Buckwheat O'Donahue want to recreate for the race competitors in 1997 and 1998. While we have an early start to the day, it is a somewhat leisurely morning. After climbing four miles up "The Long Hill," we will gather at The Scales for a photo opportunity. Then, in single file, we'll scale the vertical wall of the Chilkoot Pass. Once on top, the race restarts at noon.

ᗤᗧ

Despite all of our preparations and training, getting out of our sleeping bags to start day two of the race isn't easy. We can feel the aches and pains from the first day's hike. Almost everyone plans on travelling the sixteen miles from the summit to Bennett non-stop, so extra time is taken to reorganize packs. CamelBak water bottles are filled. Power bars made easily accessible. The smell of deep heat rub, used to ease aching muscles, mixes with the musk of the dew-dampened earth.

Breakfast is a little bigger than usual since it won't only be the first meal today; it will also be the last. "We're living on power bars, oatmeal, and pain killers today," muses Kevin McKague; "It'll help this morning, anyway." Blistered feet are patched with moleskin and duct tape. Then we hit the trail, across a small bridge, past the original Sheep Camp cabin. Cottonwood trees snapped off a few feet above the ground lie with their tops laid flat or missing altogether. A snowslide left its calling card. This area between Sheep Camp and The Scales is dangerous. Travellers venture forth at their own risk.

The worst time to be here is a warm spring day, shortly after a fresh snowfall or rain. The melting snow percolates down through the snow, infusing the many layers that have accumulated through the winter with a lubricant. The snowpack becomes an overloaded slope waiting for a disaster to happen. The avalanche can be triggered by its own weight, an earth tremor, or a loud, sharp noise. The slide races down the slope at speeds in excess of two hundred miles per hour—a rumble, a deafening roar growing in intensity, a churning, deadly wall of snow preceded by a blast wave of billowing white clouds.

Several smaller slides claimed a few human sacrifices early in the spring of 1898, but the worst tragedy occurred on Palm Sunday, 3 April 1898. Two slides in the early morning killed six men and alerted people to the greater danger. They started to head down the valley, but it was too late. Shortly before noon, an avalanche took the lives of almost seventy stampeders in the single greatest disaster of the Klondike Gold Rush. Most of the victims are buried in the Slide Cemetery, just north of the Dyea townsite.

Ione Christensen, the Yukon's senator, was having lunch with some friends just below The Scales on one of her annual hikes over the Chilkoot in the 1980s. Sitting on the rocks of The Long Hill, they suddenly froze—their mouths open, ready to receive the food held motionless in their hands just inches away. They could hear an avalanche coming down somewhere very close. "There were a few tense moments. We didn't know if we were going to be in its path or not," recalls Christensen. "We saw it later, further up the pass. We weren't in any danger at all, but we didn't know that at the time. A big rock and snowslide, one hundred feet wide, had crashed into the bowl at the end. It just sounded like a great big train."

Death doesn't always come with a rumble and a blast wave. Often it drops silently down from the sky as a white, pea soup-thick cloud. Whiteout conditions, in which the fog is so thick that nothing has distinctive shape and everything has but one colour, make it easy to get disoriented.

Fog is deceiving. It gives you a view of what lies ahead and then, while you glance quickly elsewhere, it covers up what you have seen and leaves you utterly confused. When travelling in, or above, such mountainous terrain, the loss of one's sense of direction can be fatal.

The outline of a plane used to be visible on the rock face directly across the valley from the Chilkoot summit. It was the remains of a Cessna that crashed here in the 1970s when it tried to sneak under the clouds and encountered fog. I saw it in 1979. It looked like a huge white cross on the black rock face. The propeller, cabin, and tail were still identifiable. By 1997, it can no longer be seen.

Cynde Adams and Larry Gullingsrud tackled the pass in a winter crossing in March 1998. Part way up the final climb, they looked over their shoulders just in time to see a storm sweep in to bury them in white fog, falling snow, and a wind that rocked them. They spent ten hours in the whiteout, fumbling along the trail, relying on their winter wilderness travel experience and knowledge of the trail, and wondering if an avalanche would come down on top of them, triggered by the storm. "I was a little nervous," said Adams. "I guess because both Larry and I have enough training to make us aware that little things add up. Back country rescue. First aid—it's all in the back of your mind. I just knew we had to be careful and make careful judgements."

Andy Simpson from Garforth, England, was hiking up The Long Hill when he heard someone call his name. Since he didn't know any of the racers around him, he stopped and looked around. Above him, huddled under a rock, were Fred and Dom O'Brien. They had started out about four hours ahead of everyone else, but ran into fog. Disoriented, they crawled under a large boulder and slept as well as two lost, wet, and cold men could.

Dom, a long-time fan of Robert Service's poetry, had been talked into this event by his brother over a pint of beer in a pub in Dublin, Ireland. What appealed to him was the fact that the Chilkoot Pass was one and a half times taller than the highest peak on the Emerald Isle, and the distance they would canoe was twice the length of Ireland. Besides, what true Irishman could resist rubbing shoulders with a historical ghost or two. "It was good," he told me on the summit, describing his training in the small hills around Dublin, "but nothing compares to what I did today. This is a once in a lifetime trip, you know."

Snow covers most of the approach to the bottom of the final ascent. There is a path marked across it with small flags. The Parks Service insists we are to follow them as best we can. Venturing too far off the path could potentially damage many of the artifacts that litter the ground up here. Rotting boots, broken carts, rusty picks, crude planks, bleached jaw bones of horses that met their end here, more tramway cables, the remains of buildings and cook stoves—all are buried deep beneath the snow, which will finally melt away by the end of July.

Jeff Brady, who has hiked every step of the way with us so far, is busy organizing us into an orderly line that, believe it or not, actually does have some resemblance to the one we see in historical photos. The media are scrambling around, trying to get the best shot of this moment. Some of us have dressed for the occasion. Wendy and Chris are in their cancan outfits, false eyelashes and all. Geo is wearing a gold and leather vest, with a bow tie and black hat. Michael Yee, from Skagway, is using a headband strap to carry his pack—a traditional Tlingit packing system that consists of a strap that loops across the forehead and relies on the strength of the individual's neck to bear some of the weight. Sally MacDonald, a Whitehorse doctor, climbs in a full-length dress similar to those worn by the women of the late nineteenth century and a pair of old-fashioned women's walking shoes.

John and I are beginning to understand the frustration of the stampeders who were forced to walk the same route over and over again, ferrying their outfit up the valley. To move his equipment one mile, a stampeder carrying one hundred pounds per load would have to travel a total of thirty-nine miles: twenty loads up, and nineteen trips back. We haven't had to drop our fifty-pound packs and go back for another load, but we have tramped across parts of this valley three or four times this morning.

We climb up a hillside, Brendan Hennigan filming us from below. We go back down and climb it again, with Brendan on his knees halfway up. Then again, with him standing at the top. "OK guys. I'm ready. Can we do that again. . . ." I even duct-tape my boot—the one that is falling apart—twice. Once because it is needed. The second time because Brendan thinks it would make an interesting shot. The duct tape doesn't work either time, and I continue the trip with the sole hanging an inch or so below my foot.

As the line of competitors inches forward, the modern day version of The Golden Stairs starts to take on some of the characteristics of the original. We advance a few steps. Stop. Wait for a few minutes. Start again. Stop again. After an hour of this we are still only halfway up the slope. It is easy to understand how it would take six hours for a stampeder to cover this same ground.

Looking up at the line-up stretched out above and then below me, I feel like I am standing in one of those postcard photos that show the miners suspended in icy space on this mountainside. I can see others looking up, looking down, then up again, and I believe they are experiencing the same sense of displacement.

Above us, watching our progress as we snake our way across the snow and up the large rocks and rubble, is a member of the Royal Canadian Mounted Police, dressed in his red serge uniform. The "Law of the Yukon" no longer has the grim countenance of Superintendent Sam Steele, who commanded the summit in 1897 and '98, nor does he have a Maxim machine gun aimed down the slope as he would have then to discourage undesirables and protect Canadian sovereignty. He didn't even have to climb to his lofty pedestal. He flew here in a helicopter early this morning, with Buckwheat O'Donohue and a representative of Canada Customs, specifically to greet us.

We finally top the first false summit. What looks like the summit from below is actually a short flat area that is followed by another short, steep rise through a narrow chute in the rock that leads to another small flat spot and a third ascent that does ultimately take us to the crest of the pass.

Above this chute in the rocks is a heap of knockdown canoes, carried

*Joe Bishop does a balancing act on rocks on The Long Hill*

PHOTO COURTESY OF: YUKON NEWS

here by some visionary during the gold rush, then abandoned—probably buried irretrievably beneath a snowfall. The approximately four hundred wooden frames wrapped in rotting canvas are seen by very few hikers, since they are usually concealed by the year-round snow. If we had been required to carry our own boats, we definitely wouldn't even have made it this far.

Once alongside the Parks shelter at the summit, we unload our packs and take a break. The Mountie and Customs man check the mandatory gear for the organizers and ask us the questions required to cross international borders. Once the formalities are complete, the race begins again.

For the moment, we savour the sun and the satisfaction of completing the climb. John sits in the snow and breaks out a beer. We are sponsored in part by Chilkoot Breweries, and part of the deal was that we pack a couple of bottles across the pass so they could legitimately claim that their product was "packed across the pass in '97." A birthday cupcake, full of nuts and fruit, and with a candle stuck in it beside a small bottle of brandy, help to ease the pain for Sandy Sippola. She broke through the snow near the summit and gashed her leg on the rocks underneath. "I was thinking that I would rather be somewhere else at that point," she said. Then Marjorie Logue and Roger Hanberg handed her the cupcake, which he had carried from Skagway for this occasion. "That was fun. They didn't sing Happy Birthday. I don't remember hearing that. It was a really good cupcake."

Geo brought some black sand and gold with him. He and Steve Cash walk around handing it out to the competitors, to remind them there is "Gold—Gold in the Klondike!" One of the park rangers is intrigued. "She came over so we put it in one of the pans and she found there was really gold in it," says Steve. "She had never panned gold before and, all of a sudden she's got it [gold fever]. She was really excited."

You can never take the Chilkoot Pass for granted. On a day like this, there is no place like it on earth. If there is a heaven for hikers, this is what it must be like. When the weather takes a turn for the worse, it doesn't become hiker's hell. Apparently, Hell is hot and dry. Up here, it gets cold and wet.

A year later we made the ascent in a chilly, gloomy mist that resembled a light rain shower. The cold water eventually found its way through our waterproof gear and down our arms and necks. As we clambered through the chute at the top, we were greeted by a bitter north wind that turned the mist into a wall of sleet that plastered our fronts, and turned quickly into ice.

We hunkered down behind snow walls constructed earlier that morning, the barricades barely sufficient to keep us from turning hypothermic as we changed into dry clothes and plugged the leaks in our rain jackets. The officials completed their job efficiently, then sent us on our way to get us down off the exposed summit as quickly as possible. But even under adverse conditions, that feeling of having to pinch yourself—to remind yourself of what year it is—persists. A feeling of déjà vu possessed Joe Jack: "This was, for me, the most emotional part of the trip. It took me back a hundred years. I guess if I was there a hundred years ago, I must have been one of those Indian packers. I'll never forget that feeling. I know I was there on that path in a different lifetime. . . . I know that."

# CHAPTER SEVEN

## The Chilkoot Pass
17 June 1997
Somewhere near Lake Lindeman

G o d ,   I   h a t e   my fry pan. We have been grinding away at this pace for about eight hours and, somewhere along the way, the cast iron fry pan has drifted to the bottom of my backpack. I have only one task. Find a spot to place my foot and keep moving forward. But with every step I take, it bangs me in the butt. At first, I barely noticed it. But after thousands of steps it's really starting to get on my nerves.

It's bad enough that my hips are sore. My aching feet are wet and hot—which is not a good combination for feet. My calves groan every time I step down, and my thighs scream every time I step up. My shoulders are large bruises where the straps of the backpack seem to ride directly on the bone. Physical discomfort I can handle. It's a natural part of endurance events and everyone is experiencing the same problems to varying degrees.

But it's that damn fry pan that's really got to me. The sooner we reach Bennett, the sooner I can dump it in the bottom of the canoe where I don't have to see or feel it. If we didn't have to take it all the way to Dawson, it would join whatever other relics rust at the bottom of the lake.

Why don't I just stop and move the pan? This is a race. While the pan is driving me crazy, it's not slowing me down. There's no time to waste adjusting the load for something that isn't affecting your physical performance. It even provides me with a little motivation. The sooner we reach Bennett, the sooner the irritation will stop. John and I keep moving.

Mostly we trot along in silence. Occasionally we pass, or are passed, by other competitors. Ahead of us the fastest teams have already reached Bennett, having completed the sixteen miles from the summit in just over five hours. Olympic cross-country skiing experience pays off for Todd Boonstra and Adam Verrier. They are the first to arrive in Bennett, followed closely by John McConnochie and Phil Moritz. Right on their tail are Jim Lokken and Art Ward, with Steve Reifenstuhl and Mark Gorman from Sitka, Alaska, in fourth. Joe Bishop and Thane Phillips are fifth.

*Descending from the summit*
PHOTO COURTESY OF: JOHN FIRTH

None of them stop for any longer than it takes to carry their boats to the water and load them up. They are already paddling furiously down a choppy Lake Bennett. "It's a great field," says Vern Tejas, racing close behind the leaders; "You're looking at some of the most competitive people in this part of the world."

On this terrain—the trail is loose rocks, tree roots, uneven surfaces, a series of small climbs and descents, all made slippery by mists and drizzle—you have to be aware of your footing at all times. Otherwise you dramatically increase the chances of injury. It becomes even more hazardous as evening falls. The dark of the night is more opaque—transparent enough to reveal the bigger features, yet sufficiently obscure to conceal the pitfalls.

The elite competitors drive themselves. Their legs pumping like pistons, they take on the intense characteristics of barn horses at feeding time—nothing will divert or delay them from reaching their assigned goal. The teams at the back are going too slowly to do themselves much damage. It is the teams in the middle, who may push the edge of their limits—and beyond—that are at greatest risk.

Karl Dittmar and Fred O'Brien slow down to a virtual crawl. Fred tore a tendon in his knee and is hobbling along with a bandage wrapped around it. He is also suffering from a lack of energy and an unsettled stomach. "I was really sick but, you know, it was the food. It was too rich," he determines. "You know, power bars and stuff like that. What I really needed was bacon and eggs and blood pudding."

Kevin McKague also has a twisted knee, which is making it difficult to travel. He is passed by Dr. Russ Bamford who notices him limping. "I can take care of that for you," says Russ. He finds a small pebble, presses it firmly against the side of the knee, and then wraps a tensor bandage around it. "There," he says, "that should help."

Kevin stands up and the pain is gone. It is an astonishing introduction for the schoolteacher to the basic principles of accupressure. "I couldn't believe it. It was amazing. I never had any more problems—all the way to Bennett."

Russ also stops to assist Fred. The physician from Faro, Yukon, acquires a reputation for his trailside manner and a nickname: "The Good Samaritan of the Chilkoot Trail." He desires to be competitive but surrenders positioning and strategy to the medical needs of other competitors. He attends to another hiker whose name he never learns: "I was going to trade with him. His legs were shot and his feet were okay. He was going to take my legs and I would get his feet."

Gerard Cruchon is walking like a zombie—methodical, mindless, his eyes totally glazed over. He and Jacques Chicoine are hiking with Sandy Sippola and Marjorie Logue. As they reach the top of a small hill, Gerard turns off the trail and lies down behind a rock. "I'm tired. I need to sleep. I'm stopping. I'm going to sleep," he informs the others. Sandy is a little concerned. They had received a warning about a bear being in the area from a park warden. She walks over to him and addresses him in that voice acquired by bartenders and used to wake up sleeping customers—a career Sandy had in an earlier life: "Gerard! Get up! This is enough. You know, you're acting worse than a drunk. Get your ass up and move it!"

Gerard drags himself to his feet—he knows that voice because Sandy used to be his bartender in that earlier life—but he doesn't last for long. All four of them find a level spot further down the trail and sleep for a couple of hours before continuing. There is safety in numbers when you bed down in bear country.

Word of the bear travels up and down the trail like wildfire. A park warden warns John and me about it at Lindeman. "There was an encounter earlier and some people ran. We don't like that," says the warden. "We want to teach the bear to be afraid of people. So, what we want you to do is holler and make a whole lot of noise and chase the bear away." John and I look at each other. I have no desire to chase any damn bear and have absolutely no intention of becoming tutor to one. I see similar sentiments in John's eyes.

About an hour later we pass a troop of Boy Scouts from Juneau. They are stomping along, lustily singing "ninety-nine bottles of Coke on the wall" to notify the wildlife that they are on their way. When I first hear them singing, a long time before we actually encounter them, I think I am having an auditory hallucination. It's not often one hears modified bar songs shouted out at maximum volume in the middle of the northern-wilderness night.

Being in bear country does add a little risk to the adventure. The only predictable thing about bears is that they are unpredictable. For the most part, if you do everything you can do to avoid them, they will do the same for you. Actual attacks are uncommon and rarely fatal, but very well publicized.

Thomas Tetz and Hans Gatt are both outdoor professionals. When they spot the bear on the trail ahead of them, they shout and wave their hands to scare it away. Instead of running, the bear ambles towards them. They retreat behind a huge rock and the bear follows. "This is getting a little scary," suggests Thomas, who pulls out his axe just in case it might be needed. They circle the rock once, the bear stalking along behind them. They go around again, and the bear resolutely tags along. Finally, on their third orbit—upon reaching the side of the rock nearest to Bennett—they turn tail and start to sprint down the trail. Thomas looks back and sees the bear appear from behind the rock. The next time he looks, the bear is gone.

A race volunteer is treed by a bear. It is hard to be certain that it was the same animal because most bears look alike when you're running away. The bear, apparently only in need of a caffeine hit, settles for ripping into the man's pack and eating a bag of expresso coffee beans before wandering off.

We encounter two park wardens, armed with rifles, patrolling the trail. Behind us, the park staff starts to get nervous as the light fades, and they stop teams from travelling until daylight. The wardens locate the bear later the next day and shoot it. A bear hanging around people will gradually lose its natural fear of humans—a circumstance that will inevitably prove fatal for one or both species.

When we started from the summit just after noon today it was relatively easy going. Downhill on a snowfield that, while starting to get soft and wet, was still solid enough to support our weight. I stopped to fill my water bottle from a small waterfall dropping over a rock just above me on the hillside. When I reached the rock, I found the snow had melted away around the stone to create a crevasse that dropped down about fifteen or twenty feet. It occurs to me that, even after two months of melting, there is still enough snow to cover Stone Cribbing, a platform built to anchor one end of a tramline, as well as the remnants of the tent city that populated this valley in 1897 and '98.

In 1979, we stopped at Stone Cribbing and shared a water bottle with another group of hikers resting there. In the 1990s, people drinking from the same container isn't an acceptable practice—who knows what dwells on the lips of a stranger? Don't kiss anyone you don't know. In 1979, sex was safe and hiking the Chilkoot considered dangerous. Now it's the other way around.

Your brain takes you to all sorts of strange places when you're tired and mildly dehydrated. You start to ponder the greater questions in life, like, "If you play country and western music backwards, do you get everything back?" I recall a story I once heard about an exhausted hiker trying to eat a can of sardines. To get out of the wind and cold he huddled inside an outhouse, and then opened up the can. Taking out the sardines, he laid them out neatly on the toilet seat, then proceeded to eat them. When asked why he didn't just eat them out of the can, he simply shrugged. "I was cold and tired," he explained, "and under those conditions, it just seemed to make more sense to line them up on the toilet seat."

The snow cover continued for a couple of miles, all the way to the beginning of the narrow canyon that collects the multitude of small streams and creeks from the mountains above. They pour out as a thundering waterfall that drops from under a snowfield on the hillside across the valley from us, and then turn into a small racing river. In the middle of this canyon is Happy Camp—in my opinion, one of the most misnamed places on earth.

Even on a sunny day, when the mountains above us are spectacular, the campgound is wet and dingy. There is a group of flat, muddy tent sites, a shed, a shelter, and a two-holer outhouse—one for men and the other for women. According to a sign hanging in the shelter, even the nineteenth-century occupants used the word "wretched" to describe it. The name derives from the feeling that hikers have after crossing the summit. They're simply happy to be anywhere.

Just past the camp, the valley widens out and Long Lake lies in front of us. The trail now climbs for a half-mile or so, then winds along the top of a ridge. From the top you can look across Long Lake to the mountains, down the valley ahead of you, and at the seemingly impenetrable wall of rock behind and above. The path winds and twists over the rockiest of ground and occasional snowpacks, avoiding the areas where vegetation clings to life in this moonscape. I imagine most of us believe we're pretty tough until we look at a tiny flower blooming from a crack in the bedrock. We could end its life without expending much effort at all, yet it survives year round in an environment we only dare to challenge in summer.

We left Long Lake behind, dropped down a long, barren ridge and across a grey wooden bridge to reach Deep Lake, a scenic camp spot six miles from the summit and surrounded by the first real trees we had seen since leaving Sheep Camp. Everyone who planned to make a brief rest stop today seems to have picked Deep Lake as the best place to do it. Greg Fekete and Ross Phillips were already there when we arrived. When they left, Brendan and Anne turned up. And as we departed another team was coming down the ridge.

We hear Moose Creek as it drops out of Deep Lake into a deep canyon, then plunges in a spectacular series of rapids and waterfalls for three miles, down to Lake Lindeman. The metal frame of an old canoe, some rusting and rotting sleds, and a couple of dilapidated cabins are all that are left of the thriving community that grew up on this marshy land to provide services to the stampeders and timber to the boat builders. There are tree stumps standing four or five feet high, logged when the mid-winter snow was piled up that high. The trees were dropped into the canyon to be carried by Moose Creek down to Lindeman where the builders waited.

Lindeman is a welcome sight. Breaking out of the forest on the ridge overlooking the lake, we pause momentarily to take in the view. Below us, a thick growth of trees in which we can see the roofs of buildings. There are shelters built for hikers, quarters for park wardens, and a photo museum-cum-library. Beyond the shoreline is the broad expanse of the lake itself, its surface a mirror image of the pale blue evening sky and snow-capped mountains.

Along with the site at Canyon City, this is the best camping on the trail. It is also a second wind for us. We are into the final stretch before Bennett— still seven miles away, but close enough that we can almost smell it. The lake was named in 1883, by US Cavalry lieutenant Frederic Schwatka, after Dr.

Lindeman, secretary of the Bremen (Germany) Geographical Society. Schwatka was the first explorer to accurately map the interior of the Yukon and Alaska.

In an endurance race, an individual will reach a point at which he realizes how much energy is actually expended taking a single step. He will also recognize that he is so tired and low on reserves he's not sure he even wants to take that next step. John starts to burn out over this stretch, especially on the climb just past Lindeman, which, at the end of an extremely long day, seems never ending.

John is experiencing late-run desperation—the emotional and physical letdown that occurs when you know you're close to the end. It's that point in the race when the only solution is to convince yourself to keep moving. Don't stop. You'll get there eventually. We pause at the top of each hill to get the rubber out of our knees, then stumble on down the trail. There are long hills, followed by longer hills. I'm able to convince John, who's starting to struggle mentally at this point, to keep going.

John recalled this stretch later:

> This was the lowest point of the race for me. I was losing it and I really needed to just stop. I think I would have used any excuse to take my pack off, but every time you take off your pack you feel less and less like you want to put it back on again. Your being out in front, going continually like that, was good, because it got me to where I was going. Telling me that we were almost there. It kept me going because maybe you were right. It would be pretty stupid to stop for a couple of hours, then get up and find out that Bennett was right around the next corner. I didn't know where we were because I had never been there before . . . but you had. I finally reached a point where I said, 'I'm not taking this pack off until I get to Bennett—because the next time I take it off I'm going to stop.'

It's been seventeen hours since we started this morning when we climb one last sandy rise to finally see the Presbyterian Church on the hill above Bennett, and, beyond, the narrow lake that stretches as far as the eye can see between the mountains. We trudge past the church and head down the hill towards the station. On the lake we see the silhouette of a canoe, with paddles stroking the water in harmony. On shore, a couple more canoes are being packed. We can see flashlights on the platform in front of the station. Standing on the tracks, I can see someone in a yellow snowsuit with silver fluorescent stripes down the arms and legs. As we get closer, I notice he's also wearing a blue mushers hat with the ear flaps hanging down.

"Welcome to Bennett. What team number are you?" he asks.

"Nine."

"Great. We aren't checking pack weight or mandatory gear, so you can put your packs on the platform. There's fresh water in the blue tank at this end of the station. The canoes are lined up at the other end of the building. They're in numerical order, with the lowest number closest to the building. The loo is down there too.

"If you need to get some sleep or you just want to get changed out of the wind, you can go inside. If you're doing any cooking, you have to do it on the platform. No stoves burning inside the building. Any problems, just ask for Beriah Brown—that's me."

*Boatbuilding at Bennett*

PHOTO COURTESY OF: YUKON ARCHIVES, VANCOUVER PUBLIC LIBRARY COLLECTION

As John and I cook up a hot meal, our first since about six this morning, I can't help feeling that the name of the race official is somewhat familiar. It isn't until around midnight, when I crawl into my sleeping bag for a two-hour snooze, that the penny finally drops: he has the same name as his grandfather.

His grandfather didn't come to the Klondike, but the gold rush established his professional reputation. What he did had a most profound impact on a young mining promoter having breakfast on 17 July 1897. T. A. Firth and Beriah Brown never met, but their destinies were linked. Some people make history. Others write stories about it. Brown was the reporter for the *Seattle Post-Intelligencer* who intercepted the *Portland* before it reached Seattle to determine if the rumours were true. He then wrote a career-making news story that started with this sentence: "At three o'clock this morning the steamer *Portland* from St. Michael for bound Seattle, passed up the sound with more than a ton of gold on board." These were the words that summoned T. A. here, for one final grand adventure.

8 February 1898
Bennett, British Columbia

My Dearest Delia,

We have left the world behind us on the far side of the frozen mountains that engulf this host. Manacled not only our body, but our soul to avarice so transcendent it blinds us to more pure ambition. Each day we were driven by some merciless taskmaster, endless lines of sentient puppets, all marching in the same direction on God's great stage as long as our bruised and bloody feet could stagger forward on this rocky trail. We are the children of Mammon on our journey to the promised land.

It is winter, yet all the snow has been worn away by the sheer volume of men. We picked our way over mile after mile of loose, jagged rock. I had reached a point where I no longer held much hope that we would ever finish this endless loop in my lifetime, that I had entered a timeless state of mere endurance, placing one foot in front of another until I ran out of ground or my strength failed.

Of our group, Franklin alone has not been driven to this point— where our bodies are numb to physical sensation, our memories and doubts blinded by unquestioning possession.

When we first reached the shores of Lake Bennett, we determined it was best he remain there and establish camp in a reasonable location before joining us. The tents and winter shacks built by others reached far back onto the hillsides and into the flats alongside the river that joins Lindeman Lake with Bennett. He was also to locate a source of lumber for our boat. Those who arrived before us have stripped the land of all trees for as far as the eye can see. Some are living and building their boats so far inland it is impossible to imagine how they will ever get them to water's edge.

While he accomplished those tasks, Robert, Paul, and I became links in the human train carrying outfits from Lindeman City to Bennett—an endless, mindless, slave-like chore we only completed last week. I would have written to you then, but I had no energy to record sensation. In my memory, it is the relentless agony of the labour that remains. I no doubt did have moments of joy and peace over the past two months, but they have no place with me tonight.

My boots, the ones I purchased in Dyea, are almost worn out. I do not believe I will replace them quite yet. Our budget is thin—Franklin's success did not come without a price.

Our tent is within a stone's throw of the ice. Three men built a sled topped by a massive sail, rather than a boat, and, using the prevailing wind, have already started down the lake towards Dawson. Franklin purchased their site for a dear fee. He studied how others were building their boats and where they were getting their materials. He told us he briefly considered one of the many saw-pits that have been erected around us upon which men, at either end of a long double-handled saw, cut green logs into boards. One man stands on top of a platform and the other beneath, where he is recipient to all of the sawdust that falls. Franklin told us he watched men who were almost brothers in their companionship fall out within minutes of starting the first cut and become bitter and cruel adversaries—each accusing the other of slacking, and often coming to blows after things had been said that could not be taken back.

"That's not for me," he told us, "and besides, the boards they produced were uneven, being a half inch thick at one spot and two inches at another. I could not work with those."

He has made arrangements with an entrepreneur by the name of

Rudolph, who with his partners owns a sawmill, to cut and deliver the boards he and Robert will need to build the boat—another expense that I had not allowed for, but one of the last luxuries that we can afford. We are on a long list of men all wanting the same, but have been promised our lumber will start to arrive within a fortnight.

As long as we stay busy we will not get lonely. The cold days, if there are several consecutively, get monotonous. We get cabin fever. A little cranky. Very cranky.

While we wait, we entertain ourselves by washing our clothes, ourselves, and preparing the kinds of meals we have been denied these past many months—coffee, bannock baked on our small wood stove, and a plate of beef stew. Each moment with a full stomach and a rested body I am terrified that I shall awaken and discover this is all a cruel dream. That I am still mechanically placing foot in front of foot as a witless beast of burden.

Often, in the endless, sightless night when it is so very cold, the thin walls of our shelter are all that seem to stand between us and the icy grip of the Angel of Death. If there is anything to be learned from this, it is that we are capable of enduring far more than we expect of ourselves. I do not understand what makes the breaking point for each individual man, but I now know that we can accomplish the seemingly impossible. Many things that at first appear to be limitations prove in the end to be inspirations. We can proceed then, in the spirit of one who expects difficulties and intends to surmount them.

Franklin and Robert will now spend their days designing the vessel that will bear us to the Klondike. It will be, they tell me, a thirty foot skiff capable of carrying just over three tons—which is about as much weight in supplies as we will have when spring does arrive. It was my responsibility to make sure we could survive the coming year and ensure that we brought all the tools and materials to build such a vessel. It is their place to construct it and make sure it floats—a task they have taken to heart, much to my comfort.

Paul is beginning to spend much of his time down near the waterfront, whiling away his hours in the Chop House or the Grand Palace. He bore his weight fairly, without complaint, over the past few months. But he seems at loose ends now that he has no specific chore to occupy his time. As a man who has never wanted for money,

*The trail between Bennett and Lindemann*

PHOTO COURTESY OF: YUKON ARCHIVES, ERIC HEGG FOUNDATION

he has never acquired a purpose in life and has no trade or interests beyond a burning curiousity about what is happening in the world we left behind.

This evening I climbed the hill above us and looked down the lake. It is a narrow ice sheet pinched between black towering peaks that plunge from the sky to some unknown place below and continue inland as far as the seen horizon. I saw black objects moving slowly in a steady stream along the surface until they vanished from my sight. These are men who will not wait for spring, when the ice will break and allow us unhindered access. They travel on foot, on ice-boats with sails, or by sleds pulled by dogs. It was a vision that bated my breath momentarily and kindled my imagination, for this is the unlocked door of our future. What great new experiences lie beyond that mysterious portal?

I know how hard it must be for you to wait for my inconsistent communications. It is much easier to be in the place where things are happening. I should improve in my writings for you since, not being a builder, I will now have little I can do for the coming months. A number of men have offered me reimbursement to write letters home for them so that is how I shall occupy my time while awaiting the completion of our boat and the going out of the ice.

I long for one cool, misty, lonely walk with you. I miss the vivid realization of things that come from being alone and still. You can't have everything, although I believe we shall one day soon have that.

Oh! Tell me, dearest, tell me true,
That all thy love's for me,
Oh! Let me fold thee to the heart,
So long has beat for thee.
Oh! Grant me just one look, a smile,
That beams with love's sweet glow,
'Twill ease this weary, longing heart,
This heart that loves thee so.
So tell me, yes, oh! Tell me dear,
This heart will be thy home.
Oh! Tell me, yes, do tell me that,
For life thou'll be my own.
Tommy

*Team on Bennett Lake*

PHOTO COURTESY OF: SKAGWAY NEWS

# The Southern Lakes

*St. Andrew's Church and Bennett Lake 1897*

## CHAPTER EIGHT

### Bennett, British Columbia
Wednesday, 18 June 1997

T h e   Y u k o n   R i v e r   begins its life in the snowfields and glaciers of the Coastal Mountains, fifteen miles from the Gulf of Alaska and the Pacific Ocean. The streams of melting water twist and roar their way through deep, narrow rock canyons to the Southern Lakes, a chain of long, narrow lakes linked together to form the first one hundred miles of the Yukon River. From there it travels almost twenty-four hundred miles before emptying into Norton Sound, the Bering Strait, and the Pacific Ocean.

It is fed by one of the largest drainage basins on earth, covering almost 70 per cent of the Yukon Territory, this small corner of British Columbia, and over half of the state of Alaska. While not the longest river in the world, the volume of water that the Yukon River disgorges from its mouth is second to none. Only two dams block its progress—a small water-level control dam just after the river passes through Marsh Lake, and the hydro dam at Whitehorse. There are only five bridges across it—four for vehicle traffic and one foot-bridge—all of them within the first three hundred and fifty miles. Bennett Lake was named in 1883 by Lt. Frederick Schwatka for James Gordon Bennett, the publisher of the *New York Herald Tribune*. It may have been Schwatka's respect for Bennett, who sponsored the 1871 Stanley expedition in Africa—"Dr. Livingston, I presume"—that prompted this gesture, since the publisher himself never had anything to do with the North. Prior to that time, the Tagish Indians called it Kusooa.

The former town site of Bennett is located on the southeast corner of the narrow lake. There's not much here to recall the height of the gold rush beyond a legacy of rusting tin cans. These reddish, crumbling containers are the single most widespread link to our past in the North. Everywhere that people set foot in this country they left tin cans as proof of their passing.

The invention of the tin can benefited the presence of non-Aboriginal people in the North more than any other human innovation in the nineteenth century. Without it they would have starved, since it was the most effective means of preventing food spoilage. You can buy just about anything you need in a can. Beans. Lard. Butter. Soup. Fruit. Meat. Potatoes. Cakes. Vegetables. Milk. Juice. You can leave it on the shelf for months and it'll taste exactly the same as it did on the day you bought it. People who grew up in places where they grew their own vegetables shudder when I tell them I still have a hankering for canned peas.

Canned food was one of the four major "food groups" predominant in the North until the advent of modern-day refrigerated transportation. Two others were dried goods and living off the land. The fourth food group—Sourdough—you will learn about later. It is an occasional passing fantasy of mine to produce a cookbook of recipes made up solely of those ingredients.

### The Firth Family Klondike Goulash (Recipe #1)

*Canned Goods*
14 oz can of tomatoes
6 oz can of tomato paste
can of mushrooms
can of olives (pitted and chopped)
can mushroom soup
can of niblet corn
pound of canned cheese (modern version, use real cheese)
dabs of canned butter (modern version, use normal butter—canned butter tastes awful)

*Dried Goods*
box of noodles (1/8–1/4 inch in width)
cup of cracker crumbs
Onion flakes (modern version, use two finely chopped onions)
Garlic powder (modern version, use a crushed garlic clove)

*Living off the land*
two pounds ground moose meat (if you have no moose handy, substitute caribou, buffalo, musk ox, or beef)

*Modern ingredient*
two green peppers (chopped)

Brown meat with salt and pepper. Add onions, peppers, corn, tomatoes, tomato paste, mushrooms, and olives and cook for ten minutes.

Cook noodles in salted boiling water, then drain. Put noodles in a flat dish (three or four inches deep) and pour meat mixture over them.

Heat the mushroom soup, then pour over meat mixture. Sprinkle crumbs and cheese on top. Dot with dabs of butter and cover. Bake at 350 degrees F for fifty minutes; remove lid and bake for ten more minutes.

Serves up to ten people, depending upon how hungry everyone is.

ைை

It's hard to visualize this low, flat, rocky beach hosting two branches of the Merchants' Bank of Halifax, a dozen hotels, a daily newspaper, warehouses owned by the Canadian Development Company Limited, stores, and a ship-building yard. Steam powered sternwheelers were constructed here during the 1897–98 winter from parts carried by men and horses over the Chilkoot from Dyea and up the White Pass from Skagway.

Although it was the largest tent city on earth at the time, Bennett never acquired the notoriety of most gold rush towns. Rather than frequenting the gambling establishments and ladies of liberty available along the waterfront, most found entertainment in baseball games, tug of wars, playing chess, reading newspapers that were months old, public speaking competitions, and outdoor lectures proffered by one of the odd mixture of scientists, preachers, or philosophers who made the trek.

The place was almost too nice to be true. It's no wonder it vanished. The history one finds here speaks of Bennett's demise in the years following the gold rush. On a hill providing a commanding view of the lake stands St. Andrew's Presbyterian Church. Missionary John Sinclair, believing that Bennett was going to be a permanent community, built the structure employing the voluntary labour of stranded gold-seekers. When the cornerstone was laid on 24 May 1899, John Irving, a representative of the British Columbia provincial government, made the dedication: "Years hence, as man passes through these natural gateways to the North, possibly when we may all have passed away, may this edifice still stand as a monument to the pioneers of Christianity in this wilderness of mountain, lake, and stream."

Inside the structure was a pipe organ that, when played, could be heard far down the lake. The original instrument was removed in 1900, but in 1973 country music star Sylvia Tyson tinkled organ ivory in the old church for a CBC television special. The organ she played was ferried in exclusively for the one-time performance and removed immediately afterward.

About the time that construction finished in 1900, Bennett was nothing more significant than a meal and water stop for the railroad. The church stood mostly empty for one hundred years. Boards weathered and shrank so that the wind now whistles freely in one side and out the other. The cathedral glass panes have all vanished and the windows are boarded up. Its belfry supports a crude wooden cross, and the roof is kept water-resistant by Parks Canada. The steeple is one of the most photographed landmarks of the gold rush era. I also saw an edible miniature reproduction once, built entirely out of pretzel sticks, at a craft show. Mainly used as a storage area for Parks Canada, it has occasionally been used as a church over the years. Ernest Harling, a cook with the White Pass and Yukon Route in the 1930s and '40s, gained a reputation for baking wedding cakes in Bennett for ceremonies performed in the building. Skagway outfitter Skip Burns—Jeff Brady's old boss—got married there in 1972.

Down the hill are the railroad tracks and the only other historical building that remains. The bright red train station at Bennett is host to a photo display that recalls the building's history, from its days as a trading stop for the First Nations to its current role. Ironically, while the railroad is the only reason you can still find Bennett on a map, it is also the reason that the town died as quickly as it did. When the railroad was completed through to Whitehorse in 1900, there was no longer a need for the sternwheelers to move passengers and freight down the lakes into the interior; thus, there was no longer a need for Bennett.

In the 1970s, it was to the train station that hikers came to catch a ride back to civilization. The building wasn't red then. It was off-white, with a white and green awning stretched over the platform. And it wasn't a photo display; it was a dining room for passengers taking the "History Train" between Whitehorse and Skagway. Lunch at Bennett was world-renowned. Two trains would arrive near midday and passengers were ushered into the dining halls, one at each end of the building, with the kitchen in between.

They would sit, elbow to elbow, on benches lining both sides of the wooden tables covered with gingham tablecloths. Massive white Armorlite bowls with green stripes around their tops, which probably weighed a couple of pounds when empty, were loaded to the brim with beans or stew. The staff claimed the stew was made from moose or caribou, and the tourists would dig in, thrilled at having a northern wild-game meal. The locals knew it was just beef. Juice was served in waxed cups, and home-baked buns on paper plates, both imprinted with a picture of St. Andrew's church. Formality and dining decorum were checked at the door. It was one big indoor family picnic. The only things missing were the ants.

It was company policy not to cater to the hungry hikers who stumbled in off the Chilkoot Trail—the corporate bigwigs figured their pampered train passengers wouldn't appreciate sitting down for their meal beside someone who hadn't seen a shower or bath for a week. But the staff fed them anyway, enabling the train passengers to vicariously participate in the Chilkoot experience.

The station closed in 1981 when the White Pass and Yukon Route shut down during an economic slump in the Yukon's economy. When the trains began running from Skagway to Bennett again, in the mid-1990s, the photo gallery was established in the south dining room. The north dining area is still where travellers sit to eat, but the stew and beans have been replaced by bag lunches.

Meals for hikers in Bennett reappeared for one year only, in 1997. The Chilkoot Sourdough Pancake Project offered pancakes to hikers in July and August as part of the Centennial Celebrations of the Klondike Gold Rush. A shed was set up on the actual location of the Bennett Bakery, and hikers were greeted by people dressed in period costumes. Over ten thousand hot cakes were flipped by more than twenty volunteers working twelve hours a day, seven days a week. Managing the entire operation were Whitehorse residents Judy Dabbs, Pat McKenna, and Ione Christensen—who also provided the most important ingredient, and the fourth major "food group" in the northern diet: Sourdough Pancake Starter.

"Starter" is a culture of mythical proportions in the North. An organism that is a living connection to the past, its age isn't measured in years or the number of pancakes cooked, but by genealogy. All of the Sourdough Starters are named after their current owners and can be traced back four or five generations. The Christensen Starter was once called the Cameron Starter, after Ione's parents, and, before that, the Ballentine Starter, named for her grandfather and great-grandfather who originally packed it over the Chilkoot Pass in 1897.

*Teams preparing to depart in the middle of night*
PHOTO COURTESY OF: SKAGWAY CENTENNIAL COMMITTEE

It can be frozen and thawed without any damage. People dry it out, seal it in envelopes, and mail it to friends (to reactivate it, they simply place it in warm water). It produces hot cakes that are light and crispy and literally melt in your mouth. When not needed, it sits dormant in a refrigerated jar as a thick white paste topped by a greenish liquid. When required, it is stirred from hibernation and fed.

Food for the Starter consists of warm water, flour, and sugar. Mix those ingredients with the Starter in a bowl, put it in a warm place, and it starts to boil all by itself. After a few days of bubbling and more feeding, it is ready. Some is poured back into the jar and stored away as Starter for the next batch. The rest is fried or baked into Sourdough pancakes, waffles, buns, or bread.

Sourdough Starter is to be shared with friends and strangers, but there is one inviolable rule: under no circumstances is one Starter to be mixed with another. Each has its distinctive flavour. Sourdoughs (people who have lived in the North for a while) claim you can actually taste the difference between the Christensen Starter and the Taylor Starter, a culture nurtured by another gold rush family. "Anyone who deals in Sourdough," cautioned Ione, "is pretty protective of their own Sourdough against anyone else's Sourdough."

There is neither beef stew nor sourdough pancakes waiting for me at two in the morning when I drag myself out of my sleeping bag—just another power bar and a handful of gorp (a mixture of nuts, chocolate bits, cranberries, and sunflower seeds). The floor of the waiting room is littered with black silhouettes that turn out to be sleeping competitors, wet gear spread out to dry, and backpacks.

Outside the station, the air hangs heavy and cool—hovering around that point at which the dew begins to condense on the abandoned flatcars and tankers that sit overgrown with weeds just past the station. Only the slightest whisper of a breeze disturbs the perfect tranquility. On the front deck, watching the trail and sipping cups of tea, sit Beriah Brown and Park Warden Christine Hedgecock. "Listen to that," says Beriah. "Birds. This is my favourite time of the morning."

The lake is a far cry from fulfilling its stormy reputation. Almost dead calm, with just a slight ripple marring its perfect surface. Windsurfers love this body of water. When the breeze picks up, it's like surfing in a wind-tunnel. Just don't wipe out if you're not wearing a wet suit: the water is bloody cold.

We're the only canoe getting ready at this time. Not quite like 28 May 1898, the day the ice went out on Bennett Lake and over seven thousand boats were launched within a twenty-four hour span. Just thinking about what a spectacle that must have been sends a shiver down my spine—or maybe it's just that I'm standing ankle deep in the glacial water.

As we pack up, Brendan and Anne appear to record the moment of departure. Brendan can barely function. He and Anne once again set aside the luxuries of sleep and food to continue filming. He asks me a question as I'm loading the canoe. I start to answer him, then realize he has already forgotten that he asked a question and has wandered off to film something else. It probably wasn't much of an answer anyway.

"It was important we got you leaving Bennett," said Brendan later. "It would have caused great problems in our technical structure. It was a very natural ending to the first segment of the story. We had been walking and filming for about twenty hours. We were absolutely exhausted. But then, we get there [Bennett] and we start filming. I'm trying to film this thing half-asleep. I remember it was a beautiful night. It was dark and the moon was out and there were some clouds moving across the sky."

Not everyone is thinking it's a beautiful night.

Further down the lake, Michael Yee is standing on a rocky beach wondering what happened to his partner, Kate Moylan, and their canoe. The west shore of Bennett Lake consists of mountains that drop straight into the lake, with few places to land, so most teams are travelling along the east shore. There are several shallow bays with narrow beaches near the south end of the lake, which are separated from each other by points that protrude into the lake like rocky fingers.

Shortly after leaving Bennett, Michael realizes he left his life-jacket behind. The pair decide to pull into a bay and that he'll run back along the railroad tracks to retrieve it. But as they come around one of the fingers, Kate spots movement on the beach.

"We can't go in there," she shouts back from her position in the bow, "there's a bear there." They paddle past a couple more bays before landing. Michael hops out and heads back along the tracks towards Bennett. Then the bear appears on the beach, strolling towards the canoe.

"I jump in the boat and paddle furiously back up the lake to where we originally planned to land," says Kate. When she arrives, she climbs up to the tracks, hoping to intercept Michael on his return trip, but he has already passed.

When he arrives in the cove where Kate is supposed to be, all Michael finds is his paddle still lying on the beach. "I don't see the canoe. I don't see a bear. All I see is a little bit of my gear on the shore. I'm thinking, the boat is swamped and she's drifting downwind. And where's the bear?"

"I'm imagining he's being chewed up by the bear," Kate smiles sheepishly. "He thought I was dead. I thought he was dead." Frantic, both pull out their whistles and start blowing, praying the other is alive to hear it. Eventually, Michael does hear Kate's whistle and heads back up the tracks to where she is. It is five hours since they landed.

"It was exciting," Kate will decide much later. "It was a true, honest-to-God Klondike adventure."

ᘓᘔ

The race has broken into three distinct groups.

There is the front pack—well planned, well prepared, very organized, and totally focused. They are the ones using CamelBak water bottles, lightweight hiking shoes, and spandex. There is no hesitation. They are pushing for the gold. Cathy Tibbetts thought she could be in the lead pack but was sadly disillusioned by the time she reached Bennett: "I'm a world-class marathoner and all these people were blowing past me like I was standing still."

Wendy Cairns and Christine Guenther are the first women's team through. "I became possessed by this little voice inside me saying, 'Go! Go! Go!'" says Wendy. "There was this couple who had legs twice the length of mine and to keep up I had to run. I became obsessed with catching them in a way I would never have expected of myself."

On the lake, John McConnochie and Phil Moritz glance back over their shoulders. They see another black dot on the water gamely trying to keep pace. It's Adam Verrier and Todd Boonstra who they passed shortly after leaving Bennett. Behind them, another dot has appeared. Who it is they don't know, and they don't want to wait to find out. Their paddle blades barely dipping into the water, they maintain a steady, demanding rhythm.

"It's like a bunch of alpha-male baboons," says Mark Gorman of the lead pack: "sitting around, eyeing each other, and snorting." He and partner Steve Reifenstuhl are the shadow on the water that the leaders can see behind Verrier and Boonstra. Roman Dial and Vern Tejas are fourth. Jim Lokken and Art Ward, fifth. McConnochie and Moritz don't stop at Carcross, at the north end of Bennett Lake. They barely even look up at the officials on the beach recording their passage. It's their plan to go completely non-stop to Dawson City, pausing only for the mandatory rests at Whitehorse and Fort Selkirk.

Verrier and Boonstra land on the beach, but only long enough to refill their water bottles and grab a handful of power bars before lurching back towards the water. It's like watching two drunks who have been spun around in circles and then told to walk a straight line. Bobbing up and down in a canoe for the past six hours has screwed up their equilibrium. The body has to learn how to walk on land again.

Buckwheat arrives in Carcross to a controversy. One of the teams has apparently been photographed using kayak paddles (a single paddle shaft with blades at each end), which is illegal. He groans and says he'll review the photos before the teams leave Whitehorse. If true, he'll impose a time penalty on the team to be added to their over-all time at the finish line. In addition to controversy is the worry that things are moving a little quicker than organizers expected. The Carcross checkpoint was barely open when the first team went by. Nobody is in Whitehorse yet to manage the preparations for the first mandatory stop of twelve hours. "The fast people are a lot faster than I thought they would be," Buckwheat acknowledges. "They seem to be getting to checkpoints anywhere from six to ten hours earlier than we anticipated."

The front groups begin to establish themselves in the hierarchy of the race.

Bruce Todd and Rod Leighton, looking back, see a canoe behind them on the lake. A few minutes later, Todd checks again and finds a canoe moving up to pass. In the stern is Solomon Carriere, steady and fluid at seventy strokes a minute, switching sides every ten strokes. In the bow sits Steve Landick chewing on a piece of pizza. The two Whitehorse physicians watch in shock as the marathon race veterans cruise past. "I would have liked to talk but we couldn't—we had to go," shrugged Carriere. "We planned it. I don't think they even knew we were there. We paddled until we were right behind them, pushed out of their wash, and gave a hard one to get us past them. Then Steve dropped his paddle and grabbed the pizza right away. It was perfect. We could see them fold."

The middle group are the pacers, conserving their energy and taking time to make decisions.

Juneau carpenter Michelle Ramsey has no false expectations: "After a couple of days the frontrunners will be gone and the rest of us will have a great time. It will be physically challenging, but it will be a great adventure."

Dirk Miller and Derek Peterson, another Juneau duo, feel no need to push themselves to a new high. "We'll leave that to McConnochie and the others," says Dirk; "We want to enjoy this." They have added a certain dimension to the planning process that hadn't occurred to John and me when we packed our supplies. "Dirk has signed a release form," explains Derek, "saying I can eat him halfway into the trip if I need to. It may turn into the Donner party, but at least one of us will make it to Dawson."

At the back are "The Survivors." Rosemary Matt and Paul Sargent from Juneau don't want to be any faster than this final group. Even being slower would be fine. "I don't feel like I have anything to prove," gasps the five-foot-two Rosemary from under her fifty pound pack. "It's just an outdoor adventure."

"We're not in it for the race," adds Paul. "We're in it for the event itself. We just want to enjoy the challenge and finish the race."

Gerard Cruchon finally struggles in and drops his pack in obvious relief. "Yesterday. It was real tough for me. But I made it." He and Jacques Chicoine take a while to get themselves on the lake. Their canoe has the hood ornament from a Cadillac attached to the bow and the Canadian flag flying from the stern.

Fred O'Brien and Karl Dittmar appear. While Fred laments the lack of cabbage in his diet, Karl is busy getting the canoe ready. Within fifteen minutes of arriving, they head out. As morning approaches, the weather changes. Teams leaving in the early daylight hours have a totally different experience from ours. Paul and Rosemary head out from Bennett, but the wind lashes up massive waves, pushing them up on the rocks and then ripping their spraydeck completely off the top of the canoe. "We decided to camp, dry stuff out, and wait until the wind dropped," says Paul.

Brendan and Anne considered using a conventional canoe for the race, but decide upon a freighter canoe with a small motor. It gives them more flexibility. They can film faster teams, drop back to slower teams, then zip back up to the leaders again. When they start out several hours behind us, the winds are really howling. "I was told by one of my friends who'd done that lake several times, keep to the shore," says Brendan. "What he meant was a hundred yards off the shore. Don't be in the middle. We kept to the shore . . . maybe fifty feet away. We came to a point and we couldn't get away from the rocks, so we got pushed into the shore. Went sideways. We just couldn't get out again. One of the things we know is—when in doubt—safety first. So we put up the tent and rested for about three or four hours until the wind died down."

Eventually, only Beriah Brown and Christine Hedgecock remain at Bennett. Then only the silence of our passing. There are different kinds of silence. There is the silence of a city at sleep. The silence of a morning in the forest. The silence of memories that emanate from a lifeless object, like the gaping walls of St. Andrew's, the dining wings of the train station, or a weathered 1895 nickel discovered under rocks at water's edge. These silences speak of an organ and a congregation playing hymns. Of tourists crammed in their seats around the long, laden tables. Of First Nations' packers or stampeders exchanging money on the shore, not noticing a coin fall to the ground. Of a canoe gliding gently into the bay under the murky blue of the summer night sky.

Whatever the source or circumstance, it is the essence of those who came before that lingers in the silence that follows.

*Carcross check point*

PHOTO COURTESY OF: SKAGWAY CENTENNIAL COMMITTEE

# CHAPTER NINE

## Carcross, Yukon

Canoes, bags, and paddlers litter the beach. After the lead pack blows past with all their intensity, the rest take advantage of the warm sunshine and sand. Most paddle through the night to get here, and several, like John Small, don't sleep for over thirty hours. We don't rest on the beach. After the race started, Dawn Dimond retrieved our camper from Skagway and dropped it off here for us. John and I crawl inside, heat up a dish of lasagna, and settle down for a nap away from the hustle and bustle of the checkpoint. I doubt if Delia sent off T. A. with pre-cooked meals or parked a wagon here for his comfort.

At the edge of the water, Geo Ljljenskjold and Steve Cash arrive, still hollering "Gold! There's Gold in the Klondike!" Then Steve stands on the beach, waving the Yukon flag above his head, cheering on Chris Guenther and Wendy Cairns as they come into sight. Doug Sandvik and Ken Russo nose their canoe into the shore. "We had a game plan," says Doug: "Start slow and taper off. We think we can handle that."

We're all breaking one of the commandments of marathon canoe racing. In fact, it's the only commandment. NEVER GET OUT OF THE CANOE. Not to go to the bathroom. Not to sleep. Not to stretch. When you get out of the canoe for any reason, the canoe is not getting any closer to the finish line and nothing is being accomplished. Sprawled out on the sand in the warmth of the midday sun, the prevailing attitude seems to be, "Who cares?"

Some are, for the first time, also coming to appreciate just how big the footsteps we are following in really are. They are beginning to recognize that success in the Klondike Gold Rush has less to do with equipment than it does with sheer brute strength and heart. Chris Olsen spends a few minutes staring back up the lake from which he has just disembarked. "They did it with vessels that were handmade," he notes. "Very crude raft from what I understand. I can't believe they did it. I can see why a lot of them died trying."

Karen Lester pulls a quick change of clothes, shedding clothes still damp from hiking over the Chilkoot, and made even wetter by waves splashing up alongside the canoe. "Must have been tough for them. They didn't have all the warm clothes and Gore-Tex socks I do."

The price exacted by the Chilkoot Pass is still evident. Skagway's Ken Graham is sitting in the sand duct-taping blisters that broke on both heels during the Chilkoot hike. He hasn't taken time to treat them and the red, angry sores are bloated, turning a pasty, unhealthy white. "Unfortunately, I think it was my worst hiking experience ever. We've changed our team name from 'Young and Stupid' to 'Limpy and Gimpy.' Seth [Plunkett] is Limpy because he hurt only one foot."

Sandy Sippola and Marjorie Logue just wave at the crowd on the beach as they paddle past, despite the fact that Marjorie is so tired she's nodding off and falling asleep in mid-stroke. Sandy doesn't want to fall flat on her face in front of a crowd. Her ankles swelled up at the end of the hike. Sitting in the back of her canoe, with her knees bent at awkward angles, she's effectively cut off most of the blood circulation to her lower legs. During one brief stop, further back on the shore, she could barely support her own weight. They plan on stopping further along the shore.

Where legs and feet suffer hardship on the pass, it is a different part of the anatomy that is starting to feel the stress of paddling. Roger Hanberg is lying face down on the sand with his wife, Pauline Frost, massaging the most vulnerable part of a paddler's body. Sitting on a hard plastic seat with no back support, for hours on end, can be very hard on the buttocks. "I just need a rest right now," Roger moans. "I think I'll do something easier next time—like run an ultramarathon. Forget this kind of race."

"When we got to Bennett, I was thinking, I can hardly wait to get into the canoe," says Chris Guenther. "Then, after a day in the canoe, I was thinking it would sure be nice to be back on the Chilkoot. My bum was the sorest part of my body. It felt, most of the time, like my feet felt by the end of the Chilkoot."

Eric Lidskoog has a disappointing message for the checker at Carcross. "We're going to scratch. I feel like a million bucks, but," pointing back at his partner, Scott Otterbacher, "he feels like a half-penny."

The Chilkoot Pass caught up to Otterbacher. He struggles to suppress his emotions, but his evasive eyes betray the pain. His body looks like it has been twisted out of shape. "I feel like I let my partner down. It's very competitive here and I feel we would have had a shot at the top runners here, if not winning this thing. But I used a new backpack, which wasn't too wise, and never got the adjustments right. Put my back outta wack." He glances at the lake and blinks rapidly several times: "Gold fields. Klondike. Dawson City. Not gonna happen this year."

At first glance, Carcross is not much more than a gathering of ancient cabins and shacks mixed in with modern bungalows. Viewed from the water, its most prominent features are the charred remains of the riverboat SS *Tutshi*, which was destroyed by a fire of suspicious origin on 25 July 1990, and the railway bridge that spans the narrows between Bennett Lake and Nares Lake. The bridge was designed to pivot its centre section to enable the riverboats to pass through.

In the small downtown stand the last remnants of the thriving gold rush town it was in 1898: the Caribou Hotel, a century-old structure still in use today; Matthew Watson's Store, a dusty nostalgic trip for those who remember small-town general stores with their massive cash registers and huge glass display cases; and the White Pass and Yukon Route station with "The Duchess," a diminutive steam engine long retired from service. The town's name is a shortened version of Caribou Crossing. In reality, caribou herds rarely crossed the river at this point. The main migration crossing had been a narrows at the east end of Nares Lake. The current site was originally a seasonal hunting and fishing village for the Inland Tlingit and the Tagish people.

Even though the caribou stopped coming long before the gold rush occurred, the name stuck. The exact location of the village was transient. When the mosquitoes were bad, people lived on the north side of the narrows where the breeze kept the blood-sucking pests at bay. When the winds became a hard-blowing harbinger of winter, the village moved to the south side, on the lee side of Gopher Mountain—now called Montana Mountain.

When a gold rush comes and goes, it usually leaves in its wake little more than debris. Few towns whose roots are planted in such conditions survive long enough to even claim a credible assembly of phantoms. In this hamlet, there is an eclectic collection of ghosts and memories for just about everyone. Archaeological sites near the community uncovered evidence of prehistoric bison, along with miniature stone and bone weapons that may have been used to hunt them in the years following the last Ice Age. There is little else to tell us about the hunters—the microblade people, who vanished from history as mysteriously as they appeared.

The White River Ash makes its first appearance in this area. Ranging in depth from several feet to minute fractions of an inch, it is evident in hillsides and riverbanks all across the southern Yukon. It was deposited approximately

1,250 years ago by a volcanic blast from Mount Churchill, a couple of hundred miles to the northwest in Alaska. Prevailing winds dispersed the ash across the southern Yukon, forcing the inhabitants south to escape the heavy, crystaline sand that blanketed everything. About three hundred years later, an Athabascan-speaking tribe appeared in the deserts of Arizona. They are believed to be the people who fled the ash.

When the scows, barges, and Peterborough Canoes arrived with gold-hungry stampeders in 1898, it was apparent to the First Nations that cultural conflict was inevitable. The First Nations found value in wildlife, fish, the river, and the trees. They couldn't comprehend the concept of a rock having extraordinary value just because it was heavy and yellow. The stampeders had gold fever and little understanding of the wilderness through which they travelled.

Since the easiest place for the fleet to land was the north side of the narrows, the First Nations obligingly moved, temporarily, to the south. But when Burt's Roadhouse, the Carcross Inn, the Hotel Scott, and the Caribou Hotel were built—along with a North West Mounted Police blockhouse, a telegraph office, and a railroad—the move became a permanent one.

Fred Trump, grandfather of New York multi-millionaire real-estate developer Donald Trump, spent time in Carcross in 1899, operating a hotel with his business partner Ernest Levin. They were after gold, but had no plans to dig for it. They operated a hotel at Bennett in 1898, then later opened a store in Whitehorse.

It was here that the Golden Spike was driven for the White Pass and Yukon Route on 11 July 1900, to complete the longest narrow-gauge railroad ever built.

The SS *Tutshi* carried passengers from Carcross to a luxury resort at the south end of Tagish Lake. Called Ben-My-Cree (Gaelic for "Girl of My Heart"), the resort was considered, at the time, to be a northern French Riviera and attracted the rich and famous by the boatload. While awaiting their journey down the lake, Hollywood actors, such as Robert Taylor and Clark Gable, British royalty, including Edward, Prince of Wales, and politicians—notably former US President Theodore Roosevelt—tilted a beer or six in the Caribou Hotel.

Carcross's strangest living connection to the gold rush died in 1972. Polly the Parrot was 126 years old—and misnamed for all of that time—when he finally guzzled his last shot of rum. But God, could that bird sing! His fame as a performer of opera, interlaced with bursts of fanciful profanity, was international. Entire trainloads of tourists would cross the street and crowd into the Caribou Hotel to offer their fingers to the ornery bird, which snapped at them and drew more than his fair share of blood between arias and blasphemy. This was the home of North America's top big game hunting guide, Johnny Johns, who counted among his regular clientele mystery novelist Erle Stanley Gardener, the creator of Perry Mason. His promotional brochure guaranteed good food and unexcelled hunting, but cautioned, "We do not furnish women or liquor—bring your own."

Four of the six co-discoverers of gold in the Klondike are buried in the Carcross Cemetery. Of the five who were present in the Klondike on 17 August 1896, only George Carmack isn't buried here. He died in 1922 in Vancouver, British Columbia. The sixth man, Robert Henderson—who wasn't in the Klondike when the big strike was made—was buried in Dawson City. Finding the four in the graveyard on the south shore of Nares Lake is a test of gold rush trivia.

Skookum Jim, who died in 1916, is buried under his Christian name: James Mason. Canadian Government surveyor William Ogilvie, who interviewed all the participants, concluded that Jim was the man who found the gold. Ogilvie believed George Carmack got to claim the title "Discoverer of the Klondike" because the group didn't believe white men would accept an Aboriginal in that role.

Tagish Charlie has "Dawson Charlie" written on his tombstone. When he moved back to Carcross in 1901, there was another Tagish Charlie living there, so he changed his name to Dawson Charlie. One winter night in 1911, while crossing the railroad bridge, he fell and was swept under the ice by the surprisingly strong current that runs between the two lakes.

Kate Carmack is the only name immediately identifiable. Unhappy in a foreign culture, and eventually abandoned by her husband who denied her access to any portion of the fortune they mined out of the Klondike, she returned home to Carcross in 1901. Until her death in 1920, she lived on a small government pension, supplemented by selling needlework to tourists and receiving token amounts for posing for photographs with people who knew her story.

History books rarely, if ever, mention the fifth person who was in the Klondike on 17 August 1896. Patsy Henderson never received recognition because he was, at age fifteen, too young to legally stake a claim, and thus there was no official paperwork to verify his presence, and so recorded history passed him over. When he passed away in 1966 his headstone read, "One of the original discoverers of Klondike Gold." Yet, when the Yukon Government put special plaques on the graves of the co-discoverers in 1996, Patsy's was conspicuous by its absence.

The sixth individual present—as a very young child—was Graphie Carmack, Kate and George's daughter. There is no official record of her presence either.

ოლო

In many ways, the fact that there are no records fits in quite neatly with First Nations culture. A lot of First Nations traditional ways are not written down, and so "officially" they don't exist. Their history is oral—communicated through stories and songs. The storyteller has a special status in the Indian world. Until the white man came, there was no light to read by at night, and there were no written materials with which to pass on stories. The storyteller was the educator–entertainer who spoke history and knowledge into the memories of the next generation.

Patsy, a stately man who wore a beaded caribou-skin suit made by his wife, Edith, had a tale to share with the world. For over a quarter of a century he was the entertainer–educator of the thousands of travellers who came to Carcross on the White Pass and Yukon Railroad. He told the traditional legends, sang songs, explained something of early life, demonstrated animal calls, and, using models, showed how the First Nations built and used game and fish traps. Then, in a photo gallery of his past, he would tell of the finding of gold.

### Patsy Henderson's Story of the Discovery of Gold

I am going to tell the Klondike story. Here is the man who found the first gold. That man's name is Dawson Charlie. He find gold in 1896, the seventeeth of August. He is my brother. Skookum Jim is my uncle. Another partner, George Carmack—he is a white man, George Carmack—and myself. Four of us.

Now these people all die, except me.

The time we find gold in the Klondike, I was just a kid. I am old man now.

I want to tell you a little story about George Carmack. George, when he came to this country, no white men here at that time.

*Patsy Henderson*

When he come, he married Skookum Jim's sister, my aunt. He stayed around here with Indians.

First year, he didn't understand Indians. Second year, he understand. At that time we don't work for nobody, we work for ourselves. George like this. He don't work for nobody. He stay around here five years.

He got tired around here and wife and he went down Yukon River. He never came back for two years. We miss him. We go down looking for him—Charlie, Skookum Jim, and me. When we start from Tagish, we go down river in rowboat. We row boat all way down the river. No machine. All hand work. When we come down Klondike we find him. George Carmack. We told him we come down to look for you. He tell us, too bad you fellows look for me long ways, and he tell us we can't come back until winter time. So we stay and put fish trap in water on the Klondike River.

After a while he [Carmack] tell us, one man he come up the river before you fellows. That man he told me he found gold last fall, away back, and that is where he went again, that man. That man is named Bob Henderson. He is a white man. We haven't seen him, but George saw him. George tell us, let us go look for that man. Maybe he found lots of gold. He tell us like that, so we go look for him.

Charlie, Skookum Jim, and George Carmack—three people look for Bob Henderson. That is time they find gold, but I stay home in camp on Klondike. George Carmack, he tell me, "You stay at camp and look after camp." Three people leave Klondike own camp and start off up the creek. But the first gold found eight miles from camp. Dawson Charlie found ten-cent nugget.

He didn't find in creek. Find on side hill on slide on top of rock. So we went up creek. We see gold. We pan it. But at same time they look for Bob Henderson and find him away back. Maybe forty miles from the Klondike. Bob Henderson has got a creek and he got a little gold. He stay there and he is alone. Those three people stay at Bob Henderson's camp one night. Next day, they come back. But they come back different creek, Bonanza Creek. Not called Bonanza Creek yet, but Bonanza Creek pretty soon. And they see gold again. Everytime they come down a little ways then they see gold, but they look for good large place. So when they come down half way creek they take a rest on top of bank and one man go down creek to get drink of water.

Skookum Jim go down to creek for drink of water. When he took drink of water he see gold. He call: "George. Come down here. Bring down shovel and gold pan and we try here." When George come down to the creek, "Look George. Look at gold on rock." First pan, fifty cents gold he panned. He tried a little bit above. He found lots of gold. A little below. Lots of gold. Twenty minutes, panned five dollars gold. Then George say, "I think we have a good place. I am staking claim."

Staked claim for three people. When they staked claim they named creek "Bonanza." First creek to be found in Klondike. Lots of creek after a while. Same evening they come back. They got gold and George Carmack he weighed. He says five dollars worth of gold.

When I see the gold first, just like I don't care because I no savvy. I never see gold before. Now I like to see gold all the time.

Next day we go down to Forty Mile to record the claim. We come back again. Go down one day, come back two days. When we get to camp on Klondike we move camp up the creek to Bonanza so when we get up there we build ten feet sluice box.

We start work on first day September. Worked for three weeks. We took out gold—$1,450. At that time very cold. We cannot stand it no longer. We go down to Forty Mile for winter camp. We took gold in store. We tell people we took out this gold in three weeks time.

That is the time the big rush start. No one stay home. Everybody go up. The big rush start to come up the river two years steady. Winter time. Summer time. Everyday somebody come.

ᔕᔕ

As we pack up to pull out, John's nerves are on edge. Further down the beach Ken Russo is a couple of lakes premature with his verse as he pushes off:

The wind she blows on Lake Laberge
Then she blows some more.
If you don't want to drown on this lake,
You'd better stay close to shore.

With Windy Arm just ahead, it is a warning that all of us are best to heed. The lakes show little mercy to those who fail to treat them with respect. The waters are so deep and cold they often refuse to relinquish the dead. But it is a caution not all of us will take to heart.

*Frank Farkvam approaching Windy Arm*

PHOTO COURTESY OF: JOHN FIRTH

# CHAPTER TEN

## Six Mile River
Tagish, Yukon
Thursday, 19 June 1997

There are two ways to tackle Windy Arm. Neither is the wrong option, and both have their risks. Windy Arm is a narrow part of Tagish Lake, about twelve miles in length, down which severe winds constantly blast out of the mountains. For boats travelling from Carcross to Tagish Lake, they must cross the north end of the Arm for approximately one and a half miles and are exposed to side winds from the south. The conservative approach is to stay close to the north shore—this is the only part of the lake system oriented east-west—where you will never be far from safety in the event that you are swamped by the waves. By playing it safe, you add approximately one mile to the distance because you must loop through the horseshoe shape of Suckers Bay, then paddle against the prevailing south winds to get around Perthes Point. Once past the point, you turn with the wind and an experienced paddler can steer it to his or her advantage.

Suckers Bay has claimed many victims, the most famous of which was a twenty-four foot cedar dug-out canoe packed over the Chilkoot Pass by Ida Calmegane's grandfather, Tagish John. He received the canoe as payment for work done for people at Dyea and used it for several years in the Caribou Crossing area. It was a valuable asset for a man whose livelihood depended on fishing because the boat rode well in shallow water where most traditional First Nations canoes were unstable.

One day Tagish John got caught in a sudden squall on Windy Arm; he escaped with his life, but had to abandon his canoe. The bow was visible for many years, sticking out of the water, but the relentless pounding of the breakers and the jagged shoreline eventually ground it up. Everything that goes down in Windy Arm gets devoured by the waves and rocks in Suckers Bay.

The second way you can attack the crossing of Windy Arm is to take the south shore, which is substantially shorter. Once you emerge from behind the mountains, you have approximately a quarter mile in which you are exposed to side winds, then you tuck, as best you can—given the rocks and other small islands in the water—into the lee side of Bove Island. Once you emerge from the other side of Bove, you turn your canoe with the wind and have it behind you as you paddle straight down the lake. The major danger along this route is getting swamped. If you go over, you're in trouble because you're a long way from solid land.

This is the first place where John and I disagree on strategy. I favour the south shore, while he is adamant that he won't go unless we take the north shore. "One completely endangers your life," he reasons. "The other doesn't—and that's the one I'm taking. The worst case scenario is that you're wet and cold and on shore. I have a family waiting for me at home and I'm not taking any chances I don't need to. If you want to take the other way, then you can do it with someone else."

I'm still convinced we really won't be at any greater risk by taking the south shore but it's the first test of our partnership and there's still a lot of race to go yet. The vision I had before the race started, of us sitting on a gravel bar cutting power bars in half, flashes before my eyes. It's too early for this. There are no gravel bars until the second half of the race.

"Okay," I agree, "we'll do the north route." The decision made, we head into the maelstrom. Wouldn't you know it. . . .

"One of the scenes we wanted was Windy Arm," says Brendan Hennigan:

> We got to Windy Arm and it was as flat as ice. Here we were at this famous place where we would have people in canoes, popping around on top of four-foot waves and some really dynamic possibilities for shooting. There we were and it was flat. And there was nobody around. We were sort of disappointed because we were looking for the storm scene. You know the film *Ryan's Daughter*? You know they waited six months for that storm scene? We finally bought one from the other film crew that was out there. They had Windy Arm storm shots.

They get the teapot. We get the tempest. The waves, when you can look back and read them, are simple enough to deal with. You try not to get broadside to them or they simply pour over the gunwale and swamp you. Like a surfer catching a ride, you try to make their momentum add to your own.

When the ride appears to be coming to an end, or when the direction you're heading no longer suits your purpose, you "crab" back out of the wave and set up for the next one. Every seventh or eighth wave is substantially larger than the others.

Then there are the waves that seem to boil up underneath you without warning. They break in a twisting fashion, forming u-shaped crests that turn the canoe sharply. You must react to these without hesitation because other waves are relentlessly rolling in from behind.

We are about halfway through Suckers Bay when John miscalculates a wave. We are picked up and carried towards the beach—turned into mere observers as Mother Nature momentarily has her way with us. It appears almost surreal as the wave breaks and gently deposits us on the rocks, completely out of the water. We hop out and pull the canoe beyond the reach of the waves. Right beside us is a fairly recently constructed dock that looks like it would be used to load livestock onto a much larger ship. It creates a good windbreak.

"I don't know about you, John, but I could use a cup of tea about now," I suggest.

"Sure. Why not?" John's eyes light up and he rubs his hands together in anticipation. "This isn't going to change, so we may as well have a warm cup of tea to get us through it."

When we finally cross the bottom part of the bay and turn into the wind, it gets brutal. For me, anyway. I'm in the bow, and every wave we cut into seems to end up in my face or my lap. At least I won't die of thirst. I feel like I've swallowed half the lake. John has a different view from the stern. "That was quite fun. Going around those points and going up Suckers Bay. Watching you actually paddle for the first time."

We aren't the only ones driven ashore in Suckers Bay. Michelle Ramsey and Jim Heckler are also beached by the waves. But it isn't from the water that the danger comes for them, it's the sky. They beach near a nesting area for terns and immediately come under attack by the frantic parents. A couple of birds hit Heckler, drawing blood before the paddlers scramble back onto the lake.

The south route is the gristmill for drama.

As he battles the waves before tucking in behind Bove Island, Roger Hanberg suddenly remembers he doesn't feel very comfortable in small boats. "When I got in Windy Arm it was the first time it struck me: if we got the wrong wave now, there's a good chance we could die. We could drown. We're right in the middle of freezing cold water and there's nobody else around. It hit me—that's why there are so many warnings about Windy Arm. It's a very dangerous area and we're in the middle of it."

Once past the island, the canoes can turn with the wind and it's a long two-mile run into the narrows. "You look behind yourself," says Steve Cash, "and you'd see white caps all the way up the lake. We cut straight out to the island. When we got to the island, we turned and then we just started riding. That was fun. It was the most interesting part of the whole trip."

Suzanne Crocker and Gerard Parsons find it just as interesting as Steve does, but not as much fun. "For an hour we paddled for our lives because we knew we were a long way from shore and if we went over—it was cold and we wouldn't make it."

Fred O'Brien decides he needs an umbrella as he and Karl Dittmar paddle past Bove Island. Other teams are waiting on the shore "during a storm of biblical proportions." It isn't raining, but Fred is curious. Just how good a sail will an umbrella make? "With the wind picking up I opened the umbrella and we started to pick up speed. I was happy to display the umbrella to all those stampeders on shore, gesturing to them, bravado-style, that we would see them in Dawson."

At first the umbrella keeps getting blown inside out. But Fred persists: he wedges himself into the bow and gets the umbrella stabilized. Karl digs his paddle into the water to use as a rudder—and they hang on for the ride of their lives. "I tell you . . . we were shooting over those waves," says Fred:

> It was wild. Absolutely wild. We didn't make the river at the end. We cut straight across the Arm at ninety degrees and had to beach on the east shore. My heart was in my mouth—both from joy and concern. Every time we got a blast of wind and wave I called out "Jesus. Where are we going!?"—but not too loud. I recalled St. Therese of Lisieux's reflection on the Bible story of Jesus asleep in the boat during the storm where she indicated she would not wake him. I resolved to take her advice and prayed for Karl, myself, our families, and put my trust in God.

Karl keeps the canoe on course and it isn't until they are almost to shore that their luck runs out. A wave sideswipes the canoe and totally immerses

*The salvage of a wreck 1897*

PHOTO COURTESY OF: YUKON ARCHIVES, VANCOUVER PUBLIC LIBRARY COLLECTION

them in water. They pull the canoe into a sheltered bay where they set up a temporary camp to dry out. The waves, says the stoic German, were about six feet high, but adds, "they'll probably grow as the years go by."

Their trip across the Arm nets them a one-hour time penalty from race officials for using a means of propulsion other than a paddle. It also resulted in the addition of a "Fred O'Brien Rule" for the 1998 Dyea-to-Dawson race. "It should be noted," Fred proudly points out, "that the revised rules for the race include not only a prohibition of sails, but also umbrellas."

Cynde Adams and Larry Gullingsrud start out with a fairly calm crossing, but it quickly becomes apparent that a canoe ahead of them hasn't fared so well. At first they're not quite sure exactly what it is they're seeing. The sun is glancing off the water into their eyes, making it difficult to see anything. They think they can see bags floating in the water, but they're not sure. Then they hear the cry for help. One of the "bags" is a man. The rest are tether bags attached to a capsized canoe.

The two experienced search-and-rescue experts approach the man in the water and recognize him as Jimmy Smith. They throw him a line and he grabs at it. But Jimmy's hands are so cold he can't use them to hang onto the rope. "That water is colder than hell. It didn't take long to sap the strength right out of me," he said later.

Jimmy crosses his arms across his chest and pinches the rope to his body in a death grip while Cynde and Larry pull him to shore. Jimmy's partner, Ken Brewer, is already on shore, but he, too, is hypothermic. The two had been in the water for over forty minutes.

"We were adjusting some of the gear so we could rest," explains Ken. "A wave hit us from the side and rolled us over." They first attempted to save the canoe and then, realizing they weren't going to succeed, started for shore to save themselves. Ken saw Jimmy was fading fast, but also knew he wouldn't be of much value if he tried to assist Jimmy, since he, also, was slowly dying in the water. "I didn't think Smitty was going to make it to shore."

When Jimmy does reach the shore, he is barely conscious. "He was pretty much out of it," says Larry. "He was right on the edge."

"I couldn't even drink soup," adds Jimmy. "They gave me a cup of soup, but I spilled it all out."

They strip off his wet clothes and stick him in a sleeping bag. Then Cynde climbs in with him to lie body-to-body so he can benefit from her body heat. Ross Phillips and Greg Fekete also land to assist the rescuers. Another passing canoe stops and then heads off to a resort called Ten-Mile, just a few miles further down the lake, to notify race officials. Cynde and Larry eventually go out and retrieve the capsized canoe.

"We were dysfunctional," says Ken. "There was no doubt about that. They took total control out there. They saved our lives." Almost seven hours after getting upended, the two paddlers are taken to Carcross where they withdraw from the race.

"You never really know the focus of anything you do in your life until you're presented with it," Cynde is philosophical about the entire situation. "If that was the whole reason to join this race—to be there at that time—then that's great . . . and I believe it was. The reward is that these guys are able to go home to Juneau and not be in the lake."

Past Windy Arm, the winds die and the water flattens out. As the dusk deepens we see pin-points of light far ahead of us. There are a lot of cabins located on California Beach at the north end of Tagish Lake, one of them owned by my sister Nancy Huston and her husband, David. We know she's not there tonight but we plan on stopping anyway. It'll be a place to dry out while we catch an hour or two of sleep. When we arrive, at about four in the morning, we try the back door, the garage door, but can't figure out how to get into the cabin. John and I climb back into the canoe and keep on paddling. "Did you try the front door?" David asks us later. They knew we would be there and had left it unlocked.

Around the corner, as we enter the Six Mile River between Tagish Lake and Marsh Lake, three canoes are pulled up on the sandy beach. A group of paddlers stands around a roaring fire. Sebastian Jones and Malke Weller decided the idea of a warm campfire on a cool night was just too appealing to resist. So they stopped. Wendy Cairns and Chris Guenther were next on the scene. Steve and Geo later turned up, then us.

Now, I determine, it's time for the beer I packed over the pass. It's still in the canoe, floating in the six inches of water we collected in Windy Arm. I pull it out and Sebastian's eyes light up. "I'll trade you a Jim Beam that's been carried across the Chilkoot Pass for the beer." I consider for a moment: I could always pack another beer over the pass, but, not being a bourbon drinker, it's unlikely I would carry a bottle of Jim Beam. In 1979 I tasted from a bottle of tequila that had been carried over the pass. It was, without a doubt, the best tequila I ever consumed. This might be an opportunity to test my theory that packing things over the Chilkoot improves their flavour.

I hand him the beer and take the Jim Beam. After a couple of shots to warm the blood, I hand it back to him—my hypothesis intact. The beer makes the rounds of the group around the fire.

John and I decide we will grab a couple of hours of sleep. The others want to paddle on a little further. "We were all really tired," says Wendy. "A bit delirious maybe. But we still felt we had something left, so we kept on going." One by one, they push off and head down the river.

Behind us, the full moon hovers over Tagish Lake, a double halo ringing it in the crystal clear sky. Its mirror image is perfectly profiled on the looking-glass surface of the lake. Ahead of us, the sun is just starting to rise, creating a canvas of red, gold, pink, and lavender, framed by a few scattered clouds. The fire at our feet gradually fades to a bed of red coals, while a pillar of billowing smoke climbs lazily into the still air.

As I drift off, I sense movement around the embers. No more than flickering shadows. But for those with more vivid imaginations, ghosts have gathered to share our company, and perch themselves on logs or sit cross-legged on the sand to share the warmth of dying flames.

Tagish, NWT
5 June 1898

My Dearest Delia,

We are resting safely on shore for the moment and will probably remain here for at least a few days. The North West Mounted Police have established a post here, where they number each boat as we pass by. It is, they tell us, the only method they will have to determine who will die where along the river. Last night a Customs and Excise man, by the name of Godson, came about to our fire. He checked my bill of lading from Skagway and coldly informed me that we owed the Crown $5.47 in duties. Once business was concluded, he turned out to be not a bad fellow at all, just greatly overwhelmed by the number of boats passing by each day.

Samuel Johnson once wrote that being on a boat is like being in prison—with a chance to drown. And he was writing about a much larger vessel than the one we sail aboard!

Such a sight we must be. The four of us, amateur rowers, each with our own makeshift oar, struggling to work together as one company. Our rectangular scow, seemingly with a will of its own, reluctantly co-operates with our efforts. Condensed milk and beans roll around the bottom of the boat when rough water comes with the wind, and we are pitched in every conceivable direction.

*Flotilla on Bennett Lake 1897*

Praise God indeed that we have Paul. While Robert and Franklin have built a solid-enough, seaworthy craft—when we first put it into the water at Bennett on 27 May, it didn't even leak!—I fear we may truly have floundered had not Paul been with us. He has experience sailing on the coast near New York. He assisted Robert and Franklin in the design of the masts, located the steering oars in the bow and stern, and added an odd piece on the bottom of the boat called a centreboard that he told us would help stabilize us when we are under sail. Then he attempted to teach us how to work with the wind. For him, it is child's play. For us, it is havoc.

"For they have sown the wind and they shall reap the whirlwind."

Our journey on the water has been a lot faster than we ever imagined it could be, and not without its spine-tingling moments. I don't know that I can give you any true idea of the amazing and unreal thrill of it.

The ice finally vanished from in front of Bennett on 28 May and boats by the score set sail immediately. But soon we heard that the ice still remained, a grim and dirty white barrier stretching from shore to shore just a few miles out of our sight. So we decided to wait a couple more days before disembarking.

When we finally did join the exodus of boats on 30 May, we had a stiff wind to start our passage, which then turned into squalls strong enough to blow all the stuffiness out of us. Paul took the helm and kept us going straight despite gusts that had us racing over the waves with the speed of a freight train. The waves were quite massive and the boat kept rising up one side, balancing precariously on the crest, then tipping and sliding down the far side. On the west shore there appeared to be no place at all to land. The steep dark mountains plunged directly into the white and blue waters. All along the east shore we could see waves lashing jagged rocks along a terrifying shoreline. On the rocks were many of the luckless ones who didn't have a Paul to steer them true. The bays we could see were jammed with boats taking shelter until the winds abated.

Several times we passed boxes being tossed by the whitecaps, and once we spotted the hull of a boat, overturned and barely visible beneath the surface. God alone knows how many men and women lie at the bottom of that frigid lake.

When we turned into the narrows at the north end of the lake, called Caribou Crossing, we sailed into the leeward side of a mountain and the winds vanished. The sails drooped. Paul stepped away from the steering oar, his hands frozen into claw-like shapes by the strength of his grip upon the pole.

"We need to change our means of propulsion for the moment," he informed us. "I believe that means you gentlemen will have to take up your poles and replace the wind with your shoulders. I will endeavour to thaw out my hands."

Thus, for many hours, the three of us walked back and forth, back and forth, back and forth on the deck. At the bow we would sink our poles until they found bottom, then we would walk—one pole on each side of the boat—all the way to the stern. Then, lifting our poles from the depths, we would go once again to the bow.

Lake Nares did not seem a long lake and it was dead flat. During our time there we saw nary a ripple to suggest a stir of fresh air. It has a muddy bottom and often we found ourselves ganging up on one pole to try to pull it from the muck on the bottom. It took us much longer to travel this body of water than it did for us to come all the way down Bennett Lake.

There was little room on the shore of the lake to reach landfall and not much space to maneuver on the water. We were never out of the sight of men there—of camps on the shoreline, of boats moving slowly along with us, northward to the Klondike.

We did manage to stop for one night, after passing through the second narrows that took us out of Lake Nares. When I awoke, it was still as dark as it gets here at night, which isn't very dark at this time of year. The sky was as clear as a window. I felt the stars were shifting and we were steering wrong, even though I knew we were not moving at all. Paul had told me that I might encounter this illusion after being on a boat for a prolonged period of time.

We expect many things of the heavens at night. Looking up at the moon, with its silver halo, the world seems as old as time. This must have been the way the firmament was when the waters had gone and the night of the fifth day of creation had fallen on creatures still bewildered by the wonder of their being. What is a hundred miles in a country so boundless? Everywhere we go, there is still more of it at our shoulders, behind our backs, or in front of our eyes. I sense the vastness of creation, my own insignificance in the greater master-piece. I am humbled by how much we owe God, who brought all of this harmony and splendour into being. It does not seem right that you should not be here with me to witness this.

There are qualities in men that do not stand alone, but which must be mixed with the appropriate medium or circumstance to appear. Paul's true talent before the mast, with a courage that was bred from his confidence, aided us greatly two days ago as we travelled across a body of water called Windy Arm. We did not have terrifically strong winds, but rather than coming from behind us, they came at us from the side.

Off to the north we could see a deep bay, littered with wrecks of those who didn't make it past Windy Arm. Men had salvaged what boats and loads they could and were towing their scows by rope along the shoreline towards a distant rocky point beyond which we could see open water. Beyond, to the east and directly ahead of us, another magnificent sight to note. A stupendous mountain rising like a medieval fortress from the waters.

"We will stay here on the south side of the lake as long as we can," explained Paul; "When the wind starts to push us towards the bay, I will try to catch enough of it in the sail to pull us forward as well. With luck, we shouldn't reach the north side of the lake until we are past the point. If we can do that, then the turning wind will be our ally and not our enemy."

When the wind did buffet us, Paul had us rig the sails so they ballooned out in front and pulled us forward. It took both he and Franklin to hang onto the steering oar. Robert and I had the bow oar and were sweeping with it, trying to hold the nose of the boat true to the line that Paul had given us and combat the wind's efforts to blow us north into the rocky bay. I could see the extra guy lines we had tied to the masts to give it additional support were as taut as bow strings and were stretching. But Paul never faltered. He repeatedly urged us on, encouraging us and telling us to keep it up. When one of the ropes holding the smallest sail broke away, he left Franklin to manage the steering oar (a task that even he, with his size, could barely manage for the short time he was on his own) and balanced himself perilously on the gunwale to secure it back in place.

My arms were burning and I wasn't sure how many more pulls I had in myself when we barely scraped past the ominous rocks and sailed into safer, calmer waters. We were grateful that the trip down Tagish Lake, and into the short river that brought us here, was uneventful—the water was as flat as glass. We had to row much of the distance but somehow it didn't seem to drain my arms the way that Windy Arm had.

While we travelled, we discussed our plans for the future. When we started, we were all for getting to Dawson City as quickly as possible. But now, looking around at all the other men striving for the same goal, I am beginning to doubt that we shall accomplish anything useful by being in their number. Paul is of the same mind. Franklin and Robert were all for pushing on as quickly as possible. But now that we are at Tagish, they appear content to rest for an extra day or two.

We can see one more lake ahead of us, which seems to have two names—Mud Lake and Marsh Lake. Perhaps when we reach the far end we will have determined our course.

Oh Delia, I have missed you. The days seem to slip by, all alike. Before I know it, days, weeks have gone and I have not put pen to paper to tell you that all is well with us here. There was no mail for us here although there is a post office. It is I who have been remiss in my duties to you. So today I write. And tonight I devour once again the last words I received from you and pray that all is still well.

So silent doth the hours go by,
A day seems many years;
So silent doth the thoughts to die,
Come to my mind so clear.
A message will I send to-day,
And ask her to forgive;
I cannot bear a longer stay:
In pain my heart now lives,
If answer comes, "My Heart's Still Thine,
I Love Thee As Of Yore,"
Remorse will turn to thought Divine,
We'll love till life is o'er.
Tommy

# CHAPTER ELEVEN

## Miles Canyon
Thursday, 19 June 1997

Alvin Hamilton sat alone on a bench on a cold, blustery fall day, his trademark cigar idly smoldering away in his right hand. As a senior citizen would be in this weather, he was chilly and had a massive coat drawn up around his shoulders. But he specifically dictated that this is where we were to meet. A man familiar with the halls of power, he was used to having his way.

"You know," he told me, "this is my favourite place in the North. To me, Miles Canyon is what the North is all about." At first I believed that statement to be the nostalgic longing of a old man visiting his haunts one more time before he died. But as he continued to pontificate, waving his cigar with grandiose gestures, I began to realize that even in his final years Alvin Hamilton was still an architect of dreams.

Second in Canadian politics only to Prime Minister John Diefenbaker in the period 1957–63, Hamilton was Minister of Northern Affairs and National Resources. He dreamed up the Roads to Resources election platform (or, as the federal opposition called it, "Road from Igloo to Igloo")—the first defined strategy for northern development in Canadian history. His regime resulted in the establishment of Canadian sovereignty in the Arctic and put into place the framework through which the Federal Government subsidizes those who choose to live in the north.

Hamilton learned snippets of First Nations languages to aid him in dealings with northern Aboriginal and Eskimo bands. His only regret, he often said, was that he wasn't Minister of Northern Affairs when the Russians put Alaska up for sale, because he would have liked an opportunity to bid on it.

Miles Canyon is a favourite haunt of Hamilton's, but not for its natural beauty. It is a monument to his passion. A dam built during his tenure as Minister of Northern Affairs had tamed the raging rapids. Miles Canyon is the centre-piece on which other dreamers had focused some rather fanciful schemes—schemes that a visionary could identify with, though Hamilton's was the only one that became reality.

The first to allegedly indentify the canyon as vital to the transformation

*Sandy Point in Marsh Lake*
PHOTO COURTESY OF: JOHN FIRTH

of the North was mining promoter and developer Thayer Lindsley, in the late 1940s. Apparently his plan was to build a hydro project to generate millions of horsepower of cheap electricity—power that would then be sold to feed a growing industrial hunger for energy in the lower forty-eight states. A series of dams, with one of the pivotal structures built in Miles Canyon, would create a lake that would stretch five hundred miles from the Coastal Mountains to Fort Selkirk, capture the flow of the Yukon and Pelly Rivers, and absorb all of the southern lakes. Once the water was contained, it would flow south, rather than north as it does now, through an elaborate series of tunnels drilled under the Coastal Mountains to empty, ultimately, into Taku Inlet near Juneau, Alaska.

Next on the drawing board was a plan known as the Dyea Hydro Water Diversion Scheme (in Canada), and the Taiya Power Project (in the United States) in 1950. This plan envisioned a dam built across the Yukon River Valley that would cut off the river, raise the water level in the canyon by sixty feet, and reverse the river's flow back towards Bennett. A series of tunnels would take the water under the Chilkoot Pass, spilling out near Dyea.

Both the Canadian and American governments were intrigued by the idea. Aerial photos that were taken as part of the project's research show the entire length of the Yukon River. Handwritten notes suggest constructing the dam at Miles Canyon. Maps set out plans to relocate the White Pass Railroad along the route the highway between Carcross and Skagway follows today, with a bridge to span the new lake at Gladys Point. The plan was killed by a report from Canadian Government geologist Hugh Bostock, in which he detailed his political argument against the use of Canadian water to generate power for American corporations, with little or no compensation for Canada, and his personal opposition to damming one of North America's greatest rivers.

The plan was nevertheless attractive to the American Aluminum Company (ALCOA), which attempted to resurrect it in 1954 by announcing plans to open a smelter at Dyea, provided that the dam was built at Miles Canyon. Without cooperation from Canada, however, the idea was doomed, and ALCOA gave up completely on the scheme in 1957.

The very name of Miles Canyon terrified river travellers until the Whitehorse Rapids Dam was built in 1959. The small lake created by the dam was named after Lt. Frederick Schwatka and it immersed two sets of rapids—the canyon itself, and the more treacherous Squaw Rapids that followed right after. What remains of the adjacent Whitehorse Rapids is only evident when the dam's spillways open in the spring. About sixty feet in width, the canyon is a mile-long chute sculpted by walls of perpendicular basalt columns that were formed, between six and twelve million years ago, by a series of at least fourteen lava flows from nearby Mount McIntyre. For the boats travelling the canyon, the greatest dangers came first from waves that crawled up the sides of the canyon and then spilled back into the channel's centre from above, and next from whirlpools that sucked boats down—then spat back out what was left.

Squaw Rapids combined a series of razor-edged rocks, which could slice the bottom of any vessel, and water-worn boulders that snagged boats and tipped them into the angry combers. Whitehorse Rapids was a quick drop—almost a waterfall—about twenty feet in height. Beyond it, massive standing waves, resembling the manes of white horses, could swamp any unwary crew's boat. Just past the rapids, was a wide, calm stretch of water, with a small tent city on the east bank. There, the stampeders stopped to take stock of what they may have lost in running the rapids. There were tramlines that carried men—who dared not test the waters—and outfits around the rapids;

these, also, unloaded in the tent city. At one end was a graveyard for the bodies of those who didn't survive the passage.

Not everyone is convinced that the demise of the rapids had to be the price of progress. Cal Waddington, a CBC radio broadcaster who came north in the 1950s, still questions the trade-off that occurred when construction started on the dam. "I miss those rapids. 'Well, do ya wanna look at the rapids or do you wanna turn on a light switch Mr. Waddington?' . . . It's not that easy. Yes, I can turn on the light switch, but when I see films of the Whitehorse Rapids . . . I was there. I can hear them. I can reach out and I have a part of it because I was there. They were going to be there for a long time. There was no need to think about them not being there. Who could have known they would be gone so quickly?"

The dam raised the water level in Miles Canyon about twenty feet, calming the waves and whirlpools. The current was reduced to such a degree that Whitehorse yachtsman Craig Moddle sailed his Hobie Cat catamaran upstream, against the wind, in 1998. "It's a bit tight," he said; "There's not much room for tacking in there."

Yet, for a large, unwieldy craft to make the corner at the south end of the canyon can be a challenge. On 1 July 1985, during a re-enactment of Frederick Schwatka's 1885 trip down the Yukon River, I was on a large raft that failed to negotiate the corner. There were eight of us (all dressed in 1880s US Cavalry uniforms) working the sweepers, but it wasn't sufficient—just as it hadn't been enough for Schwatka's actual crew. They, too, crashed into the wall. There was no serious damage done to our modern-day raft, just a few loose logs that followed us down river—with our deepening respect for those individuals who ran this canyon when it was still rapids.

လာ

Making the turn into the canyon is pure relief for John and me. It's been a long day since we woke up early this morning on the bank of Six Mile River. Sometime while we slept, Brendan and Anne caught up to us and are now also snoozing on the sand, a sleeping spot that would have been submerged, along with the communities of Carcross and Tagish, had any of the grand visions for Miles Canyon become reality.

All along the west bank of Six Mile River, the houses and cabins of Tagish can be seen. There are approximately one hundred people living in this area, a bedroom community of Whitehorse. As we approach Marsh Lake, a bridge

tands six foot two and was once described by a boyfriend as
ugh to hunt geese with a rake."

e of year, there is only the wind, the waves, and an occasional
to. For the competitors, paddling gets monotonous and the
wander. "You have a lot of time out there to think about
olomon Carriere, a twenty-year veteran of marathon canoeing.
ing—and you've run out of stories and jokes—you just think
g. You've got to keep your mind active. If your mind isn't active,
ts to get inactive too."

do anything like this again, I'm going to memorize the words
songs," says Chris Guenther, "so I can sing to keep myself
lon't know enough lyrics."

ee is one of those people who thinks in terms of pure numbers.
number of strokes per minute, and the number of hours he is
lding graphite paddles, at approximately eight ounces each, and
housand strokes daily, he calculates he is lifting just over twen-
dle each and every day. "And these are light paddles. I can't
the people using wooden paddles must feel like," he says.
sing wooden paddles and, while we have no idea how much
can tell him how we are feeling: pretty tired after seventy miles
ng on short rations and little sleep. He continues on into the
on one more calculation: "These paddles can move a lot more
e old wooden ones."

fter leaving the lake we come upon the first dam ever built on
ver. It is a control dam, originally constructed in 1912, designed
vater in the early spring and then release it to break up the river
wn stream. The purpose was to open a channel for the river-
h earlier than nature itself would allow. The dam has been
times over the years, with the latest version completed in the
most recently used to control water levels between Marsh Lake
tehorse Dam, which is the only other dam ever built on the
A lock was installed to enable boats to get around it.

us, Wendy Cairns and Chris Guenther shoot through one of the
ther side. The change in water level is only about three feet and,
don't collide with the structure itself, it can be done. But the
nuch wider than the canoe itself—one small miscue and you
impaling yourself on one of the bolts that stick out of the

spans the river and there is a boat marina on the east bank. This is the business centre of Tagish. A weathered two-story house sits close to the shore
promising "Caribbean Take-Out." Roger Hanberg and Jeremy Lancaster pull
into the house just after sunrise and order up grilled cheese sandwiches.
"That's all the cook would make at that time in the morning," I'm told.

During the gold rush, Tagish was the bottleneck that Canada Customs
and the Royal North West Mounted Police exploited to record exactly how
many men and boats were making the journey down the river. Prior to their
arrival, the Tagish Indians had a fishing village on the east bank, with two
large potlatch houses. There is no evidence of the village now, but there are
spirit houses that mark the burial area and the First Nations still use the area
for annual gatherings and potlatches. Spirit houses are small buildings constructed over graves—a tradition that started when missionaries, who didn't
approve of cremation, convinced the Indians to bury their dead instead.
When an individual died, all of his or her belongings were either buried in
the grave or placed in the spirit house to accompany the person on the journey after death. Rifles, pots, knives, blankets, and handmade fish spears were
items commonly placed inside the houses. Stampeders cleaned out most of
the spirit houses at Tagish before the North West Mounted Police learned
what was happening and put a stop to it.

The very name Marsh Lake, once known as Mud Lake, implies a body of
water surrounded by swamp. The first point of land you encounter as you
enter the lake would sustain such an image. Beyond it, however, there is
nothing muddy or marsh-like about it. The name Marsh was actually
bestowed by Schwatka, who named it after a Yale University palaeontologist
Professor Othniel Charles Marsh—founder of the National Academy of
Sciences.

The First Nations name for the lake, Takwadada—where sand washes up
on shore—is much more fitting. Sandy Point is, thus, appropriately named.
Approximately half way up Marsh Lake, it is the kind of sun-soaked jewel one
expects to find in Hawaii or Jamaica, not in the Land of Ice and Snow. It juts
about one hundred yards into the lake and is as wide as it is long. The white
sand is piled high and continues to run in a wide sweeping arc along the bay
north of the point. Seagulls stroll casually in the waves. Ducks float serenely
just off the shore, gently rocked to inactivity by the lazy swells.

Lined up along the leeward side of the point are white, red, and yellow
canoes. Sprawled on the beach are competitors who obviously believe their

tan is more important than their final positioning.

John and I pull in for lunch, as do Brendan and Anne. Two Skagway paddlers, Steve Jaklitsch and Jeremy Schader, turn up at about the same time. A couple of canoes pull out as we arrive. Another team is also here, but they don't hear us arrive over their snoring. For myself, it is a welcome opportunity to warm up. Sometime last night I became extremely cold because the bottom of my sleeping bag was wet. There was a pinhole leak in the waterproof bag in which it was packed. This morning I awoke congested, coughing, and could barely breathe. To top it off, my lower back has tightened up to the point that it almost forces me to walk doubled over. John is his usual sympathetic self. 'Hunchback' we call him now," he says, mimicking my posture.

John needs the break to rest his eyes. There are rules against picking up historical artifacts, but none against leaving some. John lost his sunglasses over the side of the canoe earlier this morning and has been battling the sun reflecting off the lake surface.

Two paddlers arrive with a dilemma that harkens back to the gold rush.

They aren't sure they will be able to continue once they reach Whitehorse. "We thought we would be finished this thing in four or five days. Now we realize it's going to take longer than that. But he," one points at his buddy, "has to be back for work." In the end, they decide the race should get priority as the experience of a lifetime and that "he" can probably get another job. It's the kind of decision that was made a century ago by stampeders who already knew they were too late to cash in on the gold in the Klondike, but who were determined to press on despite the cost.

Thomas Tetz and Hans Gatt also reach a conclusion on Sandy Point. Hans has pulled the tendons in his wrist, making it impossible for him to grasp the paddle. The two decide they will withdraw from the race in Whitehorse. "There's no sense to keep on going with that wrist. I need that wrist after the race, too. I can't afford to bugger it up for the rest of the summer."

While we aren't exactly sprinting, John and I are a day ahead of our original schedule—and almost that far behind the leaders. There are twenty teams ahead of us, or travelling with us, on Marsh Lake. Several more are in Whitehorse, resting. A dozen are on Tagish Lake, and two are still in Bennett.

As we approach the north end of Marsh Lake, passing through McLintock Bay, we take a break to enjoy a treat delivered to us by Brendan and Anne. They crossed the lake to Lakeview Marina, a tourist resort on the east shore, and picked up bacon, tomato, and lettuce sandwiches for us.

Brendan also tosses us a couple of b
"We have a little beer supply, so we
and sort of say, 'Would you like a b
know, they are your best friends. Y
paddle and we switch off the moto
stuff, and to know people. I'm gett
tary."

The east shore has a familiar fee
cottage there for almost forty years.
night water-skiing on this bay (lake
and occasionally playing a four-hole
that appears in spring when the ice
fairways or greens, but you certainly

In April each year, Dawn, Erin,
selves in the cacophony of geese, sw
here on their migration north each
areas for viewing the migration of n
the ice is packed with water fowl.
Tundra Swans, three varieties of
According to the information availab
Swan Haven, 10 per cent of all mig
for a day or two to feed as they wait
move on to their summer nesting
trumpeting, cackling, and quacking o

It is this annual bird assembly
for the First Nations. They had a fish
the river mouth, where they also too
waterfowl—a welcome change after
meats and fish from the previous su

My father told stories of lying on
ing squadrons of geese and whoopi
ers—the lowest were just above the
below the clouds. The flocks on the g
heat radiating from the birds simply
sleep at night for the noise of them,"
anymore. Or the geese. There's not
The skies were black with them."

Cheryl, who
being "tall en
At this ti
gull to listen
mind starts
things," said
"If you don't
about anythi
your body sta
"If I ever
to a thousan
awake. I just
Michael
He counts th
paddling. Wi
making forty
ty tons of pa
imagine wha
We are
we're lifting,
of lake paddl
river, workin
water than th
Shortly a
the Yukon R
to hold back
ice further d
boats a mor
rebuilt sever
1980s. It wa
and the Wh
Yukon River
Ahead o
gates to the
provided yo
gates aren't
could end u

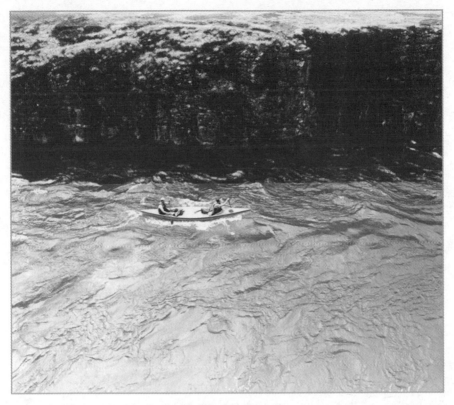

*Through Miles Canyon*
PHOTO COURTESY OF: YUKON NEWS

columns. John decides he doesn't want to take the chance, so we use the lock.

In the high clay cliffs that line almost every corner of the river we see thousands of holes swarming with swallows that congregate in great clouds over the water. It is local wisdom that the day the swallows leave each year is the day that summer ends and fall begins. We sneak up on a beaver swimming across the river and are almost alongside if before it realizes we're there and dives after sending up a geyser of water with its tail.

We reach another Canyon City—not to be confused with Canyon City on the Chilkoot Trail. This is where the stampeders stopped a mile or so before reaching Miles Canyon. Here they could elect either to hire a river guide and gamble with the rapids or take one of two tramlines that ran around the dangerous parts of the river. Remnants of several buildings, tent frames, and a fox farm can still be seen among the trees; a few of the logs laid for the tramlines can be seen along the walking trails. In 1900, when the White Pass Railway reached the Yukon River downstream from the rapids, there was no longer a need for the tramlines or the city and both were abandoned.

Each summer, archaeologists can be found digging in the earth, seeking the past that is buried here. They have pulled poker chips, coins, foil wrappers from champagne corks, and even a small gold nugget from the dirt. Below that layer of history they discovered evidence of an First Nations fish camp.

Everyone is putting out a little extra to make sure they get to Whitehorse. Some paddlers are starting to get brain cramps. Suzanne Crocker and Gerard Parsons doze off and their canoe drifts for a short period, spinning lazily in the centre of the wide channel. They awaken, disoriented, and paddle upstream for a few minutes before they realize their mistake.

Ron Theunissen almost passes out while paddling. "I almost tipped the canoe over. That's when I said, 'Okay. It's time to stop.' If we"—he and partner Eric Carmicheal—"took our time, it would probably be pretty casual. But we're trying to do as well as we can and it's pretty demanding." Ron keeps checking his watch, thinking there's something about today he should remember but he can't quite put his finger on it. It isn't until after they arrive in Whitehorse that it registers. It's his birthday.

As we paddle through the swirling water of Miles Canyon, I look up at the great black pillars I've seen so many times in the past. I see the White River Ash. I also see an orange algae that someone once told me could only be found in places where the air is free from pollution. I can't help but think of Alvin Hamilton as he must have been in his political heyday, with his cigar and his dreams for this land. Growing all by itself on a rock abutment near the water's edge, midway down the canyon, there is a solitary pine tree. I see it as one of those wonders of nature—how did a tree start growing here, and how on earth has it survived? Hamilton saw pine trees as an alternate fuel source for the North (the Japanese used pine root pitch as aviation fuel during the Second World War) just as he saw this magnificent canyon as a cornerstone of northern hydro development. In many ways Hamilton is symbolic of the human need to control the environment, but all too often without regard for the consequences that such control will effect. Sandy Point. Tagish. McClintock Bay. Carcross. Bennett. Had his dreams been realized, "Who could have known they would be gone so quickly?"

"We did a lot of stuff that we didn't realize would have an impact at some spans the river and there is a boat marina on the east bank. This is the business centre of Tagish. A weathered two-story house sits close to the shore promising "Caribbean Take-Out." Roger Hanberg and Jeremy Lancaster pull into the house just after sunrise and order up grilled cheese sandwiches. "That's all the cook would make at that time in the morning," I'm told.

During the gold rush, Tagish was the bottleneck that Canada Customs and the Royal North West Mounted Police exploited to record exactly how many men and boats were making the journey down the river. Prior to their arrival, the Tagish Indians had a fishing village on the east bank, with two large potlatch houses. There is no evidence of the village now, but there are spirit houses that mark the burial area and the First Nations still use the area for annual gatherings and potlatches. Spirit houses are small buildings constructed over graves—a tradition that started when missionaries, who didn't approve of cremation, convinced the Indians to bury their dead instead. When an individual died, all of his or her belongings were either buried in the grave or placed in the spirit house to accompany the person on the journey after death. Rifles, pots, knives, blankets, and handmade fish spears were items commonly placed inside the houses. Stampeders cleaned out most of the spirit houses at Tagish before the North West Mounted Police learned what was happening and put a stop to it.

The very name Marsh Lake, once known as Mud Lake, implies a body of water surrounded by swamp. The first point of land you encounter as you enter the lake would sustain such an image. Beyond it, however, there is nothing muddy or marsh-like about it. The name Marsh was actually bestowed by Schwatka, who named it after a Yale University palaeontologist Professor Othniel Charles Marsh—founder of the National Academy of Sciences.

The First Nations name for the lake, Takwadada—where sand washes up on shore—is much more fitting. Sandy Point is, thus, appropriately named. Approximately half way up Marsh Lake, it is the kind of sun-soaked jewel one expects to find in Hawaii or Jamaica, not in the Land of Ice and Snow. It juts about one hundred yards into the lake and is as wide as it is long. The white sand is piled high and continues to run in a wide sweeping arc along the bay north of the point. Seagulls stroll casually in the waves. Ducks float serenely just off the shore, gently rocked to inactivity by the lazy swells.

Lined up along the leeward side of the point are white, red, and yellow canoes. Sprawled on the beach are competitors who obviously believe their tan is more important than their final positioning.

John and I pull in for lunch, as do Brendan and Anne. Two Skagway paddlers, Steve Jaklitsch and Jeremy Schader, turn up at about the same time. A couple of canoes pull out as we arrive. Another team is also here, but they don't hear us arrive over their snoring. For myself, it is a welcome opportunity to warm up. Sometime last night I became extremely cold because the bottom of my sleeping bag was wet. There was a pinhole leak in the waterproof bag in which it was packed. This morning I awoke congested, coughing, and could barely breathe. To top it off, my lower back has tightened up to the point that it almost forces me to walk doubled over. John is his usual sympathetic self. 'Hunchback' we call him now," he says, mimicking my posture.

John needs the break to rest his eyes. There are rules against picking up historical artifacts, but none against leaving some. John lost his sunglasses over the side of the canoe earlier this morning and has been battling the sun reflecting off the lake surface.

Two paddlers arrive with a dilemma that harkens back to the gold rush.

They aren't sure they will be able to continue once they reach Whitehorse. "We thought we would be finished this thing in four or five days. Now we realize it's going to take longer than that. But he," one points at his buddy, "has to be back for work." In the end, they decide the race should get priority as the experience of a lifetime and that "he" can probably get another job. It's the kind of decision that was made a century ago by stampeders who already knew they were too late to cash in on the gold in the Klondike, but who were determined to press on despite the cost.

Thomas Tetz and Hans Gatt also reach a conclusion on Sandy Point. Hans has pulled the tendons in his wrist, making it impossible for him to grasp the paddle. The two decide they will withdraw from the race in Whitehorse. "There's no sense to keep on going with that wrist. I need that wrist after the race, too. I can't afford to bugger it up for the rest of the summer."

While we aren't exactly sprinting, John and I are a day ahead of our original schedule—and almost that far behind the leaders. There are twenty teams ahead of us, or travelling with us, on Marsh Lake. Several more are in Whitehorse, resting. A dozen are on Tagish Lake, and two are still in Bennett.

As we approach the north end of Marsh Lake, passing through McLintock Bay, we take a break to enjoy a treat delivered to us by Brendan and Anne. They crossed the lake to Lakeview Marina, a tourist resort on the east shore, and picked up bacon, tomato, and lettuce sandwiches for us.

Brendan also tosses us a couple of beers and lets us in on a journalistic secret: "We have a little beer supply, so we think it's prudent to pull up to a canoe and sort of say, 'Would you like a beer?' So you hand them a beer and, you know, they are your best friends. You chat for maybe twenty minutes. They paddle and we switch off the motor. We've started getting this other good stuff, and to know people. I'm getting the feeling we have a real documentary."

The east shore has a familiar feeling. The Firth family has had a summer cottage there for almost forty years. Both John and I spent many a summer night water-skiing on this bay (lake water is warmest after the sun goes down) and occasionally playing a four-hole golf course set up on the massive beach that appears in spring when the ice melts. (There wasn't much in the way of fairways or greens, but you certainly learnt how to play your sand wedge.)

In April each year, Dawn, Erin, and I ski across the bay to indulge ourselves in the cacophony of geese, swans, ducks, eagles, and hawks that gather here on their migration north each year. This is one of the most accessible areas for viewing the migration of nearly any bird on earth. The open lead in the ice is packed with water fowl. Thousands of them. Trumpeter Swans, Tundra Swans, three varieties of geese, twenty-two species of ducks. According to the information available at the public viewing platform, called Swan Haven, 10 per cent of all migrating birds in North America stop here for a day or two to feed as they wait for open water further north so they can move on to their summer nesting areas in the high Arctic. The honking, trumpeting, cackling, and quacking can be heard the entire length of the lake.

It is this annual bird assembly that made this a central gathering point for the First Nations. They had a fishing camp set up on the point closest to the river mouth, where they also took advantage of the opportunity to hunt waterfowl—a welcome change after a winter's existence sustained by dried meats and fish from the previous summer harvest.

My father told stories of lying on sand bars in the 1940s and '50s, watching squadrons of geese and whooping cranes fly overhead in multiple layers—the lowest were just above the tops of the trees, and the highest just below the clouds. The flocks on the ground were so dense one could feel body heat radiating from the birds simply by passing close to them. "You couldn't sleep at night for the noise of them," he said. "You don't see cranes like that anymore. Or the geese. There's not the [same] number of those any more. The skies were black with them." That would be ideal for Dawn's sister

Cheryl, who stands six foot two and was once described by a boyfriend as being "tall enough to hunt geese with a rake."

At this time of year, there is only the wind, the waves, and an occasional gull to listen to. For the competitors, paddling gets monotonous and the mind starts to wander. "You have a lot of time out there to think about things," said Solomon Carriere, a twenty-year veteran of marathon canoeing. "If you don't sing—and you've run out of stories and jokes—you just think about anything. You've got to keep your mind active. If your mind isn't active, your body starts to get inactive too."

"If I ever do anything like this again, I'm going to memorize the words to a thousand songs," says Chris Guenther, "so I can sing to keep myself awake. I just don't know enough lyrics."

Michael Yee is one of those people who thinks in terms of pure numbers. He counts the number of strokes per minute, and the number of hours he is paddling. Wielding graphite paddles, at approximately eight ounces each, and making forty thousand strokes daily, he calculates he is lifting just over twenty tons of paddle each and every day. "And these are light paddles. I can't imagine what the people using wooden paddles must feel like," he says.

We are using wooden paddles and, while we have no idea how much we're lifting, I can tell him how we are feeling: pretty tired after seventy miles of lake paddling on short rations and little sleep. He continues on into the river, working on one more calculation: "These paddles can move a lot more water than the old wooden ones."

Shortly after leaving the lake we come upon the first dam ever built on the Yukon River. It is a control dam, originally constructed in 1912, designed to hold back water in the early spring and then release it to break up the river ice further down stream. The purpose was to open a channel for the riverboats a month earlier than nature itself would allow. The dam has been rebuilt several times over the years, with the latest version completed in the 1980s. It was most recently used to control water levels between Marsh Lake and the Whitehorse Dam, which is the only other dam ever built on the Yukon River. A lock was installed to enable boats to get around it.

Ahead of us, Wendy Cairns and Chris Guenther shoot through one of the gates to the other side. The change in water level is only about three feet and, provided you don't collide with the structure itself, it can be done. But the gates aren't much wider than the canoe itself—one small miscue and you could end up impaling yourself on one of the bolts that stick out of the

*Through Miles Canyon*

PHOTO COURTESY OF: YUKON NEWS

columns. John decides he doesn't want to take the chance, so we use the lock.

In the high clay cliffs that line almost every corner of the river we see thousands of holes swarming with swallows that congregate in great clouds over the water. It is local wisdom that the day the swallows leave each year is the day that summer ends and fall begins. We sneak up on a beaver swimming across the river and are almost alongside if before it realizes we're there and dives after sending up a geyser of water with its tail.

We reach another Canyon City—not to be confused with Canyon City on the Chilkoot Trail. This is where the stampeders stopped a mile or so before reaching Miles Canyon. Here they could elect either to hire a river guide and gamble with the rapids or take one of two tramlines that ran around the dangerous parts of the river. Remnants of several buildings, tent frames, and a fox farm can still be seen among the trees; a few of the logs laid for the tramlines can be seen along the walking trails. In 1900, when the White Pass Railway reached the Yukon River downstream from the rapids, there was no longer a need for the tramlines or the city and both were abandoned.

Each summer, archaeologists can be found digging in the earth, seeking the past that is buried here. They have pulled poker chips, coins, foil wrappers from champagne corks, and even a small gold nugget from the dirt. Below that layer of history they discovered evidence of an First Nations fish camp.

Everyone is putting out a little extra to make sure they get to Whitehorse. Some paddlers are starting to get brain cramps. Suzanne Crocker and Gerard Parsons doze off and their canoe drifts for a short period, spinning lazily in the centre of the wide channel. They awaken, disoriented, and paddle upstream for a few minutes before they realize their mistake.

Ron Theunissen almost passes out while paddling. "I almost tipped the canoe over. That's when I said, 'Okay. It's time to stop.' If we"—he and partner Eric Carmicheal—"took our time, it would probably be pretty casual. But we're trying to do as well as we can and it's pretty demanding." Ron keeps checking his watch, thinking there's something about today he should remember but he can't quite put his finger on it. It isn't until after they arrive in Whitehorse that it registers. It's his birthday.

As we paddle through the swirling water of Miles Canyon, I look up at the great black pillars I've seen so many times in the past. I see the White River Ash. I also see an orange algae that someone once told me could only be found in places where the air is free from pollution. I can't help but think of Alvin Hamilton as he must have been in his political heyday, with his cigar and his dreams for this land. Growing all by itself on a rock abutment near the water's edge, midway down the canyon, there is a solitary pine tree. I see it as one of those wonders of nature—how did a tree start growing here, and how on earth has it survived? Hamilton saw pine trees as an alternate fuel source for the North (the Japanese used pine root pitch as aviation fuel during the Second World War) just as he saw this magnificent canyon as a cornerstone of northern hydro development. In many ways Hamilton is symbolic of the human need to control the environment, but all too often without regard for the consequences that such control will effect. Sandy Point. Tagish. McClintock Bay. Carcross. Bennett. Had his dreams been realized, "Who could have known they would be gone so quickly?"

"We did a lot of stuff that we didn't realize would have an impact at some point in the future," laments Cal Waddington. "Nobody was out to kill the river, that's for sure. Nobody understood what the impact might be. It was just the way things were done. They didn't even conceive of it."

Approaching the landing on Schwatka Lake, where Jeff Brady and checkpoint volunteer Jean Jobagy await us, we can hear Sharon, Logan, and Keiran cheering for us. Behind them, I see Dawn and her sister Mary Mae. On the road that follows the shoreline of the lake, Erin is keeping pace with us on her mountain bike. It sure is nice to see familiar faces again.

"Welcome to Whitehorse," says Jeff, clocking us in at 10:05 PM, "We've had sixteen canoes in the past four hours. You are in thirty-sixth place. Robert Service campground is hopping tonight."

I struggle out of the canoe, trying my best to look like the crick in my back is a natural part of pulling in the canoe. Of course, when I stop pulling the canoe and still can't stand up straight, everyone laughs.

I can relate to John McConnochie and Phil Moritz, who arrived in first place almost thirty-six hours earlier and crawled out of their canoe for the first time since leaving Bennett. "We haven't slept since we left Sheep Camp. Let's see if we can walk," suggests McConnochie, as his legs wobbled helplessly under him before his wife hugged him, almost as much to keep him from falling as to express her delight at seeing him again.

Jean informs us we can leave at 12:19 tomorrow afternoon—our twelve-hour mandatory stop, plus the time adjustment from the staggered start in Dyea. We head off to another modern advantage we have over the stampeders— a night in our own beds.

*SS* Casca Burns

# CHAPTER TWELVE

## The Shipyards
Whitehorse, Yukon

The best thing that happened during the last voyage of the SS *Klondike* in June 1966 was something that didn't happen. It didn't rain. If it had, there would have been soapsuds from one end of Whitehorse to the other.

My father often took us to see the *Klondike* as it inched its way down First Avenue, towed by four TD 24 Caterpillar tractors. It's not every day that a 1,042-ton, 247-foot long ship can be seen travelling down a city street. The stacks and masts towered above the buildings on either side of it. The hull, which not only blocked automobile traffic but prevented pedestrians from using the sidewalks, was cradled on four massive steel skid plates. There was little room for error: six or seven inches on either side. A slight pull in the wrong direction and the hull would open a new entrance for Taylor and Drury's grocery store. The Cats rode over huge truck tires, placed under their treads to prevent them from tearing up the pavement as they crept along. The skid plates slid along the pavement, lubricated by eight tons of Palmolive soap flakes. High above it all, fluttering in the wind, was the flag of the British Yukon Navigation company (BYN) and, at the stern, the Canadian Ensign. It took five weeks for the *Klondike* to travel the mile from the White Pass shipyards to South Whiskey Flats, where the largest of the 250-plus sternwheelers built to sail on the Yukon River was ultimately restored and designated a National Historical Site.

೧೧

The *Klondike*, actually the *Klondike II*, was built in 1936 to haul ore up the Yukon River from Stewart Island. Then it was converted to a supply barge to assist in the construction of highways—a most profitable time for the BYN. The irony is that it was the road construction that ultimately killed the need for ships whatsoever. By 1950, there were merely a handful of steamships still operating and they grew fewer in number each year. Finally only *Klondike II* remained afloat. Canadian Pacific Airlines purchased her and retrofitted her as a luxury cruise ship for tourists in 1954. The inaugural season of 1955 was sold out, but low water and labour union problems forced cancellation of the first two trips. When she was pulled from the water at the end of the summer, it was for the last time.

The land journey of the *Klondike* in 1966 was the last time a steamship was to ever leave the shipyards. The only two ships remaining in the yard, the *Whitehorse* (built in 1901 and universally acknowledged as the queen of the fleet) and the *Casca III*, both burned to the ground on 21 June 1974. When the blaze was finally doused, only a forward deck hatch from the *Casca III* survived untouched, salvaged from near the smoldering ruins.

The loss of the *Casca III* was a personal blow to my mother. It was the first ship she ever boarded on the Yukon River when she arrived in 1937 as a newly-married bride. Prepared to spend the entire journey in romantic bliss, the honeymoon couple was surprised to find the stateroom had bunk beds. "We had a good laugh about it."

The overwhelming sense of loss was no different for others of her generation. Many still dreamed of the glory days of the steamships and pined for them. I would often see an oldtimer or two standing silently by the hulks, wistfully gazing at them, a veil of emotion and time between themselves and reality. The inferno, set accidentally by transients who camped overnight in one of the hulls, ripped away that veil. It took from them the tangible evidence of their past and left them with little more than fading memories to hold the story together. "I've always thought of Dawson City as the centre of the gold rush," lamented the late historian Roy Minter, "and of Whitehorse as the centre of transportation during those days. These boats were such an integral part of all that. Today they're gone and the Yukon just lost a little of its soul."

According to lifetime Yukoner Charlie Taylor, the 1974 blaze wasn't the first fire in Whitehorse to be fueled by sternwheelers. While church bells pealed and the telegraph operator stood on top of the post office playing "Ode to Joy" on his trumpet, an abandoned river steamer was used to fuel the bonfire around which the entire population of Whitehorse celebrated the end of the Great War on 11 November 1918.

The *Keno* was the final steamship to travel the Yukon River. On 25 August 1960 it was launched from the Whitehorse shipyards and headed downstream to be dry-docked in Dawson City and restored as a museum. She was the only steamship I ever saw in action. We watched as the *Keno* chugged and huffed herself upstream, great billowing clouds of steam and smoke issuing from the tall stacks with each turn of the wheel. The orange buckets slapped relentlessly into the green water, churning it up and hurling a fine mist into the air. The white, stately superstructure and pilot house shuddered with the vibration of the engines as they strained against the river current. Finally she stopped, momentarily frozen in place, and then, with a deep-toned baying from the whistle, turned slowly in the current and rapidly disappeared downstream.

Lawyer Jack Gibben, who practiced in Whitehorse in the 1940s and '50s, used to take his teenage daughter, Barb, and climb to the tops of the hills over-looking the river to watch the boats. "My father had a real sense of history," Barb reflects. "Of course, at that age I didn't appreciate it. Didn't everybody have rapids and steamboats in their backyards? 'Remember this,' he would say, 'it's history. One day this will all be gone.' I did a lot of things with my father, but that stands out as my favourite."

The sternwheelers were the predominant feature of the river and town until the 1950s. Then, as the influence of river commerce began to diminish, the waterfront lost relevance for the residents. Becoming the territorial seat of government in 1953 created a new focus for the community that, until then, had been a company town virtually owned and operated by the White Pass and Yukon Route.

Squatters moved into the waterfront area, using the wood from many of the old sternwheelers to build themselves tar paper shacks and blockhouses with corrugated tin roofs. Old bungalows, hotels, stores, and quonset huts at the end of their usefulness were dragged into the shipyards and given a new lease on life, forming all or a portion of someone's home. The groupings of residences along the waterfront even acquired names—Moccasin Flats, Whiskey Flats, Sleepy Hollow, and the Shipyards. In the 1960s, the Yukon Government began a program to clear out Whiskey Flats and Moccasin Flats so that a government administration building could be built.

They started by removing massive clumps of willows surrounding the squatters. The result was a view of a collection of shacks and old vehicles clustered along the water's edge, surrounded by a semi-circle of outhouses that had been constructed in the privacy of the trees. I think the government wanted to embarrass the residents into leaving by exposing their toilets to public scrutiny, but it didn't work. The residents were used to strolling naked from their houses to the outhouses, and the lack of tree coverage didn't affect their lack of modesty in any way. Eventually, the government had to evict the squatters to clear the sites for development.

After the steamships stopped running, the river became little more than a part of the landscape for a brief period, but the soul of a culture cannot stay hidden for long. Gradually, its presence began to reassert itself into the community's consciousness in a different way. After a lifetime of living beside the river, my sister Nancy found herself listening to, rather than watching, the swirling current. "I've always had a lot of respect for the river and have always had a fascination with it, but I'd forgotten that I hadn't heard the river for a long time even though I lived right beside it," she notes.

The flow is like a record constantly skipping on the same note. The river has one mood, one sensation, no variation. Visually, the river changes—it has no sense of continuity. Riverbanks erode. Islands in the river come and go. But to close your eyes and just listen: there is always that sustained feeling of one living note, one that just repeats itself over and over again.

For Nancy, the sound of the river gives her a sense of peaceful emptiness without clamour or intrigue, and recalls images of her uncluttered childhood—learning how to swim in the Klondike River, drinking crystal clear water from creeks so cold that it hurt your teeth, and the musky odour of high bush cranberries.

Yvonne Harris and her husband Paul walk by the river daily, using it as a remedy to relieve workplace stress. "I find I get a real sense of peace. You can look at what's around you in terms of the beauty, so I'm really entranced by being on or around the water," she says.

Most journeys down the Yukon begin near "the ways," the ramps on which the ships were pulled from and lowered into the river. They are now rotten and overgrown by long grass and willow thickets. Much of the rest of the waterfront is still blocked off by rows of grey pilings—all that is left of the massive wharf system that stretched for over a mile along the waterfront. The docks were eight hundred feet wide and contained massive warehouses and three sets of railway tracks. Once the ships stopped operating, the docks served as a boarding ramp for commercial airlines that used the river as a runway—until the Canadian Air Force decommissioned its air base in the early 1960s. After that, the dock's primary purpose was to provide a hiding place for the partying and sexual intimacy of Whitehorse teenagers on the riverbank underneath.

Politicians love the waterfront for its picturesque setting. New Democrat Audrey McLaughlin started her journey to become the first woman elected leader of a federal political party by standing in Rotary Peace Park with a champagne glass full of Yukon River water—using one of North America's cleanest rivers to address the issue of water pollution. Canadian Prime Minister Joe Clark campaigned on the lawn in front of the *Klondike* in 1979. So did another Prime Minister—John Turner—in 1984, who shocked me with an impressive demonstration of the kind of memory a politican must have. He paused in the middle of the crowd to shake my hand and ask me, "How's your mother doing?" I had no idea he even knew my mother, but he had met her in the early 1970s when he was Canada's Finance Minister, and his grandfather knew T. A. Firth from the Klondike Gold Rush.

For twenty-one-year-old John Dines, in August 1964, the first inkling of where his river journey was going to take him came just as he prepared to launch in the early hours of a misty morning. The trip was just a lark. He was bored with his life as a heavy equipment operator: sleep, eat, work. Life in the road camps was profitable, but dull. He decided to go to Dawson City. The only question for him was how he would make the trip. He went to the shopping mall of the North—the Sears catalogue (for more up-scale families, the mall of choice was the Eatons catalogue)—and bought himself a six-foot army khaki inflatable rubber raft, powered by three-foot aluminum oars. By the time he loaded the raft with his food and gear, he had only enough room to sit in the stern and place his legs on the top of the gunwales on each side. Just as he was ready to push off, he spotted an Indian woman watching him from near the bow of the *Whitehorse*.

"Got a smoke?" she asked.

"Sorry. I just quit smoking cigarettes," replied Dines.

"Got a smoke?" she repeated. He handed her a cigarillo—a new product in the marketplace—and lit one up himself. They stood there, puffing away in silence for a moment. "I'm Mrs. M. C. Neilson," said the woman. "I'm the grand daughter of Skookum Jim."

He glanced up at the hull towering above them. After a decade out of the water, the deck planking had started to suffer from dry rot, but the prow stood resolute and proud. Even as the current pulled him downstream, he couldn't help looking back until he turned a corner and couldn't see either the boat or the woman. "Why she was down there at that time in the morning, I don't know. But I remember feeling that this wasn't a river trip *just to do a river trip* any more. It was something that I had to do to understand who I was and where I came from."

It was close to the same spot that my brother Tom, my father, and his friend Clarence "Clary" Craig launched the *Delia* in July 1970. The *Delia* was

*Moving the SS* Klondike

thirty-two feet long and four feet wide at the beam—too narrow for the lakes, but just the right width to exit the garage doors after it had been built in our basement. Painted white with red trim, it was powered by twin 35-horsepower motors. Dad was "chief steward" because there wasn't a fish he couldn't cook and because he had the best portable bar in the Yukon. Clary was "first mate" because he always carried a pair of pliers in his pocket and, when combined with a roll of haywire, there wasn't anything he couldn't fix with them. They rode in green lawn chairs side by side, each in the middle of the boat, while "captain" Tom Firth manned the wheel. For Tom, it was the first of many trips down the river. For Clary Craig and my father, it was the final voyage of life-times spent living beside and travelling on it. The Yukon Flotilla, a Canadian Centennial Celebration event, also pushed off from the shipyard on 6 August 1967. There were fifty-four boats in total—rubber rafts, canoes, kayaks, river-boats, power boats, skiffs, car toppers, cabin cruisers, and four amphicars—carrying 153 people and nine dogs. The participants were from England, Oklahoma, Oregon, New Jersey, Utah, Ohio, Quebec, Alaska, Washington,

Ontario, Wyoming, Michigan, New York, California, Wisconsin, British Columbia, Idaho, and the Yukon. It was a joint venture of the Yukon Government's Department of Travel Publicity and the Alaska Travel Division, organized to generate international interest in travelling the Yukon River as a wilderness adventure holiday and "to re-live the easy part of the actual trail of '98 to the Klondike." Since the *Klondike II* had been pulled from the water in 1955, traffic on the river consisted of people who lived along its shores and the occasional traveler like John Dines.

"For years we never saw a soul here," said Rudy Burien, a fifty-year resident of Stewart Island, eighty miles upstream from Dawson City. "Just after the boats quit we were lucky to have three or four people passing through here. We got used to it."

Flotilla chairman Derek Irons provided each boat with a forty-page logbook which contained the historical gold-rush-roots of the event, points of interest along the way, and camping spots scheduled for each day. Because of the variety of craft, powerboats had a certain number of hours each day during which time they were to drift to allow the slower vessels to catch up, to "facilitate the observances of scenery and wildlife, and to allow talk between the boats." Each morning powered craft would depart first, followed by unpowered craft.

Every night, portable outhouses parked on gravel bars marked the end of the day's travel. Evening entertainment was sandbar dancing or campfire sing-alongs.

The flotilla was one of the first major early successes of the Yukon's fledgling tourism industry—the goal of revitalizing river traffic on the Yukon was achieved. Adventurers from around the globe have turned the retracing of gold rush history into a prosperous summer industry. On any given day, seventy-five to one hundred boats can be found on the Yukon River between Whitehorse and Dawson City.

Former Royal North West Mounted Policeman G. I. Cameron, who spent seventy years of his life on the Yukon River, was thrilled to see the increase in traffic. "The steamboats were the lifeblood of the river," he said. "When they stopped, a whole way of life ended. . . . There's not many people living on the river—the small communities are gone—but to go down the river today you see kayaks and small canoes and people, dozens of them, going down. They're finding the river again."

*SS* Casca *and* Whitehorse *docked at Whitehorse. White Pass Hotel seen above.*

# CHAPTER THIRTEEN

## Whitehorse, Yukon
Friday, 20 June 1997

W h i l e  m y  f a m i l y  roots and heart are in Dawson City, it is here that most of my life's memories are grounded. Whitehorse owes its existence to the river, and its location to the railroad. The stampeders all stopped on the east bank, about where Whitehorse General Hospital sits today, and established a tent city. When the railroad arrived, White Pass figured it was cheaper to move the town than build a bridge—so that's what they did.

Until the early 1960s, the streets of Whitehorse were composed of fine silt and volcanic ash. When it was dry, a gritty dust coated everything—including the interior of Mrs. Hunter's home. The clouds were so thick on Main Street that cars drove with their headlights on so other drivers would know they were there. When it rained, cars sank up to their hubcaps in the mud and bogged down in the middle of the street.

The Whitehorse Inn stood on the busiest intersection in town. Ownership changed hands so frequently in the backroom poker games that employees never knew which player they might be working for tomorrow. I once watched the owner of a drilling company lose one hundred thousand dollars in a single hand of cards. He returned the next night and won it back. In May 1966, a miner staying in the hotel decided to prove, after drinking more than his fair share of a bottle, that signal flares don't start fires—so he shot one out his window and burned down the *Whitehorse Star*, the same local newspaper that hired me out of high school for my first job in the real world.

Down the street was the White Pass Hotel. It burned to the ground on Christmas Day, 1961, when it was fifty degrees below zero. An exhaust fan in the kitchen area shorted out and ignited a fire that, once it got into the walls, which were insulated with sawdust, was out-of-control from the beginning. The rubber overcoats worn by the firemen watering down the fire were covered by sheets of ice in back and liquefying rubber in front because of the heat of the flames. Fireman Ed Schiffkorn had his wife cut him out of the jacket because they couldn't locate the opening where the buttons were supposed to be. The blaze knocked out electrical power all over the city. Mom cooked the Christmas turkey in a wood stove in the back of my dad's office on Main Street, and the rest of the meal on a propane camp stove. After going down to watch the fire, we returned to the relative warmth of our living room. Fully dressed, we huddled inside sleeping bags in front of our fireplace and ate Christmas dinner by the light of coal-oil lamps.

The river steamer crews who stayed at the White Pass Hotel prophetically nicknamed it "Hotel Disaster"—possibly because the owner, a Mrs. Viaux, used to clean her chimneys by firing a rifle up them. More likely, it was because that is where crews would stay after their ships sank or were damaged on the river.

Whitehorse became a city in 1950, and in 1953 the Yukon Government moved the capital from Dawson City to Whitehorse. Bitter feelings between Dawson and Whitehorse residents linger to this day. The reasons for the change were easily apparent—Dawson was too isolated, and Whitehorse, because of the Alaska Highway and its larger airport, was more accessible. But Dawson residents, who consisted mainly of government employees, didn't want to leave. Dawson was their home. The Canadian Government started to apply political pressure. They delayed the construction of a highway to Dawson and held up the stringing of telephone lines, further isolating the community.

Then the government struck a deal with some key employees, wherein it offered to purchase their homes in Dawson City and build them new ones in Whitehorse. With the employees' leadership on board, opposition to the move collapsed. It was hard enough on the government workers, who had their moves subsidized, but it was a terrible burden for the private businessmen who also pulled up stakes and moved, at their own expense, in order to survive. Mom remembered being in tears almost daily at that time: "They forced people to move from Dawson City. We had to go where the population went."

ဟဟ

It may be my own bed and it may be my home town, but I'm still in the rhythm of the race. I am only able to sleep for four hours before my eyes pop open. And that is it. The rest of the time I spend reorganizing our food, drying out gear, and doing laundry. By now I realize we have over-planned. We have way too much food. There are items that we will never get around to eating, and foods we have differing opinions about. For instance, John will eat power bars, but I would prefer to starve to death before eating another, so I happily discard a pile of them.

For John, the publishing business never sleeps—and it won't let him sleep either. His rest is cut short by an urgent phone call. For some reason, a shipment of books wasn't delivered to retail outlets. John drags himself out of bed and spends the remainder of his rest time delivering boxes.

Few paddlers sleep well during their twelve-hour mandatory stop. Bill Stewart sacrifices sleep as he figures out how to take care of his right hand. He has a sore wrist that is hampering his grip on the paddle. Unless he can find a solution, he may have to pack it in, a solution he "would have felt terrible about because [he] felt this commitment to Steven." His wife, Rosemary, suggests he try some plastic casts leftover from wrist problems she had a few years earlier. One of the casts, one that had been molded to her wrist when it was badly swollen, just fits. "So I was able to put this plastic cast on and duct tape my hand up so that it was basically a rigid post, and that allowed me to continue. That and Ibuprofen," Bill adds.

Wendy Cairns and Chris Guenther can't sleep because there's some road construction going on and the noise keeps them awake. They walk a mile to town to find a hotel room—in the middle of the night during peak tourist season. Sometime after midnight, Chris finally contacts a friend who cuts her night short to take them in. "It was nice," Chris notes, "but we really didn't get enough sleep—about four or five hours."

Geo Ljljenskjold hitchhikes to Skagway to pick up his van, left there at the start of the race. He drives it back to Whitehorse and arrives just in time to jump back in the canoe.

Jeff Brady and Buckwheat aren't getting much sleep either. In addition to meeting each team as they arrive, they've finally determined who used the two-bladed paddles on Bennett Lake. Not one but two teams tied their canoe paddles together to resemble kayak paddles. Roman Dial and Vern Tejas concede the experiment probably slowed them down, but Brady decides to slow them down a little more by penalizing them one hour. Todd Boonstra and Adam Verrier, also known as "The Zig Zag Team," due to their inexperience in canoes, also have an hour added to their time.

Cynde Adams and Larry Gullingsrud are rewarded for their rescue of Ken Brewer and Jimmy Smith in Windy Arm. "We're going to give Cynde and Larry back the five hours they lost due to the rescue," says Brady.

Teams have been leaving Whitehorse for two days before John and I push

*Leaving Whitehorse, 1997. Stephen Jull and Bill Stewart.*

PHOTO COURTESY OF: WHITEHORSE STAR

off in the late afternoon. John McConnochie and Phil Moritz cling to the lead and feel strong but are concerned about the teams trailing them. Phil says, "It's still a very long race. There's some very talented athletes still out there so we by no means feel we're home free. We have a lot of good people behind us and we respect that."

Jim Lokken and Art Ward leave two hours behind the leaders, followed in rapid-fire order by Boonstra–Verrier and Steve Reifenstuhl–Mark Gorman.

There are two routes to consider when launching from the Robert Service Campground. After passing by two small islands, John and I take a quick left into a shallow channel that ultimately joins with the main current. We paddle past the SS *Klondike*, under the Robert Service Bridge, along the waterfront, and then through the shadow of a miniature steamship replica sitting on dry land in an industrial yard at the north end of the city. This is the SS *Anna Maria*, one of the Yukon's most controversial efforts to revive the phantoms of the steamships—with a fate oddly reminiscent of that of the *Klondike* under

Canadian Pacific Airlines. The other choice, which is to not make the left turn, has its risks. It carries you directly into a small set of man-made rapids, built as a training area for kayakers. The rapids aren't big, but they can be hazardous since they're difficult to see until you are virtually on top of them.

Joe Jack and Mike Winstanley felt pretty good when they set off from Whitehorse. They passed twenty-three teams on the southern lakes and were buoyed with confidence. "I told Mike I'd be pretty disappointed if we finished lower than tenth," Jack said, "but one must never get over confident on the river." They didn't make the left turn out of the campground and headed directly towards the rapids. "I just forgot they were there. I saw the fast water. Then, as we got into the fast water I saw this pile of rocks just ahead. I realized where we were and I knew we were heading the wrong way."

They skimmed past the rocks but the canoe turned slightly broadside to the current. Then the bow caught the edge of the back eddy. "It turned us over. Popped us both out of the spray deck and held me under. I remember seeing the canoe going back up. Seeing the daylight and the sky. My lungs felt like they were full of water. It just happened so fast. Something told me to stay calm. To not panic. I started back up to the surface. I remembered to breathe out, not in."

The two men were in the back eddy, but their canoe was still in the river current heading downstream. They gave chase, but the cold water started to get to Jack. His arms refused to operate. Only his life jacket enabled him to keep his head above water. Eventually his feet dragged over a gravel bar and he struggled out of the water. Further down the same bar Winstanley dragged the canoe to shore.

"How does everything look?" Jack asked. "What did we lose?" The night air was quite warm, he had dry clothes, and the chill soon started to fade.

"Nothing. Everything was inside the skirt and we only have about three inches of water in the bottom."

The only casualties were Jack's paddle (which they later found), his baseball cap, Winstanley's sunglasses, some bannock, and a bag of moose meat.

"You know," Winstanley suggested. "If we call it quits here I wouldn't take it as an insult or offensive to myself—it would be quite understandable."

"No," replied Jack. "We're not quitting just because we got a little wet. Let's get organized and get off this island before the people of Whitehorse wake up and find the chief of the Kwanlin Dun stranded on an island in the middle of the city."

The river's current is powerful and, once in its cold grasp, trying to fight it is an almost certain death sentence. It is knowing how to take advantage of the opportunities the river offers, to use the power of the current rather than exhaust yourself by fighting it, that determines who wins or loses.

Nancy Huston's son Wesley informed her one afternoon that he dived into the river earlier that day. "My heart froze. I realized he had just done what we would never have considered doing. I asked him, 'Were you scared? Did you panic?'"

Wesley looked at her over his milk shake with a quizzical look on his face. "Mom, you told me never to panic in water, so I didn't. I was scared when I tried swimming back and couldn't go anywhere. So I just swam harder across the current and made it."

Not everyone is as lucky. Helicopter pilot Peter Kelly described a search he conducted for a missing man at the request of the Royal Canadian Mounted Police one summer. "They believed he had fallen into the river, so we flew just above the water looking for the body. He had on those running shoes that pump up and most people, when they drown, float head down in the river anyway. We spotted the bottom of his running shoes floating along just before Lake Laberge and he was underneath them."

When Rosemary Matt and Paul Sargent, paddling at the tail end of the race, arrive in Carmacks, they learn that a baby has been swept away and that several boats are searching downstream. For the next two days, every boat they meet asks them if they have seen the body. "I was very distressed," says Rosemary. "Every time I went to sleep for a while after that, I would dream about babies floating in the river."

Dad, as a teller in the Bank of Commerce in Dawson City in the early 1930s, watched one hot summer afternoon as crew members dived into the Yukon River from the highest level of the steamships. He was envious. It was a typical sweltering Dawson summer day and it looked like an enjoyable way to stay cool, until one crew member dove under the water and never resurfaced. The body was never found, he told us, and nobody ever understood exactly what happened. But with a current in excess of ten knots, it was unlikely that anyone would ever find out.

"The river and land can be so calm, peaceful, and beautiful," says Jack, "but any time you become disadvantaged, it can turn into a killer. This time around, when Mike and I dumped, the river was good to us."

## The M.V. Anna Maria
## 1987–1996

It was, many believe, Yukon tourism's greatest disaster. To Gus Karpes, it was a dream derailed by government bureaucracy. The lanky river guide, with his white lambchop sideburns and French fisherman's cap, conceived the idea over a period of ten years while running Yukon River tours in the *Delia*—purchased in 1974 from my brother Tom. One of the first lessons he and partner Irene Pugh taught their clients was how to wipe their bum in the bush: "If you've never done it before, one can be quite intimidated by the whole thing." It made Gus realize that "you can't sell the river [to the tourists] unless it has flush toilets. You're looking at that age group that can't cope with camping. It's impossible to sell the Yukon to that age group of forty and beyond without having comforts somewhere along the line."

At the time, Gus took a dozen passengers on each trip and camped in tents on property he leased at places like Hootalinqua and Fort Selkirk. He asked his passengers, "If you had an opportunity to ride on one of the sternwheelers, would you?" By 1986, not only had enough of them responded with an enthusiastic "Yes!"—thirty of them agreed to be financially involved. So Gus and Irene started designing one. "I built my first boat at age seventeen," said Gus. "And I worked on the last steam tug on the Pacific Coast in the engine room, so I had a pretty good knowledge of boats."

The original plan was to build a boat twenty feet wide and sixty feet long, weighing approximately eighty tons. It would have berths on board for twelve and would be rated for twenty-eight "deck passengers," who would sleep on shore in tents. The vessel was to stand twenty-one feet tall, adorned with a smokestack painted in the colours of the British Yukon Navigation Company. The stack was purely cosmetic. They wouldn't even pump fake smoke out of it and it was to be mounted on hinges that enabled them to lower it, allowing them clearance under the Carmacks bridge. Fully loaded, it would draw just under three feet of water, about the same as the original sternwheelers.

In the first few years, operation of the boat would be restricted to the Whitehorse–Dawson run, but eventually it would extend into Alaska. This was possible because of an 1898 amendment to the Jones Act—the treaty that governs which carriers can pick up or discharge passengers while travelling between Canada and the United States. The act was waived in the Yukon River watershed in 1898 because of the cross-border sternwheeler traffic and will remain waived "until such time as the railway to Alaska is completed."

*SS* Anna Maria

PHOTO COURTESY OF: GUS KARPES

Gus says:

The boat was meant to fulfill everything the old boats did. It was supposed to be a trading vessel. We had a store and restaurant on board. Canoeists could come on board, have a beer, a meal, and go back to their tent. If they wanted to quit their trip, we could throw their canoe on top of the wheelhouse. We had a post office on board with our own cancellation stamp. We sold stamps. We carried food supplies and freight for river residents. On one trip we took a new fridge into Stewart Island. We would pull into Fort Selkirk and there would be a bunch of kids wanting ice cream. That was the whole purpose of it.

Investors' funds and bank loans in hand, the project was handed over to a contractor, Western Aluminum Products, in Sydney, BC, in 1988. It was the only aluminum sleep-on-board passenger boat ever built in Canada. It was during the construction stage that the dream started to fall apart.

"It's been long enough now," said Gus in October 2000—in the only interview about the *Anna Maria* he had granted since 1989—"that I can talk about it without getting mad and raging at the bureaucrats. Once we had the hull laid, because it was the first aluminum boat of its type in Canada, every coast guard from Halifax to Tofino got involved."

During the Falklands War, an Argentinian missle struck an aluminum-hulled British ship. The heat was so intense that the metal itself burned. "Therefore," explained Gus, "all aluminum boats were considered flammable." Coast guard officials added extra fire proofing to the boat. The deck concrete was increased to three inches, doubling its weight. Aluminum railings were replaced by iron railings, adding eighteen hundred pounds. Fire doors that weighed three thousand pounds each were added along with a twelve-inch-thick firewall at the back of the wheelhouse. "I couldn't even get into my stateroom from the wheelhouse," Gus objects.

When the coast guard realized how much weight was being added, they increased the number of diesel engines from four to six, and extended the length of the boat by five feet. When it was completed in the summer of 1988, the *Anna Maria* weighed 130 tons. The boat entered into aviation history the day it was moved to water. The *Anna Maria* is the only riverboat ever required to pay an airport landing fee—a fee of fifty dollars to Victoria International

Airport—because it had to be moved down one of the runways to get out of the factory.

The sail up the coast from Sydney to Skagway, Alaska, went without mishap. It was removed from the water in Skagway, loaded onto a trailer, and so began a 110-mile overland journey to the Yukon River under the command of Chuck Morgan—the foreman on the crew that moved the SS *Klondike* in 1967. All went well until the boat crossed the border into Canada. Then a disagreement between Morgan and the Yukon Government stopped the boat in its tracks. It spent the winter of 1988–89 sitting on blocks near the top of the Coastal Mountain Range—the highest freestanding riverboat in the world.

When the *Anna Maria* arrived in Whitehorse in the summer of 1989, the operation verged on the edge of bankruptcy. Construction and transportation had cost the investors in excess of $1.3 million—well over the original budget. Because of the late arrival, the entire first season was cancelled; over three hundred thousand dollars in prepaid fares were refunded. "We had it sold out. The marketing was done three years in advance and we sold it out. The demand was there. It just seemed like no one around here wanted it. We knew we were going to go broke before we ever got to Dawson. But I was determined that no government employee was going to stop me from going to Dawson," Gus asserts.

Kevin Shackell, a Yukon government tourism officer, was among the first passengers along with five paid fares and a German film crew. "I knew we were in trouble right from the beginning. The passengers were ready to abandon ship by the Takhini River," Shackell recalls. "The boat sideswiped the shore, and a sweeper (a tree hanging over the riverbank) shattered one of the windows and knocked a light fixture off the boat. Then the boat grounded a couple of times in the Thirty Mile.

In Carmacks, Gus decided he had had enough: "By the time we got to Carmacks I was so intimidated I decided to drop off my passengers and go back to Whitehorse—just to prove to myself we could get that boat through the Thirty Mile without any problems. There's nothing wrong with the boat. Everybody blames the boat but it was, on that first trip, the idiot behind the wheel. Everybody had me so rattled and they had that TV camera up my . . . nose."

To a novice skipper, just learning how to drive, the weight of the boat was a problem in the fast running water of the river. "The boat would go into a turn and you'd wonder whether it would make it or not. If there was an eagle on one side you wouldn't tell anybody about it. Then they would all go to one side and you couldn't control the boat any more." Like the riverboats of old, the captain needed a river pilot to stand on the lower deck and guide him through some sections of the river using hand signals. "When you're standing twenty-one feet above the water, you can't even see the water." Getting stuck on sandbars, occasionally for several hours at a time, didn't help either. "Passengers didn't care. To them it was high adventure. But in this day of modern airline schedules, you can't afford that kind of stuff." The *Anna Maria* did make Dawson City in 1989—twice—and Carmacks on three or four other occasions. The bank called in their loan at the end of the summer and repossessed the boat. Gus and Irene, financially busted by the venture, went back to taking groups of tourists on small boats. Another group of investors bought the *Anna Maria* from the bank and tried using it in Whitehorse for dinner cruises. Then an investor from Austria purchased it, apparently planning to transport it to Atlin Lake and float it there, which he never did. In 2000, an entrepreneur from Vancouver, BC, acquired it with the intention of sailing it on the Fraser River. But the cost of moving it overland to Skagway prevented him. "I think the boat is saying something to us," jokes Gus, eleven years after his dream came crashing down. "It doesn't want to go."

As the only licensed captain in the Yukon, Gus piloted his boat on two more trips to Dawson City, the last in 1996, and several times to Carmacks. Now the boat sits high and dry in an industrial yard near the north end of Whitehorse. Despite his bitterness, Gus still believes in the *Anna Maria*. "Irene and I had some great times on that boat. If we had a million dollars, we couldn't buy those kinds of experiences. But how do you pay the interest on a million bucks? If we could have had one year of operation without paying interest on a million bucks, we would have been OK. It would have been a real success story."

In 2002, the *Anna Maria* left the Yukon the same way it arrived: overland, on a trailer through Skagway, Alaska, on its way back to the lower mainland of British Columbia.

*Passing the Pilings at the entrance to Lake Laberge*

PHOTO COURTESY OF: YUKON NEWS

# CHAPTER FOURTEEN

## Takhini River confluence
Friday, 20 June 1997

L o o k i n g  a t  t h e  average world globe, everyone would agree north is at the top of the world. To get there, people starting from "down south" have to travel "up north." However, when we travel to Dawson City, we go "down" to Dawson, even though it's "up" north. It's a linguistic leftover from the river steamer era when the Yukon River was the only highway between the two communities. Dawson, despite being "up" north, was downstream from Whitehorse.

There was a time when the opposite was true. The area around Whitehorse is strewn with evidence of the north-to-south flow of the Yukon River—one of the clues being the Takhini River, an apparently insignificant stream just fifteen miles north of Whitehorse. The Takhini, which flows from the southwest to empty into the Yukon, is considered today to be an "under-fit" river for the valley it occupies. In geological terms, that means the river is too small to have made a major contribution to the valley through which it flows. The Takhini River Valley was, according to geologists, carved by a single large river that flowed from the northeast to the southwest.

To see how it happened, you have to spread out a map, step way back from it, and let your imagination run, like an astronaut looking at the earth from outer space. There is evidence to show that the headwaters of the pre-historic river were located south of Dawson City. At that time, the southern Yukon Territory was relatively flat and there were no coastal mountains to block the river on its way to the Pacific Ocean through the Takhini River Valley. The uplifting of the coastal mountain ranges occurred very recently, although "recent" to a geologist means any time in the past two million years. The rising coastline started to block off the outlet, slowing the water's flow into the ocean and partially redirecting the river further south, through the Stikine River Valley. Then the last glacial advance from the south, approximately thirty-five thousand years ago, blocked off the Stikine.

It's hard to picture what an ice age must have looked like. A solid sheet of blue ice, towering more than a mile into the sky. Had there been anyone living here at that time, it would have seemed that the ice was the sky. Slowly, persistently creeping over the land, it pushed the remains of mountains—which it ground down to mere fragments—ahead of it. The two tallest landmarks visible from Whitehorse, Grey Mountain and Golden Horn, were both covered by over two thousand feet of ice. The water that collected in front of the ice sheet formed a glacial lake named Lake Champagne. When the glaciers stalled north of Whitehorse, the ice started to melt—which added to the volume of water in Lake Champagne—and gradually withdrew south about fourteen thousand years ago. As the ice retreated, the coastal mountains, temporarily stunted by the weight of the glaciers, started to rebound, and eventually blocked any outlet to the Pacific Ocean.

Water seeks the path of least resistance. There may have been some minor flows towards the north from the Dawson area prior to the glaciers, but Lake Champagne packed a more substantial force with which it could impose change on the land. The water found the weaknesses in the earth to the north and dug out a zig-zag route with its current ricocheting its way through narrow S-bands bordered by high, steep rock cliffs until reaching the low lands in central Alaska where it slowed and spread out. When the Yukon River re-established drainage, approximately ten thousand years ago, it was flowing north rather than south.

The geologists who collected the evidence of this flow reversal from the early 1930s to the late 1990s were not the first to consider the phenomenon. The "Byron of the Sierras," Joaquin Miller, mentioned the possibility in dispatches mailed to the *Seattle Post-Intelligencer* in 1898. Considering the fallibility of most of his reports from the Yukon at that time, it is surprising that he came as close as he did to the truth. His only error was in identifying the Chilkoot Pass as the primary outlet to the ocean.

Further credibility to this theory was provided in the mid-1860s, when glaciers crept down from the coastal mountains and choked off the water's flow from the south end of Kluane Lake—a large body of water near the southwest corner of the Yukon. Until then, Kluane Lake drained to the south. The water found a soft spot at the north end of the lake and the Kluane River, which currently runs north into the White River—then into the Yukon. When the glaciers retreated back into the mountains, the lake continued to drain north.

One other legacy was left by the ice age and we occasionally see that along the riverbank. At the mouth of a small creek just a few miles north of

Whitehorse, a small patch of ice and snow shrinks during the summer but never completely melts. When the ice on top of the ground vanished, the ice under the ground came into its own. Permafrost—earth that is frozen consistently for at least two years—can be found at varying levels below the surface just about anywhere in Canada. It is near the surface where the soil is fine-grained, like the area on a river bank, that the ice and snow won't melt. Not all occurrences of permafrost are so obvious. Where the river undercuts the bank but the overhanging ground seems to defy gravity, it is probably earth that is frozen in place.

The mosquito is a product of permafrost. The ground ice holds water on the surface, creating hundreds of small ponds and lakes—perfect breeding grounds for the prolific bloodsuckers. The beasts multiply in such vast numbers that it was once proposed that the mosquito be designated as the Yukon's official bird. In 1985, however, the government decided in favour of its larger cousin—the Raven. Allegedly, this choice was made because the Raven is a real bird, whereas the mosquito simply grew in local lore to be the size of one.

The mosquito is irritating, but at least it has good reason to exist. Sex. Male mosquitoes (which don't bite) follow humans because they know that female mosquitoes (which do bite) will turn up for a drink eventually. For them, people function as singles clubs. Unfortunately for the randy mosquito, we become walking clinics for safe sex and birth control when we rub on repellant.

〜

Along this quiet stretch of the Yukon, we start to encounter recreational paddlers who began their journey in Whitehorse. There's Ben Blaremont who, each summer, paddles from Whitehorse to Dawson five or six times. Beyond him is a Japanese fellow, also by himself, who can't speak a word of English. He's obviously enjoying himself as he paddles his canoe from side to side in the wide river channel. At this rate, we figure he'll paddle the distance to Dawson three times over before he ever gets there.

This is the newest part of the Yukon River—in name, anyway. In 1843, Hudson Bay Company (HBC) trader Robert Campbell named it the Lewes River, after John Lewes, the Chief Factor of the HBC Forty years later, Frederick Schwatka renamed it the Yukon River; it wasn't until 1945 that the Canadian Government made the change official.

As we approach Lake Laberge, John and I are hailed from the river bank by Dawn. She and her friend Gail Chester have come to send us on our way with one final reminder of the culture we are leaving behind for the next few days—a fast-food hamburger, fries, and drink. We aren't the only ones stopping for a break. A short distance down the river, Fred O'Brien and Karl Dittmar sit on a small island in the middle of the river brewing up a pot of coffee over a small fire.

As we make the final turn and look down the oily-calm lake, a rainbow arcs across black and pale blue clouds behind us. It is truly a bridge to the gods. Seeming to touch the earth at both ends, the red, violet, yellow, green, and blue bands are crisp and vivid. Ahead of us the glassy water turns a lavender shade and the sun glows gold and crimson in the broken clouds above us and upon the crowns of rounded hills that crowd the shores on both sides. The sun is just starting to set. It will take another three hours or so before it finally disappears below the horizon.

One thing that everyone on earth is supposed to get in equal portions is time: twenty-four hours per day. During the northern summer, we get an unequal portion of it—the sun stays up for most of that time. As we head further north, the days will get longer and the nights lighter.

An old row of greying pilings lines the river to our right. They resemble a fence with cross pieces attached to the tops of the uprights. Black Cormorants sit on top. The pilings were originally put in to direct the main current straight ahead, and thus maintain a good deep channel available for the steamboats; now there is a gap in them and it appears that the river current is strongest flowing through it. The river chart, one used by riverboat captains to steer their steamboats, shows the channel to be straight ahead, through a wide river delta of low sandbars. John and I decide to rely on the map.

Maps are more than a visualization of a specific area at a specific moment in time. They are documents of confidence that proclaim "Trust me and I will guide you true. Doubt me and you are lost." However, the map, once drawn, never changes, while the earth is inconsistent, perpetually shifting. A single wave modifies the beach line. A gust of wind reshapes the sand dune. A river current alters course.

John and I spend a few minutes discovering our faith in the mapmaker is misplaced. We should have made the turn through the pilings. That might have saved me from having to climb out of the canoe and drag it over a few mud bars before regaining the current. Once again afloat in the river,

*Scow shooting, Miles Canyon 1897*

PHOTO COURTESY OF: YUKON ARCHIVES, ANTON VOGEE

we settle down for a long grind. Ahead of us lies thirty miles of the most fabled lake in northern Canada, and potentially one of its deadliest.

Lake Laberge, NWT
17 June 1898

My dearest Delia,

Last week, just after we finished crossing Marsh Lake, Robert shot a moose. He is an experienced hunter and had shot many deer in his youth. But even his experience in dressing an animal after the kill had not prepared him for something this large. The moose stood taller than myself at its shoulder (although Paul jokes that this is not difficult to do). Its body mass is easily six of Franklin. "What are we going to do with this thing?" I asked.

Hearing the shot, two Indians came over from where they were camped and, seeing our confusion, offered to assist—in exchange for the hide and some of the meat. An arrangement to which we readily agreed, not having any means by which to preserve that much fresh meat and being reluctant to let it go to waste due to our inexperience.

Franklin, Robert, and I find them to be a solid people. They are friendly, willing to share their knowledge. A people possessed of a wisdom unlike any we would recognize back home. With a will to work for their survival and with an abiding faith in God and the land which they inhabit. Paul views them as indolent and incapable. Even as they assisted he refused to be present, preferring his own company back on the boat.

Afterwards they invited us to their camp, a primitive arrangement of trees, tree branches, clapboard shelters and old canvas, which they are currently sharing with a Frenchman who, like Paul, prefers his own company. Life here, I believe, has never been simple for them. Hanging precariously on the luck of the hunt and the fishing of salmon. How easy my life was back home, an untested constitution and unexhausted sinews helping the brain to concentrate on armchair work. They fed us the nose of Robert's moose. Roasted on a spit. I have eaten some unusual foods in my travels, but none demanded of myself such steeling of nerves. Every part of my body rejected the very idea of eating a nose, but I feared it may be conceived as being offensive if I refused. It was tough. Much like eating gristle. It had a pleasant flavour—tasting much like a nut—although I doubt I will try it again in the immediate future. To be so polite can be draining on an individual.

As evening fell that night, we could hear singing. Walking back to the shore we could see hundreds of boats slipping lazily across the bay and into the river. The men on board were all singing the same song. "Swanee River." Their voices rang of lonliness and melancholy. Of equality, fellowship, and hopefulness. It is all we have. It is what keeps us continuing on and what will, providence willing, one day bring us back home.

We have been moving downstream with little effort, but great concern. The river is big here. There are rocks everywhere. Three days ago we encountered rapids so diabolical they could only be described as a maelstrom. There were three rapids, in fact, one after the other. Known by such innocuous names as Miles Canyon, Squaw Rapids, and White Horse Rapids. We were informed the river was considered so dangerous that passage would be barred by the North West Mounted Police unless we contracted the services of a guide. The shores and rocks are littered with wrecks, they told us. Apart from a distant roar, there was no hint of the cataract that lay beyond the corner.

This did not please Paul, who maintains he is the equal of any man on the water. This I have little reason to doubt, but the police were firm in their demand for us to hire a guide so we did. A powerful man, built like a barrel complete with the iron bands and with legs like the stumps of small trees, called Daniel. Appropriately named, one might think, for he took us into the lion's den.

He steered us into a deep, narrow rock canyon that had waves dashing down upon us from the sides and created such turbulence that it could have flung us overboard had we not been gripping our oars. The water foamed with anger and hurled great billowing clouds of spray into the air. The noise was almost unbearable. I couldn't even hear myself when I shouted. I knew Daniel was calling instructions at us only because I could see his mouth moving. He managed, to our indescribable joy, to negotiate comfortable passage past a whirlpool that was not unlike a great hole in the water. Without hesitation, we plunged out of the canyon and raced uncontrollably past rocks that could have rendered us to slivers had we struck head on. Daniel was magnificent (even Paul gave a grudging nod of his head to him) swinging on the tiller and guiding us safely through—although our hull did jolt against the shore in several places causing severe injury to the sides and bottom.

I did notice the oddest thing. Even as we careened between the rocks, there were men sitting on boxes and chairs on the side of the river—clapping their hands and seeming to cheer us on. Later we were told those were men who stopped to repair their boats or dry their outfit after completing passage. For entertainment, they go down to the riverbank and watch others come through. Their loudest cheers, we were told, are reserved for those who do collide with the rocks—which apparently hasn't often occurred since guides started taking the boats through—although they also jump to the rescue when a boat does flounder.

Daniel steered us near to the right bank and leaped ashore. "You can pull over just ahead where the river slows through the marsh," he shouted to us in farewell; "I have to take the tram back upstream."

Robert took stock of our boat and declared we were no longer seaworthy, so we stopped and, with great difficulty, pulled our scow onto a gravel beach. Franklin and Robert commenced work immediately, while Paul and I set up a temporary camp. We stayed only the one night and, much to our credit I deem, we did not go down to the rapids to encourage disaster.

Last night, just after we arrived on Lake Laberge—a narrow body of water, but one so great in length that it seems to be an endless inland sea—the sky took on a dreadful appearance and the wind became extremely gusty. A great bolt of lightning struck to the earth with a great thunder such as I have never heard. Then the skies opened and the rain fell so hard it doused our campfire. All around our tent the lightning flashed and we feared we might be hit. It was the longest night I have ever known, for it struck all around us and lasted for a long time.

The wind was against us all today and we made little headway despite what felt like unending effort. It was as if nature itself was seeking to make this most remote, legendary place to which we aspire, unattainable. Tonight we're resting in a very crowded little bay, still within sight of our campsite of last night. To reach the shore we must step from boat to boat, and other men must walk across our vessel. Above us are barren, rounded hills. Somehow the sun has found a window in the dark clouds directly overhead and highlights us with a blinding light. The shadowed hills and black skies are what look real. It is the men and boats who have become scene-painting.

Each time I stop to put pen to paper I wonder if any of my words ever reach you. Not a day passes that I do not think of you or wonder how different things might have been were we not separated by such great distances. What I would not give to feel your touch. Hear your voice. Smell your hair. I long to see you so badly. Life is too short to remain so long away from those who mean everything in life.

So silently the shadows fall,
O'er every sun-beamed day;
In silence does my heart recall
A lost love's sweetest lay.
An angry word, a jealous thought,
Did break her tender heart,

And to me grief and anguish brought,
And caused our lives to part.
My dreams are shadowed by her still,
I fancy she is near;
In happiness my heart then fills,
With thoughts of her so dear.
Tommy

*Gerard Cruchon and Jacques Chicoine*

PHOTO COURTESY OF: YUKON NEWS

# CHAPTER FIFTEEN

**Lake Laberge**
Saturday, 21 June 1997

L a k e   L a b e r g e   i s   moody. Today, the promised land, passionate, and warm. Yesterday, indifferent or cynical. Tomorrow, contemptuous and impatient. When the mood changes you can see it happen—the wind blasting down the lake—a line stretching from shore to shore and advancing rapidly. On this side, a becalmed dusty green. Beyond the line, wind breaking on the waves, an angry, dancing silver. The last time I crossed this lake I was at the stern of a twenty-foot freighter canoe powered by a small nine-horsepower motor. We started the trip in a gentle swell, but it was only minutes before conditions deteriorated. My passengers, Laura and Peter Chapman, were on their knees—Peter in the centre, and Laura up near the bow. Past Laura's head, dead ahead of us, I could look directly into Maryanne Shackell's panicked eyes—which was a bit disconcerting considering that Maryanne was lying flat on the bottom of a Zodiac being driven by her husband Kevin.

I should have been looking at the back of Kevin's head, not the balding spot on top of it, and Maryanne should have been looking at the sky, not back at me. But every time the canoe crested a wave and started down the other side, the Zodiac started climbing the wall of water in front of us and our eyes would meet across the trough. "I was scared," said Maryanne. "I was scared stiff. Those were huge waves. I had a three-year-old"—their daughter Erin was hidden under the cover across the bow of the Zodiac so that the waves wouldn't toss her out of the boat—"and I was pregnant."

Up front, Laura was absorbing a pounding. As we crawled up the side of the wave, the bow lifted out of the water, hung there momentarily and then, as we crossed the centre of balance, slapped down hard on the far side. Her knees took the brunt of the impact and, when we finally reached the safety of shore, she was unable to straighten her legs for a long time. Peter had "gunwale grip" from clinging to the sides of the canoe. It took him several minutes to pry his fingers free.

During the Klondyke Canoe Pageant, Cal Waddington came to believe that he had delivered the final radio broadcast of his life. The boat he was in had engine failure, and then was swamped by waves. A rescue boat managed to get the other passengers off; then, as Cal prepared to abandon ship, the waves separated the two boats. The rescue boat struggled to get back but the heavy seas made it too dangerous. Not anticipating a happy ending, Cal wallowed through the water to the stern, sat down, and cracked open a beer he found floating in the boat—there was no point in just being wet on the outside, he reasoned. The captain had already departed his sinking ship, but somebody had to go down with it. That was a marine tradition. Cal tried the engine one final time. It fired up. He steered the half-drowned boat to shore.

The two hundred miles of Lake Laberge shoreline are littered with the remains of its victims. The Yukon Government's Yukon River authority, Alan Innes-Taylor, took an account of the debris in 1967: "Old Tires, 5 to 10 to the mile (2000 in total). Plastic containers, 20 to the mile (4000). Plastic toys, 5 to the mile (1000). Bottles, 3 to the mile (600). Wooden crates, 3 to the mile (600)." In addition, wooden spars, beams, and boards washed up into the few coves along the shore that have beaches.

In some of the coves one finds a "Dead Man"—massive cables anchored to the rocks. Steamboats seeking shelter from the storm would tie up to the Dead Man and wait out the weather. It's a favourite prank of experienced lake travellers to step ashore and declare to rookies "I've found a dead man," and wait for their reaction.

More than one sternwheeler was sent to Davy Jones's Locker by a Laberge squall. The *Thistle*. The *Vidette*. The *A. J. Goddard*—which can still be seen under the water.

A fireman on the ships from 1937 to 1949, Lorne Coleman remembers looking up from below deck and seeing raging whitecaps rise up alongside the ship, high enough that he could see them from the bowels of the boat. Another fireman of that era, Jack Elliott, recalls looking down at his feet when crossing Laberge in a storm. "You could look down at your feet and see the waves run along [under] the floorboards. They were kind of flexible, like a snake. They were made that way."

It was some of the unique features of the wooden boats—such as the flexible floorboards and the shallow draft—that also made them virtually worthless when they sank. The hulls and cabins could be easily replaced at a lower cost than that required to salvage the wreck. Only the metal parts, such as the boilers and engines, were worth salvaging. When a steamboat sank, most of it was left to break up and find its way in bits and pieces to the shoreline.

*Steamship under power*
PHOTO COURTESY OF: FIRTH FAMILY

This lake has a haunting, timeless beauty when it is at rest, with long, narrow cliffs and utterly transparent depths of water. It changes in colour from emerald, to navy, to silver, to gold, to scarlet—depending upon what combination of shades the sun and wind wish to paint with. On the longest day of the year it is easy to lose track of time. The sun sets and rises in the same place and almost at the same time. There are no hesitant dawns in the northern summer, only reluctant nights.

Realistically, I know it is impossible; but in the immortal splendour of this place, combined with sleep deprivation and all that that entails—it would not surprise me to have figures hail me from the past, drifting alongside us in their ramshackle craft. Indeed, in the early hours of this morning, a phantom sternwheeler appears before me, its superstructure glowing pink from the sky, the orange buckets churning up the mist, and the smokestacks billowing great, white puffs into the sky where they quickly turn the same shade of gold I can see in the clouds to the north.

For a moment I hold my breath as I stop paddling and watch. Then, as quickly as the steamboat came, it vanishes. I mention nothing to John. I feel no need to speak. I saw the beauty and felt a desire to preserve it—yet knew it was impossible. The simple fact that it was even there gives the moment personal immortality.

"As I was paddling down the lake, looking at all the mountains," said Joe Jack, "it wasn't very hard to see through my mother's eyes as a young child . . .

what she saw . . . where she played. And at the same time to see through my grandpa's eyes as he paddled around the lake." Joe's grandfather was hereditary First Nations chief Mundessa, better known as Jim Boss—a legend himself on a lake of legend. When Boss heard the stampeders were coming down the river to his lake, he saw opportunity. Quick to realize that the white man put great store in cash, he went into business collecting a twenty-five cent toll from each boat attempting to cross "his" lake. He also joined up as a special constable for the North West Mounted Police, instructing them in northern survival skills. He recognized that white men measure wealth by the amount of land they can post "No Trespassing" signs on and figured if they could do it, so could he. In payment for his work with the North West Mounted Police, he accepted a parcel of land on the west shore that was named Jim Boss Town. He created a small village that still exists to this day. The chief became a fixture on the lake, piloting his spotless white boat (elders tell stories of having to remove their shoes when boarding the boat because the interior of the boat was "so spic and span"—and dirty footwear simply wasn't permitted), supplying fresh lake trout to the riverboats, or collecting his toll.

Fred O'Brien and Karl Dittmar paddle onto Lake Laberge and the moment that Fred has been waiting for all his adult life finally arrives. With a gleam in his eye, and in his most precise Irish lilt, Fred can finally deliver his favourite poem in the one place where it makes the most sense:

> There are strange things done in the midnight sun
> By the men who moil for gold;
> The Arctic Trails have their secret tales
> That would make your blood run cold;
> The Northern Lights have seen queer sights,
> But the queerest they ever did see
> Was that night on the marge of Lake Lebarge
> I cremated Sam McGee. . . .

In the stern of the canoe, Karl listens and paddles. "I like Robert Service, but I don't know him like Fred, there. He knows them all by heart—Hey Fred! It must be nice to have nothing to do but read and memorize poetry!—I prefer Jack London myself because of the adventure."

Brendan and Anne turn up to film Fred and Karl. "I would say on Laberge, when Fred was reciting "Sam McGee," we're in the middle of the lake, they're coming towards us and it's pure calm. You could sort of hear a slight echo. The moonlight. The lake summer sunset," describes Brendan. "I would say there, I just felt very connected to the whole experience of being out on the lake and the history of the thing. I definitely had the feeling that to call yourself a Yukoner, you've got to come down the Yukon River."

The key to a quick passage down Lake Laberge is to stay to the right. The river enters and leaves the lake on that side. So we paddle either along the shore or straight down the middle of the lake. Over on the left side is Richthofen Island, named not for the famous German ace of the First Great War, but for a German geographer of the 1880s who never set foot in Canada's North. The island was used as a navigational aid and as a safe harbour by riverboats, and later as a target by the Royal Canadian Air Force for aerial bombing practice during the Second World War. Deep Creek, approximately ten miles up the left shore, provides the last road access to the Yukon River for the next 170 miles. There is a government campground, from which the River of Gold Tour launched in July 1998.

Lake Laberge is named after a surveyor for the Western Union Telegraph Company, Michael Laberge. Laberge never saw the lake that bears his name, but had it described to him by the Indians in 1867 while working further north on the Yukon River. He talked so much about the stories that his boss, William Dall, gave the lake his name in a detailed report following cancellation of the telegraph line project in 1870.

The echoing cliffs, two-thirds of the way down the lake, have perfect pitch. John and I come across them in the middle of the morning. There are two or three canoes nestled in the bay below the cliffs, their occupants hooting and shrieking, then howling with laughter at the replication of their sounds, and finally giggling deliriously when their first laughter also bounces back from the stone face. Other paddlers are sprawled on the beach soaking in the sun, seemingly oblivious to the cacophony. Whatever race they may have had going has ended in gales of hysteria in this shallow harbour.

We join them for a few minutes, baying for the echo gods. It was a long painful night for myself. My lower back exists in aching misery. It's now been two full days since I was capable of standing upright. Whatever is causing me respiratory problems is also sapping my energy. After ten hours of paddling on this lake, I am either at the bottom or close to it. Self-pity is the order of the day. This is John's turn to carry his teammate. Where I had driven him on the Chilkoot when all he wanted to do was stop the hurting, John isn't letting my negative vibes influence him. "I'm here to race—to do the best I can," he snaps back at my pathetic whining. "Not finish last. You want to finish last—find yourself another partner."

Looking around for another excuse to quit, I spot a waist strap off one of the backpacks. We unloaded the packs in Whitehorse, but for some reason this strap hadn't been dumped. Cinching it up around my waist is like a new lease on life. The belt takes the pressure off my back and, for the first time since Tagish Lake, I'm not in pain. The echoing cliffs seem like a good place to celebrate.

Laberge is the longest of the lakes. About the time you think you should be close to the end, because you've now paddled the length of Bennett or Tagish, or Marsh, there is still a massive body of water ahead of you that seems to stretch on forever. John and I stop occasionally. Once, when a head-wind slows us down, we pull over and sleep on the rocky beach for a couple of hours. At another time, Brendan and Anne lure us to the shore with a pot of hot coffee, and cheese and crackers. Yvonne Harris and Kevin McKague use a bottle of Beaujolais to entice the teams of Mark Kelsey–Karen Lester, Dirk Miller–Derek Peterson, and Ed Williams–Jason Rogers to join them for a toast to the summer solstice at their campfire.

*T. A. Firth with the Bostonians, a traveling stock company in Dawson City*

PHOTO COURTESY OF: FIRTH FAMILY

Finally, a shoreline creeps closer at a painstakingly slow pace. There is no sign of the river, but on the shoreline a large, white triangle can be seen on a tripod. "That's what the riverboats used to find the channel through all the sand bars and gravel bars here," I explain to John. "They would line up on one set of markers and head directly towards them until they could see another one. Then they would change course and head for that one."

It is impossible to see the entrance to the river until you are almost in it. Almost twenty years ago, Kevin Shackell, Florent Levallier, and myself arrived here one cloudy fall night in a Zodiac. It was almost pitch black out as we steered the boat into shore. The next morning we discovered we had pulled in right over the jagged wood and iron rods protruding out of the wreck of the *Casca I*, sunk there in 1911 to form a dock. We couldn't believe that we had maneuvered through the maze of metal without impaling the Zodiac.

The *Casca* is sitting high and dry this year. We beach past the wreck and wobble onto shore. You learn to appreciate the little things in an event like this. Little things like the use of your legs. After sitting in a canoe for an extended period of time, the legs tend to freeze into one shape—usually bent at the knee. Getting them into a functional state takes a few minutes and they don't always work on your first attempt. Brenda Forsythe stood up after thirty hours in her canoe and promptly fell flat on her butt in the river. "After doing all these things I didn't believe I could do, I succumbed to canoe legs," she lamented.

Canoe legs or not, the most difficult part of this trek is behind us. One hundred miles of still-water paddling is finally finished. Grateful and tired, we are off the lakes.

## The River of Gold Tour
10–15 July 1998

They were sent off onto a slightly stormy Lake Laberge with an ominous reminder: "Remember, the musicians went down with the Titanic." People were also more than willing to remind them that, during the Klondike Gold Rush, piano players and musicians were shot by excitable patrons if they were dissatisfied with the performance.

Their flotilla consisted of a Carolina Skipper, a pontoon raft, a flat-bottom river boat, and a Zodiac occupied by representatives of the media who took on the role of "Rafteratzi."

"They were particularly shocked when they saw my raft," said flotilla-organizer Rob Toohey. They added boats as they went along, until there were twenty-seven people in a dozen craft cruising down the river. "It was kind of neat. You could go around a corner, look back, and there was this entire flotilla following behind. It was the best trip I ever made. Just the fact that nobody had any expectations made it an incredible experience."

Well, not many expectations. The musicians—Wyckham Porteous, Lenny Gallant, Dave Haddock, Scott Sheerin, The Skydiggers, Bill Bourne, Rebecca Campbell, Ian Tamblyn, and Daniel Lapp—had never slept under the stars. All urban personalities, they were more accustomed to First Class—getting off the plane before everyone else, no luggage to handle, fruit baskets and champagne in the hotel room, and chocolates on the pillow.

They quickly learned "First Class" out here meant carrying your own bags, jumping out into cold water to tie up the boats, splitting and packing wood for campfires, and setting up your own tent. They didn't have to cook—the trip was catered—but they did have to help with the dishes. One woman, when presented with a bowl of porridge, asked how it was supposed to be eaten. It was, possibly, the first experience that forced them out of their metropolitan comfort zone and into a situation that, by its very nature, was threatening and terrifying to them. "The most disturbing moment," said Porteous, "was when we discovered we weren't going to be changing from the open boats to nice, comfy houseboats when we reached the end of the lake."

The organizers of the twentieth annual Dawson City Music Festival had decided that 1998 was going to be different for the "outside" performers. All of the performers had done gigs in the North, but they were usually quick trips that combined a short local sightseeing tour with a performance or two. None of them had ever stuck around long enough to understand anything about the country they were visiting. The trip down the Yukon River was intended to give them that unique insight.

Entertainers have travelled the Yukon River since the gold rush when a bevy of marginal stage personalities headed north to mine the miners, although there is only one landmark to commemorate their passage. Scatter Ass Bar was so labelled after a ship loaded with dancehall girls floundered near it in 1899 and the cargo disembarked onto the small, rocky island to await rescue. The Bostonians, an ensemble from Boston, Massachusetts, was one of the better-known performing groups to travel the river shortly after the end of the Great War. In the 1940s and early 1950s the Alaska Music Trail, a group of communities in northern BC, the Yukon, and Alaska,

*Supply raft loaded with musicians and support crew*

PHOTO COURTESY OF: PETER CARR

brought professional performers to tour the North, using steamships to get the musicians from Whitehorse to Dawson. The River of Gold Tour was just the latest in a grand tradition.

Most of the performers knew each other professionally, but not personally. They were just as nervous about living together for five days as they were about the wilderness. But that started to change on the first night as they sat around the campfire and jammed. After all, Porteous observed, "It's good to play for audiences, but it's not very often you get to play for each other."

They were also subjected to medical experiments—i.e, Dr. Suzanne Crocker's theory that a tennis ball, when taped to the middle of the back, will prevent an individual from sleeping on his back and snoring. Dave Haddock proved you can snore in any position and that it didn't matter where the tennis ball was taped.

They witnessed random acts of beer. Toohey floated up beside a canoe in the river. "Here," he called to the occupant of the canoe, "have a beer."

"Thanks mate!"

"You Australian?"

"Yeh."

"Then you get two."

CKRW Radio announcer Peter Carr and his partner, Annabelle Bennetts, whipped around a corner in their Zodiac and received a less-than-happy look from a couple in a canoe rocking uncomfortably in their wake. They circled back, passing them again, though this time much more slowly, and tossed a couple of apology-beers into the canoe before continuing on their way.

The tour included five concerts. One in Whitehorse before they left, then in Carmacks, Minto, Fort Selkirk, and at the Music Festival in Dawson City. Whitehorse was OK. The Carmacks concert was good, too, but it was in Minto that it really started to come together. It wasn't the size of the audience that night that inspired the performers (there were more people behind the stage than there were in front of it). "The Minto concert was the best," said Carr. "There was something magical about that night that just gave it that extra special quality."

"It was a great concert," remembers Porteous. "Everyone was really into being on the river by then and it was such an incredible location." The next day, they gathered in the restored Anglican Church in Fort Selkirk and sang gospel—finishing off the day with "Swing Low Sweet Chariot." Toohey, as admiral of the fleet, had been asked to marry two people during the performance in the church. But the couple bowed out, leaving the admiral at the altar. "It wouldn't have been legal in any sense of the word anyway," Toohey acknowledged.

The final show, a six-hour musical marathon in the waterfront gazebo in Dawson City, they called "The River Concert."

The difficulty that last day, added Porteous, wasn't being on the river—it was getting off the river. "It made one uneasy . . . going back into their regular lives. There are experiences beyond your own that open up things that you had forgotten, or weren't even aware of. Getting back to our lives was a cathartic moment: 'Should I keep doing the things I do? Hold the values I hold? Or could I do something better?' These were people who have seen a lot in their lives. Had a lot of experience. Have travelled all over the world. Some of us had been raised near water, on the ocean, some of the great rivers of North America. But all of us, without exception, said this was the trip of a lifetime."

*Kurt Bringsli and Tony Arcand at Minto*

# The Yukon River

*SS* Evelyn *on Shipyard Island*

PHOTO COURTESY OF: JOHN FIRTH

# CHAPTER SIXTEEN

## The Thirty Mile
Sunday, 22 June 1997

T h e   T h i r t y   M i l e is actually thirty-one miles long. But it's best not to let facts interfere with a good name. It's the distance between Lower Laberge, the abandoned community at the north end of Lake Laberge, and Hootalinqua Station, a former North West Mounted Police post and town where the Teslin River joins the Yukon. Officially designated as a Canadian Heritage River, its current snakes through a narrow channel bordered by high clay and gravel bluffs. Disturbances on the water's surface give the illusion of speed, like a toboggan ride down a water slide.

The water is a transparent Mediterranean blue and looking down we can see the river bed. There is the occasional bumpy ride as we cruise through some riffles but we are in no danger of making contact with anything that can upset us.

When the stampeders came through, their boats were larger, drew more water, and were much less maneuverable. A moment of inattention and they found themselves fighting for their lives. According to the *Klondike Nugget* of 31 May 1899, a fisherman, Charles Gisetti, was spear fishing on the Thirty Mile. He didn't catch any fish, but he did snag a satchel containing a Bible and the personal effects of Michael Torner. Exploring a little further, he discovered bags of flour and a small iron stove—remnants of a previously unknown wreck that had claimed at least one more victim.

The steamship captains called this the most treacherous piece of river in the world. There are gravel bars and rocks named after the boats that had encounters with them. The Domville Bar. The Casca Reef. Many of the features were given traditional names—Cape Horn, Rock Point, Anchor Bar, Short Bend—so ship captains could identify their location by a name common to all the river charts. When communicating with a ship coming from the other direction, they would be able to calculate where and when they would meet.

Lower Laberge was the first wood stop for the boats after they got off Lake Laberge. At one time the trees were clear-cut for miles from the river's edge to feed the insatiable appetite of the river dwellers. The boats burned timber. The crude cabins on shore were built of logs and heated with wood stoves. There are still few pine or spruce trees around today. Willows dominate the townsite, growing freely between the remaining buildings.

We walk among the few standing structures, wandering through the doors, taking in the large iron stoves—too big to be packed off—and the floors twisted and broken by years of neglect and frost heaves. Sun shafts pry through cracks and gaps, touching the chimney, the door, the floor. Dust particles hang motionless in the sunlight, sparkling like miniature diamonds in the air.

Is there any building technique that identifies a life style in the way that stacking logs together to form a shelter can? The river has always been a destination for individuals looking for or running from something. In 1898, they were running from hopelessness and looking for gold. Today, they seek solitude and simplicity and are fleeing the complexities of modern society. Log cabins mark the passage of both rites.

As we linger, there is a whispering, a vibration we can't place. Something brushes past me, touching so lightly on the arm, the neck, the face. For a moment, all the childhood superstitions that I buried as an adult bubble back to the surface. I raise my hand to clear it away and it is nothing more than a spiderweb or dust bunny. Anywhere else, just a source of irritation. Here, a reason to believe the dead want to keep us close to them.

Rebuild the ruins in your mind and envision the town intact. Storekeepers counting change over the counters. Dock workers sitting idle on the deck of the sunken *Casca*, rolling their own cigarettes, waiting for a steamship to call them to action. Mothers walking their babies, and children playing on the waterfront. An old Ford truck, coughing and sputtering its way along the dusty, rutted trail from beyond the buildings.

The telegraph office is sealed tight. Once there was a log in the back wall that someone shaved flat. Then he or she took a knife and pencil and etched the date into the wood: "Oct. 8, 1952." Below it they wrote, "All of the stations along the river are now quiet. The telegraph line, in many places, now lies on the ground. It is a quiet river. There is no sound of the axe. No sound of the saw. The woodcutters are all gone. Many of them buried along the river."

Two weeks earlier, at 4:30 PM on 24 September 1952, the last telegraph operator on the Yukon River, Hughie Birch, recorded his final sign off: "Good-bye my happy home for over twelve years." It was only fitting that the

*Telegraph building at Lower Lebarge*

PHOTO COURTESY OF: JOHN FIRTH

final farewell be sent over the wires. The telegraph kept everyone along the river—Indian villages, trappers' cabins, trading posts, police stations, wood cutting camps—in touch with each other and the outside world.

"It was a family of friends that lived 450 miles up and down the river," said former White Pass employee Chuck Beaumont. "People used to attach hand crank phones to the telegraph lines. Not much visiting otherwise. You could go one way pretty good. But going the other way, upstream, was a pretty tough racket. It was a good community. It was a sad thing to see it go. But of course, progress is such—you can't always keep things going."

It is rare that a pair in a canoe leaving the lake doesn't stop here for one reason or another. Stretch legs. Bathroom break. Catch forty winks. A team slides by as we pack up to get back on the river, but we find them camped on the shore, already sound asleep, just around the first corner. A few miles further on we come upon Brendan fly fishing in a small creek on river right. As we paddle by, he hooks an Arctic grayling—a good eating, rainbow-coloured fish exclusive to northern waters.

I'm sure the recreational river travellers find us quite odd. We travel at all hours of the night, some of us at tremendous speeds. We don't stop to fish. We rarely eat or sleep. They have an image of the wilderness and we don't seem to fit into it. Joe Jack and Mike Winstanley stopped to share a meal with a group of German canoeists. "They wanted to meet a real live Indian and they were quite happy to meet an Indian Chief. I think they were shocked when the Indian Chief pulled out his business cards and started passing them around."

Twenty years ago I recall meeting an Austrian camper near here. We set up camp and prepared our "wilderness" meal of spaghetti, Caesar Salad, garlic bread, red wine, and beer. When we invited him to join us, he looked up from where he was lying beside a small fire and pointed to a small tin can balanced on the stone in the middle of the flames. "No thank you," he said, "I am okay. I have my food here." In the can I could see rice boiling. The look on his face suggested he considered us to be a travesty of the wilderness experience.

In hindsight, I understand him. In Europe, the rivers and lakes, for the most part, are over-crowded and the riverbanks privately owned. Travellers need permission to camp on the shore. The freedom, wildlife, and scenery we take for granted is, for them, perhaps the last true wilderness left on earth. That solitary individual was bound and determined to challenge it as best he could. If that meant eating one meal out of a can and using that can as a cooking pot for the rest of his journey, then that's what he intended to do.

As we approach Hootalinqua Station, the water beneath us changes from a clear blue to a cloudy brown. Off to our right the Teslin River enters the Yukon bearing tons of microscopic silt—a reminder that the responsibility of rivers is to wear down mountains and carry them elsewhere. I read once that patience is the ability to move a mountain, one grain of earth at a time. It was probably in such a place as this that the author of that wisdom achieved such enlightenment.

There's not much left at Hootalinqua. A large outhouse and two deteriorating cabins, one of them with a white sign that identifies it as the "Hootalinqua Roadhouse, North West Mounted Police Headquarters." When the steamships were at their peak, this was a thriving hub of commerce—but it withered and died like everything else when the buckets were stilled in the 1950s. When the *Delia* arrived in 1970, my dad was able to recognize several structures, including the Hotel Balmoral and Hootalinqua Hotel, that no longer exist. The ground here is always damp and things tend to break down and rot away faster than in other places.

The fry pan I loathe buys itself some forgiveness. Brendan uses it to cook up the grayling he caught. We toast John's birthday with a shot of Scotch and a small cake, somewhat the worse for wear but still recognizable. His present is a large yellow plastic water pistol with an orange handle that, Brendan tells him, is for finishing off our competitors as we move up through the field.

We miss our first opportunity to test its effectiveness. Sandy Sippola and Marjorie Logue paddle past. "We passed seven or eight canoes in that stretch that night and they never got by us again. We would see a canoe on the shore and people sleeping there and we just were real quiet. We saw you guys at Hootalinqua." No water pistols in their strategy, just stealth and treachery.

Fred Farkvam wanted to see the *Evelyn* on Shipyard Island, one of the largest shipyards on the river and just a short distance further downriver. The *Evelyn* was hauled up on the ways in 1923 for repairs and never re-floated. We spent a few minutes checking out the horse-drawn winches still wound with thick ropes, the massive iron spare sternwheeler parts and paddlewheels scattered through the brush. The superstructure of the ship had almost completely rotted away. The hull looked to be intact but sagged at odd angles. The smokestack leaned over and was heavily rusted.

We were fortunate to even see the *Evelyn* in 1998. In 1997, a lightning bolt ignited a fire just fifty feet from the ship. Fire has always been one of the worst enemies of history, destroying it without conscience. Most fires are manmade, but lightning runs a distant second.

Brendan and Anne are on the island taking a break from the race. "The funny thing is," says Brendan, "that I'm thinking about my family. They were shipbuilders and I'm smelling peat. Peat, to me, is Ireland, because I used to go to Ireland when I was a boy. I start to day dreaming about the peat bogs and my relatives over there. And I'm reminiscing about Ireland and thinking about the peat fires and I hear this 'Can you help us guys?'"

They join a family of tourists already engaged in fighting the fire that has crept to within twenty feet of the hull. Using small trenching tools they turn the edges of the blaze in on itself and throw pots of water on the peat ahead of it. Unable to make headway towards the ship, the flames attempt to get into the trees, but the newly enlarged crew turns it aside time and time again. For the first hour it is all they can do to barely slow the fire down, but then the soaked peat finally refuses to burn. The fire sputters, then is starved into submission. "If those people hadn't been there," says Brendan, "the *Evelyn* would have gone for sure."

*The hull of the SS* Klondike I

PHOTO COURTESY OF: JOHN FIRTH

# CHAPTER SEVENTEEN

## On the River to Carmacks
Monday, 23 June

T h e   a r t   o f   passing in marathon canoe racing has been polished to the point that it is more than just a physical action. There is a protocol to follow. Initially you are supposed to be friendly and courteous. "How's it going?" asked Ontario's Bob Vincent when he and partner Gwyn Haymen caught up to Washington's Tom Feil and Jeff Mettler. "Really good," responded Feil, "until you guys turned up."

There is a strategy to follow. When you realize you are catching up to your competitor, the first thing you do is slow down. This gives you the opportunity to gorge yourself on power bars, sport gels, and sport drinks—food supplements designed for immediate, intense, short-term physical activity. You switch to the equipment that can give you any small edge. In paddling, the professionals carry various paddles for specific occasions in the race. They vary the length of the shaft or the size of the blade. Other advantages include the use of tubes to drink water from containers under your seat rather than pause for a single stroke to hoist a water bottle, or the use of a catheter to drain your urine through the bottom of the boat so you don't have to break your rhythm to pee.

Once your preparations are complete, it is time to make your move. The trailing canoe tucks in behind the intended victim, catching a free ride in the wake, or "riding the wave." The objective is to ride the wake of the lead canoe for a couple of hours and let them do the work while your presence wears on their emotional edge. If the lead team decides to sprint ahead, you can decide whether to go with them or let them go and catch up later. Either way, the trailing boat dictates the pace to the lead boat and gains both a physical and a psychological edge.

Now there is a message to deliver. Using the extra speed provided by the opponent's wake you slingshot forward. With two or three powerful strokes you draw even, then pull ahead. The idea is for the passing boat to make the pass as quick and dramatic as possible, leaving no doubt about which of the two canoes is superior. Now that you have the lead, you must maintain a stroke count that is rapid enough to make it virtually impossible for you to go any faster. The boat behind you can now use your wake and potentially make use of your efforts to slingshot themselves back into the lead. A chasing canoe, at the elite level, can force the pace for an hour or more. Paddlers who can most efficiently process the food supplements into energy will ultimately prevail. Yet, even as the chasing canoe starts to fade, you can't drop off the pace. If you permit the other canoe to keep up, it provides them with the opportunity to potentially regain the lead and make a statement of their own.

All through the night and day, Jim Lokken and Art Ward stalked John McConnochie and Phil Moritz. The two hunting buddies feel they should be able to catch the leaders as they stroke their way down the river between Hootalinqua and the next official checkpoint at Carmacks, one hundred and twelve miles away. After Jim, a school teacher in Fairbanks, Alaska, decided to enter the race last fall, Art called him up. "I'll be your partner," he offered, "if you teach me how to canoe." They spent the winter doing ultra-marathon ski trips to develop their endurance and the spring months paddling upstream on the Chena River.

The team ahead of them has a similar history. John McConnochie had never been in a canoe before training for this event. "When we decided to do this last fall, we got some videos and books and read about it. We're self-taught."

"Knowing how to do a long wilderness race would be my advantage," Jim Lokken predicts. "There is no other race like this." But they can't seem to make any ground on McConnochie–Moritz, who still hold a two-and-a-half hour lead. It is important, Lokken believes, to chase down the leaders in this stretch of water. Don't worry, he reassures Ward, strange things can happen in a race this long—and if they do, then we have to be in a position to take advantage of it. Even so, as they race into their second night since leaving Whitehorse, he is gradually losing his confidence and becoming resigned to a second-place finish.

Then it happens. Just moments after passing under the bridge to arrive at the Carmacks checkpoint, the leaders are down. McConnochie, who earlier said—that provided everything held together—he and Moritz would be the first into Dawson, has pushed his body past its limits. Dehydrated and exhausted, he has to call it quits. When Lokken and Ward arrive, they discover the gold is theirs for the taking. But Boonstra and Verrier, ninety minutes behind in third place, have beaten them in endurance races before and there is still a lot of river to go.

"You can't ever truly prepare for a race like this," Solomon Carriere says. "You can't go out and train for twenty hours in a row. Who runs a marathon for twenty hours in a row—or in any sport, for that matter? You can keep yourself in shape and hope for the best."

While the jockeying for position goes on up front, there are, behind the lead pack, smaller, shorter races developing inside the main event. "It's amazing. It's really very competitive out there," says Russ Bamford. "You pull up beside a canoe and say 'hello.' They pick up their pace a little. You pick up your pace, and the next thing you know you're racing down the river. Nobody expects to win the race, but nobody wants to be beaten by anyone else either."

Some adopt the approach that age and treachery will beat youth and exuberance every time. When Cathy Tibbetts and Dan Morrison are ready to leave Carmacks, they hide the paddles of friendly arch-rivals Mike Staeck and Deana Darnell, then flee after leaving instructions with race staff to delay revealing the location of the gear.

Knowledge of the river is helpful in those little sprint races. John and I catch up to Sandy Sippola and Marjorie Logue a few miles upstream from Carmacks, and for a while, we pace each other. Then, as we start into a wide sweeping turn to the right Sandy steers their canoe close to the bank, out of the main current. As we paddle past, they turn and vanish into a gap in the willows. When we complete the corner, we see them emerge from the willows a mile or so ahead of us and we don't catch up to them again until Carmacks. "How did you know about that channel?" I ask Sandy. "I travel up here by motor boat lots," she responds, "so I know all these sloughs and I've been through them." There are more short cuts between Stewart and Dawson, she adds, but declines to elaborate on exactly where they are.

The trial of long hours without sleep, of not eating or drinking properly, and of being confined in a small space are starting to take their toll. "The greatest challenge, once past Lake Laberge and on the Yukon River," Jeff Brady had warned, "will be staying awake."

"Today started a long time ago," says Suzanne Crocker. "We haven't been out of the canoe since yesterday at nine—more than twenty-four hours. You can move around in this boat. Pull out the sleeping bag. Eat. We can do anything in this boat now."

Reinald Nohal looks totally confused when we come upon him and

Hanne Raab. They are drifting in the middle of the stream, their canoe sideways to the current. Fatigue causes reality to become suspect and it has been thirty-eight hours since they slept. "The river went down. It went up. It went sideways. Islands moved," describes the owner of Berlin's world-famous restaurant Paris Bar. "Everything that could move—moved. Everything that couldn't move—moved anyway."

Sleep deprivation manifests itself as hallucinations. As befits a wilderness race, most of them have a nature or marine theme. Imaginary moose. Imaginary boats. "I kept seeing logs that looked like canoes," said Yvonne Harris. "And after a while the logs had racing numbers on them." Dolphins jump out of the river. Polar bears or black bears chase teams in the middle of the river.

Jason Rodgers of Barrow, Alaska, almost launches himself out of one side of the canoe when a jelly fish emerges from the depths to steal his paddle. "I love watching him hallucinate," says partner Ed Williams.

"Canoes with milkshakes," describes Michael Yee. "Big milkshakes, the size of people. Lined up in the canoe. It could have been a dream because we were starting to nod off . . . but there they were. Milkshakes."

Bill Stewart spots a medieval castle ahead of his boat, crimson in the setting sun. His partner, Stephen Jull, also sees the castle, only his is grey. "What I found interesting about the experience," says Stewart, "was how Stephen and I were even beginning to neurologically function in synchrony. We were hallucinating the same visual images."

Joe Bishop and Thane Phillips arrive at the checkpoint, complaining about the constant buzz of a chain saw they have been hearing for the past several hours. Where is this mad trapper cutting down all the trees, they wonder? Another paddler swears that he passed a barge with a full orchestra on it. Dwight Lambkin and Russ Bamford watch a large house cat chase a bird across a mountainside. They also receive directions from a hallucination: a large yellow arrow, about twenty feet long, indicates the location of the main channel through a labyrinth of islands. It turns out to have been just a downed tree, but it was still helpful. "Luckily it was pointed the right way. Under fatigue circumstances, the geography and the signs pointed to what we wanted them to say. So we saw the arrow."

While we are paddling I hear John suggest to me that we should change places. When I look back over my shoulder, he is laid back over the stern of the canoe, paddling awkwardly and looking a little panicked. "Look at how steep this river is. It's like a giant slide," he says. "I'm afraid if I sit up I'll fall right past you out of the canoe."

The Klondike Gold Rush was predicted in visions that may have been hallucinations or prophetic dreams. Skookum Jim was hurrying from Tagish Lake by foot, to visit his mother who reportedly was seriously ill in Carcross in 1895, when he fell asleep in a bush camp a few miles from the village. In his dream a beautiful woman visited him. She asked him to marry her. When he declined because he already had a wife and children, she handed him a walking stick with a tip of gold. "You're going to find the bottom of this walking stick. You're going to find it this way," she said. Pointing east towards Atlin Lake, she told him to look that way. He could see a stream of light pointing into the sky. "That's not for you," she told him. "That's for somebody else. You go down this way," pointing north, "and you're going to have luck." A year later he headed north with Tagish Charlie and Patsy Henderson to find George Carmack.

In June 1896, while travelling near Forty Mile, Carmack was going through a financial dilemma. His trading ventures had failed and he was at loose ends about what to do next. One night, he claimed, he had a bizarre dream in which he saw graylings schooling in a stream of clear blue-green water. Then two king salmon came upstream, scattering the smaller fish. Instead of scales, the salmon were armoured with gold flakes, and their eyes were gold coins. He and Kate headed upstream towards the Klondike River, which was the only stream he could think of that resembled the one in his dream.

There are those who simply don't get sleep deprived. Lucia Misikova and Martin Misik, from Brataslava, Slovakia, alternate sleeping in the canoe. "The scenery is so beautiful, so vast," said Martin, stroking lazily down the river while Lucia dozes in the early morning sunshine. "We saw a bear a while ago. A little black one. There is nothing like this in Europe."

Will Miles, a Methodist Minister from Wasilla, Alaska, finds the whole thing exhilarating. "We do find it spiritually renewing to travel outdoors. Get in touch with something beyond yourself." But, he has to confess, he didn't realize that yesterday was Sunday. "It's a blur, just like any other day. I've prayed three times a day and I have the Methodist superintendent"—canoe partner Billy Still of Anchorage, Alaska—"with me in case we need higher spiritual direction."

Beriah Brown, manning the checkpoint at Carmacks, has developed a quick means to assess the condition of the paddlers. "I ask them to name four animals in the zoo. It's a fairly easy question, but it's not in what they say . . . it's in how they say it."

He approaches Jason Rogers. Rogers is wearing a heavy coat and a toque despite the fact that the day is sunny and hot. "Name me four animals in the zoo." There is a long pause, then Rogers responds, "Like . . . which zoo?"

When we see Beriah, as he stumbles out of his sleeping quarters to check us in, he is the one who needs the personal assessment. It has been almost forty-eight hours since he last slept. Whoever was supposed to assist him at the checkpoint has been called away and the rest of the organizing team is well down river trying to keep up to a race that is moving faster than anticipated.

I'm often a competitor in these events but rarely a volunteer. I mostly wonder who these people are who deprive themselves of comfort for countless hours just to check in a bunch of strange people paddling absurd hours for nothing more than personal adventure, and why they do it. It constantly amazes me that there are individuals prepared to donate acts of kindness and generosity, a part of their lives, to allow us to realize our dreams. I wonder if they realize how much we appreciate them, how much we see them as being a vital part of what we're doing, even though we are usually incapable of voicing that at the time.

The history along this stretch of river is right in the water with us, yet most of the racers pass artifacts and places with hardly a sideways glance. Just past Hootalinqua the hull of the *Klondike I*, sunk there in 1936, is still visible at low water. In 1998, Fred Farkvan and I spent a few minutes prowling its two hundred and ten-foot deck, which is remarkably intact considering the years it has been subjected to the river.

Cassiar Bar, now only visible at low water, as well, was another minor Yukon River gold strike in 1886—producing little in terms of nuggets, but surrendering copious volumes of flour gold. It was worked by hand until 1898, then dredged until 1901. This was possibly one of the many bars that T. A. Firth stopped to mine on his way to Dawson City. If you dipped a pan into its gravel today you could probably still discover some gold. Not much, but enough to give you the same shiver of excitement that the stampeders got when they washed out their first colour.

Two gold dredges, abandoned in 1940, can still be identified by deteriorating wooden frames, large sprockets, buckets, chain links, boilers, and rusty Caterpillar engines at the water's edge. The map shows wood camps all along the banks of the river. Lakeview. Bayer's Camp. Erickson's Wood Camp. Twin Creeks. To look at the wood camps today, you wouldn't think that anyone had ever been there. All are mostly overgrown, with only vague, mossy outlines on the ground to identify where someone's home once stood. In the early part of the century, 20 per cent of the Yukon's population—one person in five—lived in cramped quarters along the solitude of the river. By 1964, one of the things about the Yukon River that struck John Dines was the absence of people: "I never met anyone else at all on the river. Nobody was on the river in those days."

Three major events decimated the river population in the first half of the century. The sinking of the SS *Princess Sophia* in 1918, the 1918–19 Spanish Influenza pandemic, and the Great War of 1914–18.

The sinking of the *Sophia* on 24 October 1918—the most devastating single calamity in northern history—was also the worst marine disaster on the Pacific coast of North America. Three hundred and forty-three people, including five riverboat crews, telegraph operators, woodcutters, traders, and their wives and children, were drowned when the luxury cruise ship sank after hitting Vanderbilt Reef in the Lynn Canal between Skagway and Juneau, Alaska. In a single night, 5 per cent of the Yukon's population was wiped out.

The influenza pandemic killed 20 million people worldwide in less than eighteen months. Nothing in history—neither war nor plague—has killed so many in such a short period of time, and it struck the First Nations population along the Yukon River with a vengeance. It virtually annihilated the people of Little Salmon, one of two major villages between Hootalinqua and Carmacks, and the surviving members of the Tage Cho Hudan "Big River People" fled to Carmacks.

When the call to arms came in 1914, over six hundred Yukoners flocked to the colours. Most expected to winter in Europe and return for break-up the following spring for the gold mining season. Few survived Vimy Ridge, Gallipoli, or the Somme to see their homes again. For those who did come back from the trenches, mud, and blood of the Western Front, it was many gold seasons later, and they were no longer young. Some would walk off the steamships to find themselves the sole surviving occupant of what used to be a small village. Many turned around and left on the next boat. Others stayed.

Robert Service called them "The Men That Don't Fit In." On the river, a person could be whatever he or she wanted to be. A poet. A drifter. A loner. Some remained for holistic reasons—they sought a simpler life. Others

*Jim McConnochie and Phil Moritz lead the race into Caramcks*

PHOTO COURTESY OF: WHITEHORSE STAR

stayed for the challenge of coping with the basics of a living-off-the-land existence that hasn't changed in one thousand years. Like many who continued or came later, "Coffee John" Bodnarek had darker reasons for seeking the seclusion of the river in the 1990s: "I trust bears and wolves more than people. They don't cheat you or lie to you. They don't bite you like people do."

"This sort of a life would terrify people," said Athol Retallack, who lived on Stewart Island in the 1950s. "Some people are just born to live that kind of life and make the most of it. Either it makes you a bigger person—you find resources—or it would shatter you. I never said to people, 'You should come up north and live my life,' because I think this is something the individual has to know about him or herself—whether they can cope with it or not."

Women found it particularly trying. My mother spoke of the housewife's lot in the isolation of the river. Often they would have one or more children right away, and then be required to raise them singlehandedly. The men worked long days cutting wood and had no time to look after home and family. Some of the women thrived on raising their children without the companionship of other women. But the primitive conditions, severe climate, and loneliness wore many down. They waited on the opportunity to escape. "The women saved the money and the men wanted them to have a trip back 'outside.' Their first trip after travelling to the Yukon. And they never came back. I don't know how many men were left alone and the wives never came back. It was a tremendous number," said my mother.

The woodcutter left behind in his ghost town fell into a daily ritual. First thing in the morning he started his fire, dressed, shaved, and prepared a good breakfast. Then he brought in wood for the cook stove and the little airtight heater in the sleeping area. Shopping in the Sears Catalogue, perusing week- or month-old newspapers, and reading his Bible came next; then he sawed and split wood for a few hours before lunch. In winter, after doing the lunch dishes, he went to work hauling wood to the riverbank. In the summertime, according to former wood camp operator Johnny Hoggan, "You'd sit and watch the river go by. When you got tired of that, you'd rest." When darkness fell, he cooked supper and did the dishes. If it was time, he would fill a wash tub—one kettle of hot water at a time—and soak away a month or so of grime. The lettered man wrote entries into his diary about the weather, sunrise, sunset, and minimum and maximum temperatures before turning down the oil lamps for the night. The rules were set. Discipline must be maintained. The only variation was the occasional visitor. "They were always glad to see you when you came by," said Alan Innes-Taylor, a former North West Mounted Police officer who patrolled the river in the 1920s; "but there was a limit to the welcome, and the time came quickly to go on. In a way, I guess we disturbed their life."

My father would go hunting on the Yukon River every autumn with his best friends: Joe Redmond, Franklin Osbourne, and Charlie Rendell. They made a point of visiting everyone on the river and carried a case of whiskey to make their welcome warmer. Never sure what kind of reception they might get, they established a set procedure. One of the four got out of the boat and walked a short way towards the cabin, shouting, "Bill! Bill Smith! It's me. Frank Osbourne." Then he retreated and waited until the cabin's occupant made an appearance. Only once did Dad recall being greeted by a shot over their heads, and that because the old boy in the cabin was hard of hearing.

Once recognized, they were invited in for coffee. When the coffee appeared, so did the whiskey, which was added to the coffee for seasoning.

One man they visited added a little to his coffee, then emptied the bottle in one gulp before it could get to anyone else. They finally figured out he was just making sure he got his fair share in case the bottle didn't make it back his way again.

Another loaded bowls of cereal from a huge bin, dumped in some milk, and tossed them on the table for the four men. There were bugs and spiders trying to escape out of the cereal, and mouse turds floating in the milk. Dad felt his gorge rise, but, given the circumstances, felt it was best to be neighbourly. So he ate it—all the time fighting the urge to throw it back up. Even so, it was probably an improvement on what they might have eaten had they visited "Coffee John." Also known as "Starvation John" because of his appearance—bone-rack thin and frail—he would "go hungry half the time. In wintertime," he explained, "you eat birch bark and garbage like that. But to me it's worth it. Pig weed is very healthy food." The other "treat" that visitors could look forward to was home-brewed rhubarb wine—described by the last surviving member of the North West Mounted Police, G. I. Cameron, as "the vilest concoction known to man." It was easy to make. Nothing else grows like wild rhubarb along the river. It was usually still fermenting in the bottle when uncorked, and one man had to hold a bucket under the bottle to catch half the contents as it frothed up and spilled out. It was pretty active stuff, and two glasses, said Cameron, "could result in a man breaking into song."

"Those guys"—woodcutters— "were like hermits," recalled John "Jack" Elliott, a fireman on the riverboats, who said they wouldn't come out when the boats arrived to load up with firewood. Often the captain would send a crew member into the camp to find out if the woodcutter was still alive. Occasionally, he wouldn't be. "If you got cut up or sick you'd take a day off or someone would doctor you up. You get cut up, as long as you could stop the bleeding, you could survive. You got too sick, you just died. That's all," said Johnny Hoggan. The same diary that logged the weather and sunrise was also the record of their lonely demise in the same abbreviated fashion.

"Wednesday, the 26th. I have been sick since Tuesday the 25th."

"Thursday, the 27th. Very bad. Pain is unbearable. No one came by."

"Sunday, the 30th. I can barely stand. It took me half a day to crawl down to the creek for drinking water. I'm dying by inches."

"Wednesday, the 3rd. I've been trying to die for the last three nights and I can't make it. I take the last dose of lead for my medicine."

There were no church bells. No fine eulogy. Just a chance discovery by a passing stranger who dutifully dumped the body into a hole before rummaging through the cabin. He would borrow what was useful for his own survival, safely package what obviously needed to be forwarded to a child or a long-departed wife, and leave the rest. Others followed, gradually stripping the place of its stoves, tables, chairs, lamps, until there was nothing left but an empty log shell. Eventually the roof collapsed, then the logs disintegrated, and, after many years, there was just the outline of the foundation barely discernible in the heavy green moss of the forest floor.

In their later years G. I. Cameron and Alan Innes-Taylor could indicate any point of land along the Yukon and provide the name of a prospector, woodcutter, or trapper buried there by them. You couldn't bury them in winter, said Innes-Taylor, so they would wrap them in skins and stick them up in a tree. When summer came, they returned to bury them. "We'd mark the grave with a board or something, and put their name on it," explained Cameron, with whom I spent several evenings listening to memories and watching old home movies that showed spasmodic slices of life in Fort Selkirk in the 1930s and '40s. The physical requirements to be a member of the North West Mounted Police must have been imposing. Even in his nineties, he stood ramrod straight and his shoulders filled any door he passed through. "And that was it. There was nothing else you could do." He had a slightly skewed approach to caring for the dead during the winter months. "We left them out by the wood pile until they were frozen good and solid. Then in the spring, when the ground softened up a little, we sharpened their feet and drove them in." The men had chosen to live and die in their lonely homes, according to Cameron, so "We buried them right where we found them."

*Buckwheat greets Steve Landick*

PHOTO COURTESY OF: WHITEHORSE STAR

# CHAPTER EIGHTEEN

## Carmacks

A l l   i t   t o o k   was a bottle of whiskey, a spelling error, and Carmacks had the wrong name. According to Frank Goulter, who arrived in the town in 1905 as a member of the North West Mounted Police, the town was called Tantalus at that time. It had been named after the massive butte just upriver a spell, which was an underground coal mine from 1903 until 1978, when an underground fire resulted in the shaft being permanently sealed off. The coal seam had allegedly been discovered by George Carmack, but Goulter loudly refuted that story. Carmack was a subsistence fisherman-cum-prospector seeking gold, Goulter claimed: coal wouldn't have interested him. The legend persisted, though, and eventually triumphed.

The bottle of whiskey was shared by Seymour Robinson, owner of a roadhouse, and another man—whose last name was apparently Dixon—in 1908. By the time the final fingers of Scotland's finest were poured down their gullets, the two had decided to rename the town "Carmack" after the alleged discoverer of the coal mine at Tantalus Butte. They ordered a sign to hang on the front of Robinson's business, but when it arrived it read "Carmacks" instead of "Carmack." Rather than order a new sign, Robinson hung it over the front door to his roadhouse and the name stuck.

Carmacks is one of those places you can visit but come away from with little sense of understanding it. It seems torn between past and present. Had Carmacks relied solely on river trade it would have shared in the fate of the other wood camps. But the Canadian Development Company pushed a stage road past the community in 1901, and the roadhouses catered to the traffic on the CD Trail as well as to the steamships. When the all-weather highway from Whitehorse to Mayo and Dawson City was built in the early 1950s, it followed the route of the CD Trail. Modern conveniences built on the side of the road relegated older facilities to the remote corners of town. For much of the latter part of the century, Carmacks turned its back on history and the river.

෴

In the twilight of the millennium, there seemed to be a renewed will to revive the past. Historical buildings were cleaned up and identified. A river walk was constructed so that residents and visitors could stroll the banks in safety and comfort. The First Nations built an interpretive centre to speak of their history and pre-history with the river—Carmacks had been a fishing and hunting camp before the arrival of the white man.

It was almost a physical manifestation of the cultural disaster that befell the First Nations people who lived along the Yukon. In an interview shortly before his death in 1989, Elder George Dawson, with weathered eyes of experience behind rimless spectacles, and a powerful voice that still resonated with the passion of youth, told of how his people almost lost the river. "It was a tough life for the Indian prior to the arrival of the white man. When meat was scarce, people starved and died. The river acted as a highway for the white man who set up trading posts and stores on the banks. In years when fur was plentiful but meat was scarce, the white man's trading posts and stores saved a great number of Indians from starvation." But, he qualified, the white man also brought many bad things.

The Indians, George said, viewed the gold rush as a passing event. The stampeders would be here today and gone tomorrow, then life would go on as before. For the most part they were right. There was some displacement of Indians, especially in the Dawson City area, but the stampeders were mostly gone within four years. Traditional values still existed for the First Nations— their language, their games, their way of life. The Indians continued to use the river as their main trade route and food source. "The river gave Native people a purpose."

It wasn't the gold rush that eroded First Nations culture, he claimed. It was the steamship. Without raising a hand in violence, the boats destroyed First Nations society as completely as any physical disaster could have. They provided an alternative lifestyle—working for a wage rather than subsistence trapping and fishing. George himself worked on the riverboats as a young man, making his last trip up river in 1927. A lot of young Aboriginal men and women would have gone out to trap and fish, but there were few elders who could teach them how. There was no more need for traditional vessels such as moose skin boats (a hull formed with moose skins stretched over a birch and willow frame, then waterproofed with spruce pitch and grease). With the need for them eliminated, the art and craft involved in their construction was also lost. When Wilfred Charlie of Carmacks decided to build a moose skin boat in the early 1990s, the only guide he had was a weathered frame abandoned almost forty years earlier.

The steamship culture introduced First Nations to racism. Early white men appreciated the First Nations values, but the stampeders, for the most part, ignored the First Nations almost as much as the First Nations ignored them. The steamships catered to the social insensitivities of some passengers who thought it was fine to have an Indian working on the boats, but didn't want to share their meal with one. Indians often rode below decks or on barges pushed ahead of the boats, or they were refused passage altogether.

Before the riverboats stopped running in the 1950s, the First Nations people had lost much of their respect for the river. The wage economy was now tied to the land highway. But they found no relationship with the road such as they had with the waterway. "When you don't respect something, according to Native people, you are going to lose it. If you do not respect something, the spirit will not return," said George.

It wasn't until the 1990s that the Yukon First Nations began to realize it was possible not only to establish a place for traditional knowledge and culture within the Western scientific box, but to package it in such a way that visitors to the North would buy it. The river provided them with the opportunity and the substance to teach people that this land had a "long ago." The First Nations culture, they proudly proclaimed, was one with the land and the river before the stampeder came. Resorts, modelled on traditional Indian fish camps, were established along the river and marketed to the tourism industry as an opportunity to experience life before the gold rush.

We have a two-hour mandatory stop in Carmacks. Too short to sleep, but long enough to stretch our legs and have a real meal. John and I, existing on gorp, dried fruit, and chocolate bars, arrive just after midnight and are greeted by my brother, Tom, and his wife, Bea—there in their camper to cook us a steak dinner. However, those who don't have a support crew must walk close to half a mile to reach a facility of any type other than an outhouse or cook shack.

Roger Hanberg and Jeremy Lancaster make the long walk to a restaurant where they order up a steak dinner "with potatoes, vegetables, soup, roll, salad . . . the whole deal. It was nice." They haven't gone high tech with their food, carrying dried Caribou meat rather than freeze-dried meals and energy supplements. Jacques Chicoine and Gerard Cruchon also avoid packaged foods, preferring instead to dine on eggs, ham, sausage, and salami.

Christine Guenther and Wendy Cairns start out with a supply of pre-prepared meals comprising curries with chutneys, fresh produce, bannock, and pancakes. "We never got around to eat any of it," laments Chris. "We just got caught up in race fever. Who would stop to cook when other people would pass you?" They settle for cheese and crackers, raisins, jujubes, fruit leather, dried fruits and chocolate bars. "I was so sick of chocolate bars when we finished," she continues. "We ate a lot of chocolate bars."

Thane Phillips and Joe Bishop are experiencing the same distaste I developed for power bars. "Your system is pissed off this is happening. We were nauseous at times," says Thane. "You just couldn't eat but you knew you had to, so you're forcing it down." At one point they discovered a box of crackers in the bottom of their food bag. "That was like those Klondikers finding gold . . . we were so happy. We were—like—'Oh my God! Different food!' And we felt better and the world was a happy place to be again."

A "magic cocktail" powered Mike and Steve Varieur in 1998. Two Tylenol 3s, some Naprasin, two wake-up pills, Coca-Cola, and fried chicken: "Good for four to five hours of solid paddling," claimed Steve. Bill Stewart and Stephen Jull are living on cans of Ensure. "We anticipated we would need about ten thousand calories per day, but we figured that because your heart rate is going to be quite low, maybe in the 110–120 range, you're going to burn mainly fat calories. We were carrying cases of it in the boat. They were really calorie packed but they did make us very heavy."

Solomon Carriere and Steve Landick survived on cold pizza that was stored in specially designed containers in the canoe, and sucked on bags of tapioca pudding taped to the gunwales so they could be grabbed and opened without disrupting the stroke.

Brendan Hennigan made the stroll into town, but not for food. He put through a call to his sister, Andrew Simpson's mother, in Leeds, England. "Don't worry," he reassured her. "I got Andrew past all the dangerous parts." There was a moment of silence before she asked, "What dangerous parts?"

Andrew was attempting to put the race into context with distances that people back in England could relate to. The entire race, he calculated, was the equivalent to paddling from Land's End (at the south end of England) to John O'Groats (the north end of Scotland). Today they travelled from Manchester to Leeds, and tonight they would go to Birmingham. The journey was far beyond anything the auto mechanic and recreational soccer player had ever anticipated. "It's tough, but it's an incredible experience. To see Moose.

Bears. Eagles. That's not stuff that people back home will ever see. There was a large eagle that flew from tree to tree alongside the river while we were paddling. Then he just soared and swooped down low right over top of us. God, it was exciting."

Once past Carmacks, the river, which has already been meandering a lot, gets really crooked. At one point, above the highway north of town, you can stand on a hilltop and look at the river flowing into Carmacks to your left and out to your right. Overland there is not much more than five hundred yards separating the two, but on the water you travel almost two miles to get from one side to the other. There is a bend just past Carmacks where the riverboats heading upstream would unload their passengers onto the bank and then continue without them. The passengers strolled along a path through the trees back to the river, then had a picnic while waiting for the steamship to catch up.

The wandering water can lull one into a sense of complacency, but at the end of twenty-two miles of wide sweeping turns lurks one of the more formidable obstacles on the river. In the later years of his life, Frank Goulter used to sit on the dyke in front of his home near the mouth of the Nordenskiold River. As the tourists drifted by in their canoes they would call out to him, "'How far to the Fingers?' That used to scare them more than anything."

*SS* Whitehorse *coming upstream through Five-Finger Rapids*

# CHAPTER NINETEEN

## Five Finger Rapids

At first, when you sweep around the corner and face the Five Fingers, there appears to be a solid, red rock wall barricading the river. As you move further around the long corner that carries you into the rapids, two channels become visible. A wider one to the left and a narrow one to the far right.

There are actually five "fingers" of water created by four massive, irregular blocks of conglomerate rock that date back to prehistoric times, when they were part of an alluvial fan formed by rivers flowing from mountains into a tropical swamp. They provide imposing proof that the Yukon River once had a closer resemblance to the Amazon River than it does to its current state.

The Fingers have a reputation that approaches mythical proportions. Whenever you talk about the Yukon River, inevitably the conversation moves around to Five Finger Rapids. Voices become hushed with dreadful respect and novices hang on every word spoken by the veterans who survived the deadly waves. Three of the channels are angled in such a way that anyone who attempts them has a good chance of being driven into one of the columns by the force of the current. The widest gap, The Canoe Channel, has a large whirlpool, and a hydraulic wave behind it, that poses a grave danger to the unwary or weary. The right hand channel is the safest. In low water it is considered a Class II rapid—with waves up to three feet in height and some maneuvering required. At high water it becomes a Class III—high, irregular waves capable of swamping a canoe.

This isn't the same set of rapids the stampeders were warned of when they passed a sign nailed to a tree suggesting they "Look Out for the Rapids." The Canadian Government blasted away part of the most easterly of the columns in 1899 and 1900 to widen the right hand channel for the riverboats. According to Gus Karpes, who sounded the depth of the water in the right hand channel, there is a rock reef just four and half feet below the surface. Plenty of room for a canoe, but it only gave the steamships about eighteen inches of clearance.

Thousands of canoes, rafts, pontoon boats, barges, and craft of every size and description have safely shot the rapids, leaving many to wonder what all the fuss was about after they bounced through. John Dines let the current carry him through in 1964. Because a rubber raft tends to float right on top of the water, he experienced none of the turbulence that other vessels are subject to; however, he did notice the crashing of the water against the rocks. "It's pretty noisy in there."

Not a single steam ship sank at Five Finger Rapids, but the fearsome reputation does have substance. An 1898 North West Mounted Police report indicates that seven men lost their lives while trying to negotiate the Fingers. The chief engineer for the Canadian Government's Public Works Department, Louis Tache, drowned in the Canoe Channel in 1899. Frank Goulter remembers standing on the bluff taking pictures of a canoe going through the Fingers at high water. Just as he snapped the photo the boy in the canoe stopped paddling, removed his hat and waved it at him; moments later, the canoe swamped and the boy vanished under the water. In 1986, five German paddlers perished while trying to shoot the Canoe Channel.

The towering walls of rock on either side seem to constrict the passage until it appears there is barely enough room to squeeze our canoe through, far less a steamship. When coming upstream in high water, the ships did have to be pulled through by winches. The change in the level of the water from the downstream side to that of the upstream side was great enough that the paddlewheels were briefly lifted completely out of the water as the ships were winched through.

John, who once shot the rapids of the Fraser River in southern British Columbia, frets constantly as we approach. He shrugs off my reassurances that there is nothing to fear as long as we take the right channel. He looks back and forth, scouting out the nuances of the narrow passage ahead, and I wonder if he's looking for a likely beach in case he decides to bail out. From a vessel as close to the water as a canoe, it is virtually impossible to identify where the river turns from smooth to turbulent until you are on top of it. It's a quick transition, and for about two hundred feet past it we bounce through a series of standing waves and then slide into a fast but relatively calm current.

Yvonne Harris started to get nervous as she approached the Fingers. "I didn't know how Donna [Dunn] would react to Five Fingers. I hadn't been through any rapids with her. I got increasingly concerned—this is really strange for me because I don't get nervous about any rapids at all. I was concerned and she was concerned. So we stopped and put on wetsuits. She puts on this pink wetsuit and it was too tight and it was very hot. After about a half-hour she said, 'I just can't paddle any longer.' So we stopped again and she got a different wetsuit. So we went through in these wetsuits—all ready for the worst—and nothing happens."

As far as Mike Winstanley was concerned, Joe Jack was taking the whole Five Finger Rapids thing a little too lightly—especially when Joe suggested they go through backwards to make it more of a challenge. "Don't worry," Joe reassured his nervous partner. "I go through them all the time and it's hard to get wet."

"We got one star on the Chilkoot," retorted a testy Winstanley, "and another in front of Whitehorse. I don't think they'll let us get away with three!" In Whitehorse, Winstanley's wife had spotted a couple of stars by their team number on the official time sheet. "What are those for?" she asked. "That just means we should keep an eye on these guys for their own good," responded the official.

The unexpected can occur. As Bill Stewart and Steve Jull get into the rough water the blade snaps off Jull's paddle. Throwing the shaft into the canoe he grabs the blade and tries to steer the boat. "He was in the stern at this point," says Stewart, "and he steers us through the rapids with just a blade. I mean, we bobbed through like everyone else, but it was a rather tense moment."

Heather Birchard and Tara Wardle found themselves hurtling through the Canoe Channel, but managed to miss the whirlpool and hydraulic. "When we went through Five Finger Rapids we ended up sitting in water up to our knees," recalled Birchard. "We thought we were headed off to the side but somehow ended up going straight through the middle. There were three foot waves and we took on a bunch of water." An emergency support boat positioned at the rapids approached the two women. "You two OK?" asked volunteer Barry Enders. "This is a hoot!" responded a thoroughly drenched but obviously elated Wardle.

Even more confounding than the reputation of Five Finger Rapids is the reputation that Rink Rapids, just six miles down river, doesn't have. Rink Rapids is another of the many geological features that were named after someone totally irrelevant to Yukon River history. Frederick Schwatka named it to honour Dr. Henry Rink of Denmark, director of Denmark's Royal Greenland Trade.

From the canoe, it appears as a white line that stretches unbroken from shore to shore. But as we get closer, we pull over to the right side where a passage was blasted for the sternwheelers and skirt around the hundred or so feet of standing waves and choppy water. Even with the passage, Rink Rapids can lay claim to being the more perilous of the two. Karpes also sounded Rink Rapids and the water is more shallow there than at the Fingers. "It's inevitable you're going to touch a prop."

On river left, in behind a small island, are the rotting remains of the *Casca II*. It sank there in 1936 after hitting the wreck of the *Dawson*, which went down in mid-stream in 1926 following a collision with the river bottom. For those in a canoe, Rink Rapids poses little danger—although Art Ward will probably argue with you on that point. Art dozes off in the bow of the canoe, leaning forward over his knees, and Jim Lokken takes them straight down the centre of the river.

"The water's real high," Lokken explains. "I saw all these whitecaps and then I went over the lip and saw they were six foot waves. I got over to the three-footers but didn't have a chance to warn Art. They just rolled across the deck and drenched him. He woke up and he didn't know where he was. Didn't know he was on a canoe in the middle of the river. He just woke up screaming because he thought he was drowning. He was dog paddling and jumping all over the canoe and we almost tipped over there."

Fred O'Brien and Karl Dittmar also tackle the centre and fill their canoe to the gunwales with water. "We managed to keep it upright, paddled to shore, lit a fire, hung everything to dry, and bedded down for some hours," says Fred.

A few minutes after going through Rink Rapids we pass "Sam McGee's Ashes," a white crescent-shaped deposit of the White River Ash on the river-bank. The name derives not from Robert Service's poem but from an entre-preneurial enterprise operated by "Kid" Marion, the purser on the *Casca II* from 1914 to 1926. Marion was a source of Yukon folklore, most of which he concocted himself. When the passengers spotted the ashes Marion would recite, "The Cremation of Sam McGee," but he moved the *Alice May* from Lake Laberge to this point on the river (it probably drifted during Spring break-up). The deposits, he said, were all that was left of Sam and *Alice* and, for twenty-five cents each, they could own a small glass vial of ash from the site collected by the "Kid" himself.

Other Marion gambits included convincing visitors that the condensed milk served in the ship's dining room was actually real moose milk: "Try a lit-tle bit—you mightn't like it but it's an experience." Or "accidentally" dropping gold nuggets (actually pieces of brass) out of his pocket and into the river, and then dismissing the loss with a quick "Lots more in them thar hills." A graveyard by the river's edge gave him his most inventive tale. In the riverbank below the graveyard he hammered two sticks and tied a pair of miner's boots to them so that they resembled a pair of feet sticking out from the earth. On each trip past, the "Kid" strolled on deck and pointed them out to the passengers. "Look there," he would say, "By golly, the river's eating right into the graveyard. That's old Sam—they buried him with his boots on, y'know. Shame isn't it. Sliding right down the bank like that."

"I used to tell them the truth," claimed Marion, "but they wouldn't believe it. They're much happier now when I tell them lies."

ᏳᏝᎧ

It is near midnight when we arrive at Minto Landing where Tom and Bea await us with Guinness and hamburgers. In this race we are meant to be self-sufficient. I justify being dined and beered in Minto by rationalizing that everyone has a different perception of self-sufficiency. For instance, in the city, a person has money in their pocket. There's a McDonald's. They buy a hamburger—by themselves, for themselves—using their own money. That, also, is self-sufficiency. Brendan and Anne join us and any guilt I may feel is swept away by the diffusion of responsibility.

Joe Jack and Mike Winstanley pulled off the river at Minto Resort, about a mile upstream from the landing, and marched up to the restaurant for banana cream pie. "I was tempted to lodge a complaint with the organizers," said Joe, "that this race wasn't hard enough. We were putting on too much weight." This can be a tricky place to get off the river. There's a large back eddy—an area of calm water at the river's edge where there is a slight upstream current—and the transition can be hazardous if you hesitate even the slightest amount at the wrong time. As the canoe crosses the eddy line the bow is pulled slightly upstream by the back eddy and the stern is driven hard downstream—perfect conditions for capsizing a canoe. The trick is to shoot across the line quickly while making a half-turn to accommodate the two opposing currents.

Wayne and Michael Gregory misjudged the landing. "The area to land was in a back eddy with a strong eddy line," explained Wayne. "We were simply too fatigued and not prepared for the sharp eddy turn and dumped a few feet off shore." A few hours later, Tony Arcand and Kurt Bringli did a copycat

*Team clearing Five Finger Rapids*
PHOTO COURTESY OF: JOHN FIRTH

performance in exactly the same spot.

"It's a danger you talk about a lot," says Buckwheat, "but it doesn't happen that frequently." It did happen to him on one trip in early October 1991. The air temperature was below zero. The creeks were frozen and shore ice blocked off Buckwheat and his canoeing partner from landing along most of the river bank. "The water was so cold, it hurt to breathe."

The two pulled themselves and the canoe to the shore, where they built a fire and changed into dry clothes. "Everything obviously worked out, but still . . . losing gear . . . trying to save the canoe . . . trying to find a camp spot in the dark. I could easily relate to those guys from Juneau"—the Ken Brewer–Jimmy Smith team that capsized in Windy Arm. "That scared the hell out of me because I had been there."

There's not a lot to Minto. A few old cabins. An airstrip with a windsock. A picnic shelter, and a pump that looks like it hasn't drawn water in many a year. At one time this was a fairly large First Nations village. But a series of unsolved murders in 1954 convinced the people a killer was living in their midst, so they abandoned the village and moved thirty miles up the highway to Pelly Crossing. Most people, seeing the name on a map, expect a town when they arrive and are always surprised at the empty space. "I've lived here [in the Yukon] for only four months," said race volunteer Janet Ryan, "and everybody talks about places like Minto and Lower Laberge like they're places. I drive into Minto. There's the windsock so this has to be Minto. But where's everything else? There's no people. There's nothing. I was expecting something. . . . Anything. . . ." All around the airstrip and buildings the land is virtually denuded of life. It is covered with a fine black and grey ash, and what used to be trees are now charred, limbless posts sticking into the sky.

We noticed helicopters carrying water buckets yesterday, and all the signs of a nearby fire were apparent although we couldn't see the flames themselves. You can smell a fire first. It's like a campfire smell, but stronger. Then the smoke drifts in—high in the air during the heat of the day, settling into a valley fog in the cool evenings. Then you notice the heat haze in the air, where the air itself seems to bend and wave. And finally, you can feel the intense heat. Eighty per cent of fires near communities or recreational areas are caused by humans. Eighty per cent of fires in remote areas are caused by natural means. When there is lots of fuel—old dried trees and brush lying around—all it takes is the right combination of humidity and air temperature to ignite.

"When your humidity is lower than your air temperature," said Gord Mitchell, a twenty-year veteran of fire fighting along the river, "the fuels all turn almost gasoline-like." In 1995, the temperature was in the high 20s. The percentage of humidity was in the single digits. Two small fires ignited by lightening didn't seem to be threatening enough to worry about. When there appears to be no threat to human life or property, the fire watch will often just let them burn.

A fire that's up and running can literally fly through the forest, crowning from tree top to tree top at speeds of up to forty or fifty miles per hour. The two small fires ignited in 1995 moved faster than expected, joined up, and swept past both Minto and Big Salmon, threatening Carmacks and Pelly Crossing, and consumed an area larger than the country of Scotland. "The Monster," "The Dragon," or "The White Buffalo"—the names by which fire fighters know the fire front—ran for miles without a break and the flames shot over one hundred feet into the sky. The 1995 blaze was a "Campaign Fire." It refused to be tamed and had to be conquered over a period of months. In the end, it was the fire itself that decided to turn away from the communities and head towards alpine areas high in the remote hills. There, it gradually ran out of fuel and was conquered by the ultimate fire-fighting vehicle—winter.

I was mesmerized by the sight of trees exploding, blasting out sparks and burning particles. The windstorm created by the intense flames hurled burning sticks the size of coffee cups up to a half mile away. It was easy to understand how a formidable barrier, such as the Yukon River, was hurdled as easily as it was in 1995 when the fire leaped back and forth effortlessly, searing massive tracts of land on both sides.

It is the lifelessness of the desolation that is most overpowering. It makes one fear that what has been lost can never be recovered. Yet, it is with the brutal destructive power of fire that nature completes its natural cycle. In death, there is life. The first to appear is the fireweed—beautiful to behold in its late summer fields of pink and red, functional in it's ability to rejuvenate the dead soil. The mushrooms follow. Then poplar and alder trees. It will take up to fifty years for the area to reach the status of a mature forest, populated by spruce and pine trees. And, in another century, it will probably burn again.

In a way I envy the forest. It will relive its past over and over again, just as it has always done. We, on the other hand, can only hope to recapture just a bit of what this journey meant to those who preceded us. They had so much more at stake than we do. Their entire future hinged on what they would find at the end of the rainbow. We, on the other hand, risk little. When we reach Dawson City our lives will go on, outwardly, much as they did before we started. I have a sense of being excluded from the ghosts with whom we travel. As if I am doubly a foreigner to them. I am not a stampeder. I am not dead. But the river does have something to offer us modern-day adventurers. Only by experiencing it can we make our day-to-day life more satisfying. Wilderness stretches the spirit. A lifetime never exposed to this silence, this vastness, is a life not fully lived.

# CHAPTER TWENTY

## Fort Selkirk
Tuesday, 24 June 1997

Fort Selkirk has her vanity. For over a century she was the crown jewel of the Yukon River, and at one point was poised to become the capital city of the territory. Perched high above the river on a packed gravel terrace, the oldest community in the Yukon was centrally located for life on the river. The Chilkat Indians came from the coast with walrus ivory, seashells, seal fat, and clamshells to barter for furs, hides, and clothing from the Northern Tutchone. In the 1790s they started to bring guns, tea, and tobacco for trade. The Tutchone were familiar with the wares of the white man long before they ever actually encountered the people. In the cemetery behind the town are graves of First Nations people that predate the arrival of Hudson's Bay Company (HBC) trader Robert Campbell in his birch bark canoe in 1848.

HBC traders were usually the first white men encountered by First Nations people, which has thus lead to a misconception among Americans that, while the United States was established on the principles of brotherhood, equality, and liberty, Canada was founded by a department store. It was Campbell who named the future town after Thomas Douglas, Fifth Earl of Selkirk.

The Chilkat Indians took exception to Campbell setting up shop in what they considered their exclusive trading area, so they burned his trading post to the ground in 1852 and sent him down the river on a raft. It was forty years before another white man, Arthur Harper, arrived to build a store. Once he was established, others followed. When the stampeders stormed by in the years 1897–98 the population increased to over two thousand. Visitors could stay in the Savoy Hotel or the more upscale Occidental. They could purchase goods at Taylor and Drury's or Scholfield and Zimmerlee. (The HBC didn't return until 1938.) There was a one-room schoolhouse, a post office, a Roman Catholic mission. At the south end of town a stockade enclosed the quarters and parade ground of the Yukon Field Force, a military body assembled by the Canadian government to establish and maintain sovereignty during a gold rush held on Canadian soil but populated primarily by Americans. When Dominion Day and Independence Day rolled

*Paul Sargent mans the checkpoint inside the cooking cabin*
PHOTO COURTESY OF: JOHN FIRTH

around, the bureaucrats celebrated on July 1st and the people on July 4th.

The federal government was prepared to name Fort Selkirk the territorial capital, but it decided not to because the gold was in Dawson City, along with most of the territory's population. When official word came that Fort Selkirk was to be overlooked by the politicians, many of the residents and the Yukon Field Force moved to Dawson. Eventually, only about one hundred permanent residents remained.

The community continued to thrive as the major stop on the river for steamships. In summer, there would be three or four boats a day tied up along the waterfront. When the all-season highway from Whitehorse to Dawson was completed in 1954, the paddlewheelers, which had steadily declined in number over the past decade, stopped coming. The First Nations people moved to Pelly Crossing, thirty miles away, and everyone else went to Dawson or Whitehorse.

It was as if the people had simply vanished overnight. Danny Roberts, a wood cutter who had been working down river when the end came, returned home to a scene that could have come from one of the horror/sci-fi films that were just starting to become popular at the time. He and his wife clambered up the gravel bank to find a city devoid of human life. In the empty cabins, tables covered with cloths, and set with cutlery and china, lacked only steaming food and hungry mouths. Beds were turned down in preparation for children's nighttime stories. Coal-oil lamps waited for darkness. Tools hung orderly and ready for the craftsman's hands. That was the way people moved in the North. They couldn't take much more than would fit into a couple of steamer trunks: it was too expensive to ship things. What they couldn't pack they would give away, sell, or simply leave behind for whoever moved in behind them.

The Roberts remained in Fort Selkirk as caretakers. But one man couldn't do it all, and gradually the jewel of the Yukon River became tarnished. Time is a great healer, but a lousy beautician. Weather beat down the walls and roofs. Grass and trees crowded out the buildings' foundations. Piece by piece, river travellers packed off items and used wood from the buildings to fuel their campfires.

In 1970, when Dad, Tom, and Clary Craig arrived in the *Delia*, grey wood and rusting barrels were barely discernible in the long grass between the thirty-or-so decaying and partially disassembled buildings left on the site. Danny showed them two piles of weed—covered stones just up behind his house. This was all that was left of Campbell's original trading post, he said. They stumbled upon an old truck whose vintage and make were undecipherable, but the name of "Taylor and Drury" was still imprinted on the door. The wooden floorboards had long ago rotted away. Fireweed grew up through the springs of the seat and stood tall in the steering wheel. The single building that defied the natural deterioration of abandonment was St. Andrew's Anglican Church, built in 1931 with material scavenged from the Yukon Field Force barracks: its fir paneling had resisted time and its high stained-glass windows were still unbroken. "Still looks as good as new," dad noted in his river journal; "Other buildings in poor shape."

The staccato sound of hammers and the buzz of power saws could be heard there in 1979. A cross-Canada youth exchange program, Katimivik, decided to restore the buildings in Fort Selkirk as part of its mandate. A crew arrived from Quebec and Ontario to work on sealing the buildings off from the environment to prevent further deterioration.

Danny was more than happy to show off the interior of the one-room schoolhouse. "This is my school," the short, wiry man wearing the steamship-captain's hat and tooth-gapped grin proudly declared. "I learn English here." While it didn't have the eternal dignity of St. Andrew's, it did appear to be the only other building that hadn't been victimized by river travellers. Old medicine and alcohol bottles of various colours, sizes, and shapes lined the windowsills, diffusing dusty sunbeams into rainbows. Rays of light pried through gaps in the sagging log walls and stabbed down towards books lying on open-top desks with ink-wells and attached seats. A cobwebbed map of the Holy Land hung on one wall. A newly crowned Queen Elizabeth and Prince Phillip gazed at us from another.

A long time ago, children shut their texts for the day and carried home their homework for tomorrow. But tomorrow never came. The books lay patiently, harbouring a lesson that was never taught. Now, Danny told us, those children were returning. They were First Nations elders who came to linger wistfully in their childhood once again. Many of them, he added, could even identify which desk had been theirs.

The Yukon government and the Selkirk First Nation from Pelly Crossing took over the restoration project from Katimivik. "Fort Selkirk is probably the most historically significant site in the Yukon," Yukon government historic site co-ordinator Bruce Barrett told Fred and me. "It was a traditional trading area for First Nations. It was the first place in the Yukon settled by Europeans. The one-room schoolhouse is the oldest standing building in the Yukon. Originally built in 1892 as an Anglican church, it became the school when St. Andrew's was completed a few years later. When we started into this one [the schoolhouse], there were pencils and paper here from the last day of classes."

The decision was made to restore the community to the way it was in the 1940s. They jacked up buildings to replace the old rotting logs in the foundations. Then they lowered the walls back down, put in new flooring and restored the roof shingles, replicating as well as possible the colours and designs of the original artifacts.

෴

It is early morning when John turns us into the narrow back eddy in front of Fort Selkirk and I leap from the bow of the canoe to pull us ashore. The bowman's job is to be the first one out of the canoe and look good doing it. Then Brendan and Anne appear with their camera gear. "Sorry guys," says Brendan. "But we were up by the campfire and missed your landing. Would you mind doing it again?" We drag the canoe a hundred yards or so back upstream. "This is the weirdest thing we've done on this trip," mutters John. We haven't slept in twenty hours, and we spent the last two battling fire-hose-force headwinds and sheets of rain on the river. When we touch the shore my body jumps up but my legs refuse to cooperate. I stumble drunkenly onto the gravel under the relentless gaze of the camera. "Thanks guys," says Brendan. "That was great." Glad he thinks so.

Just outside of Fort Selkirk, Sandy Sippola and Marjorie Logue spot lightning and hear thunder. They decide to pull up on shore and swing towards a high grassy bank. As Sandy steers the canoe into the back eddy Marjorie leaps out to pull them ashore—and misses the edge of the bank. Sandy looks up as her canoeing partner disappears under the water. "Oh yeah, great!" mutters Sandy and wonders if she should get out and help. Then Marjorie surfaces, climbs out of the water and stalks off into the bush. "She was a little upset at the time. She was soaked. She was cold. We had life jackets on but they were the kind you need to inflate. It really freaked her out because she was so tired and neither of us were thinking very well. I got out and looked for some dry clothes for her. Once we got her into dry clothes she warmed up. When we got to Fort Selkirk she was pretty exhausted."

Across the river I can see The Palisades, a million-year-old volcanic wall that looms high above the river for twelve miles down river from Fort Selkirk. Caribou bones dating back 1.3 million years were discovered emerging from below the rampart. A tool made from a caribou antler, discovered just a few miles to the northeast, has been dated at 11,300 years old, and a couple of miles upstream were stone tools close to seven thousand years old. Fort Selkirk is approximately where the glaciers of the last ice age stopped advancing almost twelve thousand years ago. The clues suggest that people have lived in this region almost continuously since that time, which would make it the oldest constantly inhabited region in North America. There are two huge round dents in the wall, compliments of two practice cannon rounds fired by the Yukon Field Force in 1898. At the south end of the Palisades, the Pelly River joins the Yukon and doubles the volume of water. What has been a wide river riddled with a multitude of islands doubles in width, and the current increases dramatically in speed and power. G. I. Cameron was the North West Mounted Police officer stationed in Fort Selkirk when Tom Drury met his end on 13 April 1933. He and all the others on the shore watched in shock as what should have been a humourous incident suddenly turned tragic. "He was a boy of about nineteen. He was decking on the boat at the time and somebody looked up and noticed he was in the water. He had fallen off the front of the boat and everyone started laughing. He was a fine swimmer. They threw him a life preserver. He started swimming for it, then threw up both hands and we never saw him again. He drowned right there in front of Selkirk. There's a stained glass window in St. Andrew's Church that was donated by the Drury family in memory of their son."

"It constantly amazes me just how unforgiving the river can be," said Jerry Dixon. "Its speed and strength are constantly being underrated." Jerry worked as a River Ranger near Eagle, Alaska, for six years in the 1970s and '80s. It was part of his job to interview witnesses and retrieve the dead from the Yukon River. Such as the Frenchman who took his bride-to-be on a romantic pre-wedding trip, only to have her knocked off the raft by a sweeper and vanish into the murky depths. Or the recreational fisherman who, while standing mid-thigh deep in the river, slipped and was dragged under when his hip waders filled with water. "There is not a year that goes by that someone doesn't die in this river."

Fort Selkirk is our final mandatory stop in the Dyea-to-Dawson. We must stop here for at least eight hours. Maria (pronounced ma-Rye-ah) Van Bibber is the historic sites interpreter for the Selkirk First Nation, and also the official signing us in. "You can leave just after eight this morning. You can camp anywhere in the designated camping area over by the picnic shelter."

Maria was born and raised in Fort Selkirk, although she now lives in Pelly Crossing. She was hired by the First Nation in 1995 to take over for Danny Roberts who, though still alive, is getting pretty old. "Feels like I'm coming home when I come back here. I like it here. I think it's one of the most beautiful places on earth," she says, pointing down river towards a hill named Victoria Rock (viewed from the side, it resembles a profile of Queen Victoria). "I remember that bluff since I was growing up. Looks like a picture of a wolf to me." In 1998 she took Fred and me over to the house where she had been born. It is two very small rooms under the same roof. At one time seven people, two adults and five children, shared the cramped quarters. She smiled constantly as she talked about the years she spent in Fort Selkirk, occasionally bubbling with girlish enthusiasm that peeled the years from her.

> I loved Saturday night. We used to play Canasta. Have you ever played Canasta? Now people have to do things like drugs or drinking. Back then, everything was fun. Nobody drank. You could have fun doing simple things. People were a lot different then than they are now. A lot nicer. A lot friendlier.
>
> Saddest times I had as a girl was when the last steamboat of the year would go around the corner away from Fort Selkirk. They would blow their whistle and all the dogs in town would howl. The happiest times I had was when the first steamboat would appear.

The dogs would start to bark and howl. Then we could see the smoke and steam billowing out over the trees. We could hear the chuffing and then they would blow the whistle. Everyone would run down the river bank and yell, "Riverboat's coming!" Those feelings I remember today as well as I felt them back then.

⌇

Then she told us about the race ahead of us. "I think that first team was going to win. It was like they had a motor on their canoe. The three teams behind them were going pretty fast too." Danny Roberts had watched them also. "They're crazy," he concluded. "They all want that gold, I guess."

Gerard Cruchon and Jacques Chicoine arrive a few hours ahead of us to discover some friends from Dawson City flew into Fort Selkirk to greet them. "They brought some wine, some homemade bread, and pâté. One of the ladies, she's a very, very good cook and she make these little things that I can't remember what they are, but they were very, very good"—Gerard pinches the tips of his fingers together, brings them to his lips, then tosses a kiss into the air. "We cook some mushrooms in garlic and butter. That was the first time I use the fry pan we carry over the Chilkoot. And we have a feast. Then I have a cigar. And some wine. It was a really, really good evening. Jacques went to bed after we eat. I thought he would give me shit because I stay up so late."

"We get to leave at 3:30," says Jacques. "I don't know how we're going to do that. I don't even know what time it is now."

Dan Morrison and Cathy Tibbetts arrived in Fort Selkirk as a warm breeze whipped up a light fog in front of them. "It was magical," Dan recalled, seeing the river bank and buildings loom up without warning out of the mist. The two of them had spent the past few hours cruising through the braided channels of Hell's Gate, a stretch of the river where the riverboats occasionally needed "dead men" and cables to winch themselves over the sand bars hidden under the water. The anchoring rings used to secure the cables could still be seen on one of the islands. There, Dan and Cathy had found themselves in "beaver heaven. There must have been a beaver, beaver house, or beaver dam every fifty or one hundred feet."

Morning at Fort Selkirk is a matter of perspective, based upon your arrival time. Officially for us it is just after eight in the morning. Sandy and Marjorie get their morning at about lunchtime. For Yvonne Harris and Kevin

McKague it is 10:00 PM. It's hard to remember times when you're not even sure what day it is.

All that matters is the original time clock. Sunrise to sunset. Daylight is just daylight, coming or going. Days no longer have names. Being on schedule means arriving before or after dark.

We don't so much go to sleep as we go comatose, for as long as we have to be there. Morning is when someone else who you know is close to you in the standings gets up. Even asleep, you hear their voice, recognize it, insert it into whatever dream you are having, and start to climb towards consciousness.

Then the aroma of breakfast lures you back into the land of the living. Steve Cash and Geo Ljljenkjold both wake up craving fried eggs for breakfast so badly that they can almost smell them. In fact, they can smell them. Gerard and Jacques are frying eggs on the table right beside their tent. Beside the French Connection are Yvonne Harris and Kevin McKague. In addition to preparing Eggs Benedict, they are frying up pancakes and bacon. Preparing the better breakfast also means being the better boat in this race.

Outclassed in backcountry cuisine, Gerard throws down the gauntlet. "We are going to paddle straight through to Dawson and we are going to arrive before you." The moment he turns his back, Yvonne and Kevin cut their breakfast plans short. As they load up their gear and scurry towards the riverbank, Yvonne casts a sideways glance at Gerard who pretends to be oblivious to the activity. "We've got to get a good lead on them," she mutters.

Stewart City, NWT
28 July 1897

My Dearest Delia,
Words I hoped I would never have to write. It is with the most profound sadness that I inform you Paul passed on two days ago. We are still not sure exactly what happened. He had been sick for a brief time, but appeared to be feeling better and was preparing to get back into our journey. He even had the energy to make light of his condition.

"It really doesn't matter what you do with me when I die," he told Robert that last night. "Throw me in the river if that seems fitting."

One cool evening I went into his tent and he appeared deathlike, his appearance pale and gaunt, no breath seeming to come from his lips. I touched his face, finding it very cold. "He's dead," I told Franklin.

*Wilderness grave*

PHOTO COURTESY OF: JOHN FIRTH

"Not yet," responded Paul, "but I shall be shortly unless we get some heat in here."

Later I asked him if there was anyone I should write to should he die. After a moment, he answered me, "No." In some ways I believe he considered being deprived of life a happiness rather than a misfortune. Even so, it was a shock to awaken that morning and find him gone.

People should die when they are old. They should have time to say farewell and tell us stories of their lives. Paul did not speak of his life and it appears there was no one to say good-bye to. We must accept unquestioningly that everything that happens is essentially good and eventually everyone dies of something. Despite the anguish aroused by the unfairness of it all.

I lie here in my tent, with my eyes closed, and I can see him in his heavenly robes. He sits in a lovely, soft armchair reading a good book with all the poets in it. Around him, a warm cabin. In front of him, on a table, a peaceful meal. Beyond him, a bountiful bath. These are the furnishings of heaven. When we join him there, he will be the spirit of hospitality. His inquiring nature will take interest in the world always. It seems that when you are on your deathbed you have more interest in what has happened recently in this life than what may happen in the next. Would that be so different in the afterlife?

Is this what makes death so hard—curiosity unsatisfied? For a good story we will receive a hot bath and civilized tea—free from floating pine needles and drowned mosquitoes.

I will sleep tonight, not from the loss of vigour caused by a day of hard work, but the weariness of grief. We buried him on the river bank out here, on the edge of the world, with only a crude wooden cross bearing his name, "Paul Reddington," and a covering of spruce boughs as his shroud.

We have been slowly working our way down the river, stopping on sand-and gravel bars to pan for colour. Franklin, who has become a master with the gold pan, has also convinced us on more than one occasion to travel up some of the tributary streams and rivers to mine their bottoms for flour gold as well.

To go upstream with our scow is the hardest work any man can do. Three of us, Franklin, Robert, and myself, go onto the shore. Two of us pull on a line attached to the bow. The other holds onto a line rigged about one-third of the way along the gunwale. Paul would push the boat into the current, then rush to the stern to man the tiller and keep the nose pointed into the current.

The river current holds the boat away from the bank and the men on shore drag it, one agonizing step at a time, upstream. When our way on land is blocked, we climb back on board the boat and row madly across the current to more passable terrain on the other side. It is like taking one step forward and two back when we do that. The river current would push us back downstream and we would have to recapture the lost ground before making headway.

However, even in the most remote corner, we find we are not alone. Other men have the same folly as ourselves—if there is gold in the Klondike, there must be gold elsewhere as well. The next strike might be on that creek, or this one. Or it may be right beneath my feet.

I found a small amount of colour on a gravel bar just a few miles up the Stewart River—a stream that is greater than the Ohio, with hundreds of gulches and side streams. It has allegedly produced adequate amounts of flour gold. As I looked at my pitiful small amount, I found myself questioning if this tiny residue of gold was worth all the misery and anguish. We had dragged our boat up this river for an entire day to reach here and this was our reward—not even enough to buy a loaf of bread. I considered the farmer who probably held in his hand no more seeds than I have grains of gold, and from those he produced the loaf of bread we cannot afford to purchase.

Tomorrow we set off again. There is talk of a strike on a small creek just a few miles down stream and we dare not delay since we have learned that the bulk of men arrive at those places after the best ground has been staked.

One should think that after so many years in this business of mining that I would know better than to chase dreams. But small strikes are reflections of our obsessions of the moment. We disbelieve the rumours. We distrust the men who tell of them. Yet we still go—just in the off chance that this one is the real one. I am unable to deliver myself of the need that drives us from creek to creek, even though— as a member of the literate fringe of the working class—I earn more for the writing of a single letter to a loved one somewhere other than here than we do for the days of back breaking misery on the bars. I am not ready yet. I must test all the bars before I shall be satisfied.

Despite my exhaustion, I have waited until the others have gone to sleep before sitting down to write to you. There must be some privacy, even in the closest friendships. Some secrets left. Some things we do not wish to share with or know about each other.

I still have the Bible you gave me. It is much battered now, but the comfort I feel as I read the passages is testament to the affection we share. A reminder that even though we are in our separate places, we can still see each other as we wish. With eyes closed, I see a woman. Lovely to behold. Gracious and valiant to stand by such an unfettered man as myself. I am heartened and privileged by your presence in my isolation. This vision I keep to myself. It is my secret. Not a day passes that I do not think of you.

I'll give thee to my love tonight,
The fairest ever seen,
Canst thou not tell her that my love,
For her has ever been?
Electrify with sweetest thoughts,
Her mind in perfect bliss,
And impress for me,
Upon her lips,
Thy perfumed tender kiss;
Tommy

*The great flood of 1925*

# CHAPTER TWENTY-ONE

## Split-Up Island
Wednesday, June 25

M y  n i g h t m a r e  i s  just a few miles ahead of us. The gravel bar—where, in my dreams, John and I have that final falling out and divvy up the gear to the point of sawing the canoe into two pieces (although I had never resolved whether we cut it widthwise or lengthwise)—is creeping ever closer.

Not that we currently have any differences. We did have our moments earlier. On the Chilkoot, when John was at his lowest. On Laberge, when I hit bottom. And when we considered how to tackle Windy Arm. But by this point in the race we have no conflict. "Look at this," I ask: "we've travelled together . . . ten feet apart for seven days. Bonding in such an intense manner. What could possibly undo this?"

"Seven more days," he responds.

It's the gravel bar itself that's getting closer. Split-up Island, at the mouth of the Stewart River, was so called because it was here, during the gold rush, that men and women who had been partners, lifelong friends, lovers, or blood relatives, grew to hate each other with irrational passion. Few forces on earth are more destructive and corrosive than bitterness bred by familiarity forced through close association. On that island, grown adults became as spoiled children, their actions crossing the border into sheer stupidity. Partners divided supplies down the middle, with neither conceding an inch of intelligence. If there were three bags of flour they took one each and cut the third in half, not considering what was spilled on the ground except to argue that the wastage was part of the other man's portion. Tents were cut down the middle. Metal wood-burning stoves were disassembled into an equal number of useless parts. Boats sawed in two. As a final parting gesture to the partnership that enabled them to get this far, they'd roll on the ground and flail away at each other with their fists in white-hot anger.

It was not just Split-Up Island where these events occurred. Reports from various individuals during the stampede witnessed it happening everywhere from Dyea to Dawson. This island earned its label because it happened here so often that estranged partners built a small shantytown while having their disputes. There are no remains of any kind now, on the island of that bizarre community. What structures they built were subsequently dismantled and used to construct boats.

If we are going to faithfully replicate the gold rush it is inevitable that some of that emotional babble should reappear. "Some partnerships are meant to break up," believes Jeff Brady. "It's tough being in a canoe together for a week, ten days . . . however long it takes. Some people were just thrown together and should not have been. Some of those partnerships ended early. Some stayed together and shouldn't have."

Right from the beginning, Steve Cash and Geo Ljljenskjold have different agendas. At first the race is fun. Racing over the Chilkoot Pass, shouting, "Gold! There's Gold in the Klondike!" The novelty and exuberance of the event overwhelms small disagreements. As they paddle through the lakes it becomes apparent that Geo doesn't like the fact that this is a race. In his view, a race doesn't fit with what it was like during the gold rush. He is content to sit back and relax. Steve, on the other hand, wants to be as competitive as he can be. He hammers it out as hard as he can, but becomes increasingly frustrated by his partner. The first major rift develops shortly after getting off Lake Laberge. Rather than sleeping during the twelve-hour mandatory layover, Geo hitchhiked back to Skagway to pick up his van. When they leave Whitehorse he hasn't had any sleep at all, dozes in the canoe, and contributes only sporadically. Steve paddles virtually solo until they are in the Thirty Mile River. Upon awakening, Geo still feels frazzled. He doesn't cope well with sleep-deprivation and lashes out at his partner: "Why didn't you stop me from going to Skagway? Why didn't you try to persuade me not to go?"

"I'm not your mother!" Steve snaps back, himself exhausted and resentful. Geo, he feels, hasn't been pulling his weight and he lets him know about it. Periods of stressful silence start to dominate the conversation, and when words do pass between them they are increasingly vitriolic. By the time they close in on Split-Up Island, Geo is sullen and uncooperative, refusing to paddle. Steve is ready to pull the plug on the partnership: "I put up with it. I shouldn't have. Even at the start. I should have pulled it right there. But I didn't because we were in the thing together. I let him get a little closer to me. He put me down. He'd attack me for something. There was no question in my mind. He was getting out of that canoe on the next island."

Wendy Cairns and Chris Guenther paddle up behind Geo and Steve's canoe. "It was a really intense time," says Chris; "I knew there was tension between them but I hadn't realized the extent of it. I guess at that time the tension was really building. They pulled into the riverbank and I thought it was literally going to come to blows." The two women land—effectively aborting any violence, since neither Geo nor Steve will fight in front of them—and offer to trade canoes. Geo can paddle with Wendy. Steve with Chris.

Steve turns down the offer. To change paddlers will disqualify both teams and—as hostile as he feels—he still wants to finish the race. "You're," he shouts, pointing at Geo, "coming with me. And I ain't going to let you play your little games. We're going to town." They climb back into the canoe and complete the race in silence. "Welcome to Dawson City!" howls a delighted Buckwheat as they draw into the finish area. To complete the race they must set up token claim posts on the riverbank. Buckwheat holds a claim post out to Geo, "You going to . . ."

"No," interrupts Geo, "I don't deal with claim jumpers like you." And walks away.

Further back on the river, Brendan and Anne decide to shut off their motor and paddle for a couple of hours just to get a feel for what the other competitors are going through. The arguments start almost immediately. "We were bitching to one another," says Brendan. "Let's go this way. Let's go that way. Do it in this stroke. We had to switch on the engine again and we think, my God, we're bitching after two hours of paddling. What have these other people been doing for four or five days?" Even with the engine running they're not immune to being pigheaded. Neither has slept for a long time. On one stretch of the river, Anne is driving the boat. Brendan asks her to pull over to the shore so he can take a pee. Anne refuses. A while later, she steers the boat to the shore. "I needed to take a pee an hour ago," grumbles Brendan. "I don't want to take a pee now." They change positions and Brendan drives awhile. Eventually Anne asks him to pull over so she can take a pee. Brendan refuses. "I went ashore when you needed a pee."

"You did not!"

"I did so!"

"You're being a jerk," confesses Brendan to himself when Anne is out of earshot, "and you don't want to admit it. She's being a jerk and you want to broadcast it to the world. It's right there over the canoe. A great big sign. You look up and see the worst of yourself in technicolor."

Mark Kelsey is more than casually interested in Karen Lesley, and she in him. As part of the fledgling courtship, Mark invites her to partner with him

*The ice goes out on the Yukon*

in the 1997 race, which he is also covering as a journalist for the *Juneau Empire*. Everything goes fine until they reach Bennett. The relationship and the race go downhill from there. Karen has limited experience on the water and simply isn't comfortable in the canoe. The high waves on the lakes wear on her nerves, and she's not thrilled with the way the boat turns sideways in the river when neither of them paddle. She takes her jitters out on Mark and he, frustrated that this romantic sojourn isn't working out quite the way he planned, strikes back. At Carmacks they are ready to brain each other with their paddles. Karen climbs out of the canoe, grabs her gear, and stomps towards town. She finds a ride to Whitehorse and doesn't come back.

Left at the riverbank, Mark and his father, who is helping with the Carmacks checkpoint, decide to drive to Dawson City to help set up the checkpoint there. "When I arrived, there was Jeff and Buckwheat and a canoe had just arrived. I thought to myself, 'We should have kept on going.' After that, every time one of the canoe teams arrived they would ask how I did and I would have to tell them I got a ride from Carmacks. It was really tough to say that." High on his list of important things to do before he leaves the North, he adds, is a canoe trip from Carmacks to Dawson City—a form of closure. "I have to do that one so I can say I completed it."

Whitehorse psychologist Bill Stewart points out that the potential for minor differences to get out of control in intense situations is very high. But it can be overcome, and the victory over rampant emotions actually enhance the challenge. Bill reflects:

> There were times when the last person we wanted to sit fourteen feet apart from was the other. But we had to do it and we had to work that out. I like the intensity of these sorts of races. And wrestling with Steven [Jull] around what we want to accomplish and how we're going to do that, then trying to evolve a common direction we can move in. I think that was part of the richness of the race. It's the most satisfying aspect of the race: trying to sort out all of the personally exclusive agendas and then finding a way to satisfy them—to find the common point where they all come together.

ෆ

It wouldn't have been half the race if it had just been me running over the Chilkoot and hopping into my own boat and paddling. I think it created a kind of bond that will probably endure for the duration of our lives even though we may not have a lot of contact. Our lives will move in different directions, but there is one thing we did together and we couldn't have done it without each other.

ෆ

No problems here. John and I paddle on into the twilight, marking our progress on the old river channel maps produced for the steamship captains. Unless you know the names of the creeks and pay attention to the chicken scratches on the map, you can't tell the differences between them. A newly painted sign on an island informs us that at least one creek will be different from the others. "Baked Goods at Kirkman Creek," it reads. Although we're not operating on a clock they probably are—and we don't stop since we're cruising by long after business hours. Kirkman Creek is famous for its hospitality and sand bars. First inhabited in April 1914, when stampeders arrived for one of many minor gold rushes that followed the Klondike discovery, it later became a sheep farm that produced Merino and Oxford wool, as well as mutton.

In 1948, Jack and Hazel Meloy moved to Kirkman Creek; they had been made Coffee Creek refugees by the annual floods that kept swamping their home. They remained here for sixteen years, developing a reputation for beautiful gardens and their generosity to river travellers.

Visitors were scrutinized carefully by Hazel, who then invited them in for a meal. Once in, they were not only provided with one of the best feeds along the river, but the long evening was spent with a leisurely cup of coffee over which Hazel and Jack regaled them with stories of their thirty years on the river. Life for the Meloys was seldom boring.

Hazel, in particular, achieved Olympus-like standing in the mythology of the river. She operated her own trap line, ran her own dog team, and few could equal her skills in the bush. Legend had it that she once killed a bear with an axe. There was little doubt about her physical prowess. When riverboat crews unloaded stores for the winter, they packed two hundred-pound quarters of beef down the gangplank. Two men wrestled with the meat and placed it on the beach. Hazel then hoisted it onto her shoulders and carried it the rest of the way to the house.

It was her don't-mess-with-me approach to life that sealed her place in river history. She never feared voicing an opinion and, when drastic action was called for, she didn't hesitate. To hail a steamship, one placed a flag on the riverbank; the crew on the boat spotted the flag and pulled over to collect the mail or passenger. One afternoon, Hazel placed her flag and waited for the next ship. When the boat appeared, the crew either didn't see her flag or decided to ignore it. Annoyed, Hazel grabbed her rifle and put a shot through the rigging on the bow. That got their attention.

☙❧

When we stopped at Kirkman Creek for the night in 1979, owner Linda Taylor offered us a bed in the old Post Office, which she used as a guest cabin. It worked fine for keeping off the rain, but there was a hole somewhere in the wire netting and the cabin filled quickly with mosquitoes—so many they made sleep impossible. It reminded me of tales about poking rifles into dense clouds of mosquitoes to make a hole into which one could spit. Or swinging a knife through the air and slicing open so many bugs one had to clean the blood off the blade. We finally set up our tent in the middle of the cabin and crawled inside.

The sand bars in the river just below Kirkman Creek were notorious for shifting almost daily in the river current, and when the steamships ran rarely a day went by that one wasn't grounded. One summer day there were several ships stuck, and only one was able to complete the journey into Dawson City that night. When asked how he did it, the captain replied, "Every sand bar had its ship, and all I had to do was avoid the ships."

⌘

The Scot in me is aroused as we slip past Thistle Creek—named after the Highland emblem. This millstream was mined by men with monikers like Murdock McIver. I fancy I can hear bagpipes playing back in the hills. In the dusk of midnight I see the dark outline of a house now closed to the weather and prying eyes. This was one of our mail drops in 1979, and when I scrambled up the riverbank that summer I came upon one of the most vivid memories I have of any person. It was one of those hundred-year hot days that follow short and furious midday cloudbursts. When I reached the top of the bank I looked out across a drenched field in which played short mud creatures that looked a lot like children, goats, chickens, and dogs. The rain had hit the ground so hard it had splashed dirt up the side of the house and covered all the barrels, boxes, boats, and sleds stacked around the place. There wasn't anything in sight that wasn't hot, damp, or dirty.

Then the door opened and out stepped a vision of clean and dry. It was as if she was walking in an aura. Everything that fell inside her influence became instantly spotless. Even the children who gathered around her to gawk curiously at the unwashed stranger with the bag of mail seemed to lose their mud cover. Maybe the heat was getting to me, or maybe we hadn't gotten enough sleep the night before. Or it could have been that she seemed so much in control of the chaos around her. But for the past two decades whenever someone mentioned Thistle Creek that image came to me.

"You probably just caught me on a cleaning day," laughed Jan Couture when I described the first time we met. She had no recollection of it at all. Muddy, sunny days along the Yukon are a dime a dozen, as are river travellers. What she does remember is gradually becoming "Yukon tough"—as opposed to "wrong side of the tracks tough"—over the sixteen years she and her husband Gerry lived at Thistle Creek. "I gained independence. The ability to look after myself and care for others. I became physically fit for the first time in my life. . . . What did I lose [being so isolated from everything]?

Contact with my family maybe." It was a far cry from her fifth-story walkup in New York City, from which she ventured to go to the ballet and attend the theatre.

Fleeing an unhappy marriage, she ended up in Whitehorse in the early 1970s. "I was just floating around. A lot of people were doing that in those years." There she met Gerry, an aeronautical engineer who wanted to learn how to fly helicopters. Exactly how and why they ended up at Thistle Creek isn't exactly clear, since it has little to do with either New York society or helicopters. But once there, they opted for the frontier life. They built a home. Jan cultivated a massive garden, collected livestock, and looked after the children. Gerry became a commercial fisherman.

It wasn't an easy life. Openings for commercial fishers were infrequent and short. When one occurred, Gerry tended his nets twenty-four hours a day, harvesting fish every three or four hours. He pulled in between one hundred and 125 fish each day, selling them to restaurants, private buyers, and other river travellers, giving some to people who needed them but couldn't afford them, and putting the rest into his own freezer. "Nobody in my family now likes fish. The fish the processors didn't want . . . the big ones—and in those days we caught a lot of big fish—we would eat ourselves."

In 1979 they learned there was a dark side to the Yukon River.

In spring, when the ice is sandwiched between the snow melting on top and the water levels rising underneath, it rots and finally breaks up. Yukoners run an ice pool lottery in which people have to guess the exact time the ice will "go out" in front of Dawson City. Since 1896, a Union Jack is frozen in the ice on the river with a trip cable running to a clock on shore (in recent years, the flag pole was replaced by a tripod). When the ice shifts sufficiently to trip the clock the person who has guessed the time closest to the actual time wins a sum of money.

When the ice starts to move it breaks into huge four-foot-thick green, crystalline blocks that are tossed around and dragged downstream by the surging river current. The thundering crack and rumble of the blocks smashing, shredding, and grinding over each other can be heard for miles like a constant series of muted explosions. They spin, swirl, and crawl over top of each other until there are so many jammed together that they come to a shuddering stop—grounded on a gravel bar or a rock. The water builds up behind the ice dam, climbs to fifteen or twenty feet above its normal level, and overflows the banks on either side. The water uproots trees and chews away at the matted grasses still prone from survival under the weight of the winter snow. Then the water finds a weakness in the ice. Without warning the wall gives way, and the mass of ice is sent spinning and flipping once again, a ponderous battering ram propelled by the tremendous volume of water finally released from behind it. The sudden release of water is much like flushing a toilet. The pans and floes of ice race in their panicked flight until another gravel bar dams the way once again. Everything that is caught in it— buildings, trees, boats, moose, dogs, people, the riverbank itself—gets sucked down the river and into the grinder.

On the maps, Stewart Island, a mile or so downstream from Split-Up Island, covers forty acres. When we pass it in 1997, it only has about three acres left. The spring floods have ripped away the rest of the island and carried it off downstream. "The river put it there," said Rudy Burian, who owned a home and store on the island for sixty years, "and I guess it'll take it away. There's nothing we can do about it."

The first flood for the Coutures was in 1979. The water rose slowly, giving them plenty of warning. They moved further inland, up a small hill behind their property, and built a sandbag dam around the house. Then the water level dropped quickly and the danger passed. Further downstream, the people of Dawson City went to bed dry and woke up floating in six feet of water. The water came in so quickly it wrested houses off their foundations and tossed them around like so many bathtub toys. "I thought that was a big flood until the 1982 one," said Jan.

She was ready to serve up dinner—a pot of freshly-made pea soup and a pan of cornbread cooling on top of the table—when she glanced out the kitchen window and saw a mountain of ice come to a shuddering halt just in front of the house. "We gotta get out of here," she said; "Get your sleeping bags and get up the hill." By the time the children were out the door the water had started pouring over the riverbank. "I didn't realize it would come up that fast." There wasn't enough time to get to the hill, so Gerry threw the kids up on the roof of the house then helped Jan untie the dogs and goats so they could escape the rising water. Finally, they pulled themselves onto the roof with the kids. It had been less than fifteen minutes since Jan had seen the ice stop on the river. A few minutes more and the water was lapping at the eaves. "I don't remember ever being so cold. After being in that water with all the ice slivers. It was like swimming in a frozen daiquiri. Then crawling up on the roof in your wet clothes. . . ." When exhaustion started to overtake them, they nodded off and started sliding off the roof. "We had to stay awake to make sure the kids were safe."

They watched as the large fishing boat sailed away downstream. They never saw it again. A smaller boat drifted inland and got caught in the top of a tree. When dawn came they could see the ice dam and water were gone. Gerry climbed down and found dry clothes in another shed. The main house had shifted on its foundations. The only thing that prevented it, and them, from getting sucked down the river was a recent addition more securely anchored to the ground. They discovered one of the dogs hanging upside down high in a willow tree, its hindquarters caught in a Y-shaped branch.

When they tried to get in the house they were unable to open the door. The house was full of ice chips. It took the two of them an entire day to shovel them out. The kitchen table had floated across the room, but the pot of soup sitting on it was undisturbed. The pan of cornbread had floated from the table to the warming oven of the wood stove, but it also was dry. It was to be the only food they had for the next two days. "If we'd had a boat the next morning, we probably would have gone and probably never gone back. But because we had to stay there for four days, and because we had three kids, we didn't have time to sit down and feel sorry for ourselves. We had to feed and clothe and make them comfortable. We got through that time where we wanted to leave and decided to stay."

# CHAPTER TWENTY-TWO

## Yukon River just upstream from Dawson City
Wednesday, 25 June

Agnew Slough, a placid moose pasture near the mouth of the White River, was where almost everyone from Dawson used to go to hunt. The hunters, Dad told me, used to line up on the edge of the river, then wait for the sun to rise and the morning mist to lift away. There, only a hundred yards or so in front of them, the moose grazed. Standing knee deep in the marsh, their great jaws chewed in a circular motion on a mouthful of roots, water ran off their jowls, and their ears flapped to chase off early morning mosquitoes. That mouthful completed, they ducked their heads under the water for another.

Then the shooting began. The hunters blazed away at the animals until two or three had fallen and the rest had fled. The pile of spent shells would, in some places, be this high, he used to say, indicating with his hand a level about midway between his waist and his knee. Exaggerated of course, but possibly not so far off the truth as one might suspect.

*Black bear on the Yukon*
PHOTO COURTESY OF: JOHN FIRTH

While human inhabitants along the river are often at a premium, there is always a lot of wildlife. In 1937, caribou herds, in such numbers that it often took four or five days for all the animals to swim across the river, were reported at Lake Laberge and in the streets of Dawson City. "Caribou used to come through by the thousands," remembered G. I. Cameron; "I saw fifty to a hundred go right through the middle of Fort Selkirk. People would stand in the streets and shoot at them." They were, in the words of Captain Bill Bromley—skipper of the SS *Klondike*—"like cattle in the barnyard." The steamships coming downstream would blow the whistle to alert the passengers, then turn off their engines and just drift through them. The upstream ships would find a place to tie up and wait for the crossing to be completed. Even then, such massive caribou migrations were rare in the central and southern Yukon. According to Hugh Bostock, the last time the First Nations elders had seen large herds this far upriver, prior to the 1930s, was in the 1870s.

Johnny Hoggan said there was plenty of food along the Yukon River in the 1930s and '40s. Rabbits. Gophers. Squirrels. Moose. Caribou. Bear. Marmots. Beaver. "I've even eaten muskrat. They're good. You're never out of fresh meat or things to eat."

Fred Farkvam and I once paddled past a porcupine swimming across the river. It kept going under the water, then resurfaced. We worried about whether or not it was going to make it but declined to attempt a rescue. A panicked porcupine was not a good thing to have inside a canoe only eighteen feet long.

Cynde Adams and Larry Gullingsrud drift up on a lynx who apparently doesn't see them coming, even though they float just five feet behind it. "That was really wild. That's a wildlife sighting you don't normally get," Cynde says.

Just past Minto, several paddlers report Dall Sheep on a low mountain alongside the river. One night Gerard Cruchon hears a hawk diving and looks up just in time to watch the predator snatch another bird out of the air. "I hear that noise like that thing was diving. He swoops like a bomber, you know, whistling. His wings they were folded back. Then whap! He caught the bird when he was flying."

John and I hear, before we see, a pair of gyrfalcons alternating dive-bombing runs at a Mallard duck, which dives under the water to escape. Each time it slips under, the predators hover and call back and forth to each other. Each time it resurfaces, they attack again. Finally the duck turns tail feathers and flees to the safety of thick brush. Deprived of their fun, the falcons head off in search of other amusement. For a long time after, drifting by, we hear the duck complaining loudly.

The one animal that everyone seems to want to encounter is the moose. Tall, ungainly, with a goofy face that only a mother could love and (on the bulls) horns that shamelessly broadcast sexual prowess to any cow who happens to be in heat. In Russia, they tried domesticating them as dairy animals and draft moose. In North America we are somewhat less ambititous: we use them to make jewellery. Just about anywhere on the continent, stores carry moose dropping earrings, tie clasps, and key rings. One can even find "Mooseltoe" during the festive season. It's an industry that, with the right promoter—say T. A. Firth, for instance—could rival gemstones for dominance in the jewellery business. There is an unlimited supply of "moose nuggets" available, with an average moose producing two hundred pellets per drop. They are simply lying around on top of the ground. A Klondike just waiting to be discovered!

The best place to see a moose is while it is standing on the riverbank. If he or she gets in the water with you, the potential for disaster increases substantially. Any canoeist who finds him or herself on a collision course with a moose in the river is wise to steer clear. It isn't the possibility of the moose turning on you and attacking. It's the probability that they may not even be aware of your existence and make no effort to avoid contact. A moose outweighs a canoe by several hundred pounds, and it's usually the boat that loses in such contests.

While paddling late at night, I was sure I could hear a strange sound, like a swimming dog trying to keep its nostrils clear, but in the dusk I couldn't see anything. "Do you hear that?" I asked. Fred Farkvam listened. The night was quiet. "No," he responded. Just then a moose stood up in the water right beside us, water running off its back onto the sprayskirt of our canoe, and walked up onto the riverbank.

You don't want to come between a cow moose and her calf. Greg Tibbetts and Larry Seethaler, at one point, ducked out of the main current and into a slower-moving channel behind one of the islands. "There's a calf," said Greg, and at that moment Mom Moose popped out of the bush and spotted the intruders. Her hackles up, her ears laid back, she started trotting along the riverbank—easily keeping up with them. The two men picked up the pace. So did the moose. She turned and leaped off the bank—landing on and breaking in half a large piece of driftwood—and started pursuing them in the

*Successful moose hunt on the Yukon*
PHOTO COURTESY OF: FIRTH FAMILY

water. "In that water," said Greg, "with no current, I wasn't sure we could keep ahead of her." Paddling furiously, they gradually pulled away until Mom decided they weren't a threat any longer and broke off pursuit.

There are conflicting feelings about the bear. Everyone desires to encounter one, but nobody wants to. It doesn't matter if it's a little black bear or its larger, hump-backed relative, the grizzly: the bear encounter is the one that everyone loves to fear. Juneau's Michelle Ramsey and Jim Heckler crawl into their tent on an island just fifty miles downstream from Fort Selkirk. There aren't any trees on the island in which they can hang up their food bag, so they leave it on the beach beside the canoe. It doesn't take long for a black bear to sniff it out and walk away with it before either can react. They are still two days from Dawson City and have only one can of soup, a package of M&Ms, and a five-pound bag of beans left. "Just when you think it's as bad as it can get, it gets worse," says Ramsey. A while later, after a brief rainstorm, the bear returns and starts to nose around pushing its snout into the wall of the tent a couple of times. "He really sniffed us out." Bored with the tent, the bear chews up their water bottles. It finally ambles away when

Heckler unzips the tent door. They break camp quickly, with Heckler occasionally shouting expletives at the retreating bear. "We grabbed all our stuff and the tent and threw it in our canoe and just left," he says. "That bear is just waiting there," Ramsey says, "for us or for someone else to turn up."

⧢

For the most part bears try to avoid human contact. Usually only when they're extremely hungry, or they become "garbage bears," do they venture close. There's something particularly tragic about watching these magnificent animals—with their glossy fur rippling over their massive legs and their great heads swinging ponderously from side to side—using their claws to paw through rotten vegetables and the mouldy remnants of a dinner that was scraped into the trash last week. Such bold or human-dependant behaviour can ultimately have only one ending: death.

If there is one place where bears frequently come close, it is to fish camps along the river. When Gerry Couture brought the fish to Thistle Creek, they cleaned them along the riverbank in front of their home, then filleted the flesh on wooden cutting tables. The entrails they cooked into a stew and fed to the sled dogs. The odour of fish attracted bears from miles around. They prowled around so close to the buildings that even a trip out to the outhouse warranted an armed guard.

⧢

Tom Randall and Elsie Wain, two Dawson residents, were visiting Jan Couture one night while the Coutures were still building their home and outbuildings. Before heading to bed, Jan and Elsie decided they needed to make a trip to the outhouse. The outhouse was mostly finished, with a door that locked, a proper toilet seat lid, and two walls. The only part still to be built was the back wall. Jan went in first while Elsie stood guard with a rifle out front. Suddenly Jan let out a shriek and exploded out of the outhouse with her underwear still down around her ankles. She headed straight for the main house. Elsie, stunned because she hadn't heard or seen anything, backed up slowly towards the house shining the flashlight towards any little sound she heard—prepared to fire on anything that moved. She had still seen no sign by the time she backed through the front door. "What the hell was that all about," she demanded; "I didn't see anything."

"I don't know," replied Jan, "but something licked my butt."

## A Fish Camp on the River
23 July 1981

"It seems that once you know fear," said Faye Chamberlain, "it comes back. I have a tremendous fear of bears in the summer—especially for my children. If I ever met a bear right in front of me again, I think I'd be shaking too hard to shoot it." She takes a long hard look at her hands clasped tight on the table in front of her and holds her breath for a moment. "I don't know how I'd handle it. It bothers me sometimes."

Seventeen years since that night on the riverbank. Seventeen years of emotional turmoil and nightmares that still jolt her awake in the middle of the night. The physical scars have mostly faded, thanks to six months of reconstructive surgery, and time. There is only a suggestion of an imbalance in an otherwise striking face. "I looked like hell then and I don't particularly like the way I look now . . . but hey. I'm alive. I felt guilty for a while. I thought that if I hadn't woken up this wouldn't have happened. But obviously she would have walked around that table and walked right on top of us. There really wasn't enough time for anyone to react. To use a rifle or get involved. Any bear I've ever seen shot . . . doesn't die right away. There's no doubt in any of our minds—all three of us—that one of us would have died if Billy had been able to shoot the bear."

Raised in northern Quebec, Faye had been heading to New Zealand in 1976 with her boyfriend. The plan was to buy a sheep ranch, but that took money. There was a pipeline boom going on in Alaska. That's where they headed first, but they never arrived. "Got to Dawson and never left," said Faye. "I was a vegetarian when I arrived in Dawson. Two weeks later I was shooting caribou and squirrels for food. Living off the land. It's funny how being broke makes you do the things you have to do to stay alive. The crowd I was hanging around with—we spent our time in the bush, just surviving. Eating mushrooms and whatever edible plants we could find. Hunting and fishing. We were just into seeing if we could do it."

The boyfriend vanished somewhere along the way, and, in 1979, Faye moved out of Dawson City to try a subsistence lifestyle, fishing in the summer and trapping in the winter. She hitched up with a trapper, Richard, for that first winter on the river, and "by springtime I had fallen in love with the place. Great country. Great gardens. Great fishing. It had everything I wanted living out in the bush. With a little ambition and energy you could live off the land out in the bush. There weren't many women who ran a trap line back then."

That July morning she and Richard started downstream from Dawson City where they had been visiting some friends. They planned on stopping at a fish camp owned by two brothers, Billy and Jack Borisenko, for the night. About a mile upstream from the fish camp they spotted three Grizzly cubs strolling up the beach and could see a large Grizzly sow on the ridge above them. "They looked so awesome. The two-year-olds were so healthy. The sunlight was shining right on the fur. You don't see four Grizzes together too often." The bears were heading towards the fish camp.

When Faye and Richard arrived at the Borisenko camp Faye mentioned the bears coming down the river. "Yeah," responded Billy, showing little concern, "that sow was hanging around last summer." Bears around fish camps were fairly common and river people tended to take them for granted. "We were pretty complacent." The Borisenkos had a couple of dogs and they were generally pretty good at keeping bears away from the camp.

There was another couple also visiting: Zeke and Carol. The socializing didn't end until around two the next morning when the coffeepot was retired and the rum bottle was empty. Zeke and Carol crawled into their own tent. Faye and Richard spread out their sleeping bags between the two tents occupied by the Borisenkos. The area was roofed with a tarp and a picnic table sat in the middle of the space; along one end a set of shelves contained cooking gear and dried goods. One of the dogs curled up at Faye's feet.

It was the dog growling and barking that awakened her. She shook the sleep from her eyes and watched as the dog trotted out of the enclosure and towards the beach. "Oh shoot," she thought, lying back down and closing her eyes, "there's probably a bear down there. The dog'll probably drive it away." But the barking kept on and she sat up again. On the other side of the table was the dog. She rubbed her eyes and looked again. The dog stuck its nose in the air and Faye realized it wasn't the dog at all. The Grizzly sow was on the other side of the picnic table. "She had been sniffing the air, then she caught the movement of my head. Then our eyes connected. When you look at a Grizzly—that size and that close—and she's got a look on her face . . . it's terrifying."

She opened her mouth to shout at the bear but could only manage one word—"Hey!"—before the sow was across the table and had snapped her jaws shut on Faye's head. "She connected behind my ear, then closed down across my face. She split my nose in half. Broke both of my jaws. Pulled my eye out. Twisted my ear canal out." Faye passed out as the bear released her head and started biting her in the back. The noise woke up Zeke. He looked out and saw the bear, but couldn't see Faye. "Oh my God, Carol. There's a bear out here." "Throw something at him Zeke," responded Carol, still burrowed in her sleeping bag. Zeke grabbed a cooking pot and hurled it at the bear. The bear turned from Faye and charged Zeke. He was already hampered by a broken leg suffered in a recent car accident and couldn't retreat fast enough. The bear grabbed his good leg and pulled him out of the tent. Carol scrambled out of her bag and scooped up their two children just as the tent collapsed on top of her.

Behind the bear Richard was now awake. He stood up and lifted Faye to her feet. All he could see was blood. He could smell the blood. He could smell the bear, but wasn't quite awake enough to figure out exactly what was wrong in all the confusion. He turned towards the noise and found himself face-to-face with the sow who had released Zeke, spotted Richard, and sat back on her haunches to assess this new threat. Richard punched the bear several times in the face. The bear responded with a single swipe of her paw that sent Richard flying into the night. Then she followed, biting him in the head and ripping a massive V-shaped gouge out of his scalp.

Zeke crawled to safety under the picnic table. The sow picked Richard up in her mouth and hooked a paw onto Faye, then started dragging the two of them out of the camp. "I was naked at the time and she dragged me through a rose-hip patch. Then she reached some deadfall across the trail and couldn't get over it with both of us. So she let go of me, dropped Richard, and started running."

Billy scrambled out of his tent with a rifle but the bear was out of sight. Less than two minutes had passed since the sow had launched herself at Faye. Billy walked down the trail towards the bear, finding Richard and Faye torn up and covered with blood. "They're dead," he wept, and returned to the camp. "They're both dead." Then out of the darkness crawled Richard, who slumped on the bloody sleeping bags. He could barely breathe. The jaws of the bear had collapsed one lung when she had carried him out of the camp.

Out on the trail Faye was conscious and alive: "I remember lying out there in the rose-hip patch and thinking all I wanted was for someone to throw a blanket over me. I thought I was going to die. I thought my neck was partially broken because she had bitten me in the neck. I was covered with scratches. Thousands of scratches. Billy has always said, 'Man. She sure picked a good pile of rose-hips bushes to pull you through."

Bear biologist Barney Smith noted later that the bear didn't use its claws

*Young grizzly bear*
PHOTO COURTESY OF: JOHN FIRTH

to attack, it used its mouth. When a bear is scared, he explained, it bites. When it's angry, it claws. The bear, he said, was probably surprised by Faye's presence. Hemmed in on three sides by tents and shelving, she probably felt trapped and went for her only route of escape—through Faye.

The attack changed life for everyone along the Yukon River. "All that happened that night," said Faye, "changed the attitude of people who lived on the river. For one thing, a lot of us just had tents at our fishing camps. Everyone started putting up shacks and cabins of some sort. Anything more substantial than a tent. A few bears habitually hanging around fish camp sites were shot."

Two years later, despite the chronic pain and the nightmares, Faye returned to the Yukon River. "I made a decision. I love the lifestyle. I love the North. I decided to go back up the river. I think that was the best thing I could have done." Three bears had moved into the country around her cabin while they were gone. "We had to deal with that. I would go to the creek to get water and there would be a bear. Sitting there. Watching me. I was a nervous wreck. I can remember literally vibrating at times."

༄

When my father, Joe Redmond, and Franklin Osbourne travelled the river there was one old timer who used to come down from his cabin and greet them from the river bank. One afternoon, he didn't show up, so the three men walked into the cabin. The old timer was sitting at his kitchen table, with a pot of tea, a bottle of whiskey in front of him, and a blood soaked bandanna wrapped around his head.

"What happened to you?" asked Franklin.

"Had a slight encounter with a bear," replied the old timer. Both he and the bear had been shocked to find the other on the trail the day before. The bear recovered from the surprise first, swatting him across the head and knocking him cold. The next thing he knew, his dog was standing on top of him licking his face. When he reached up to check the damage done by the bear, he discovered he had been scalped by the blow that felled him.

The old timer read somewhere that tea bags helped to prevent infection, so he made a tea bag poultice and tied it to his head with the bandanna. His story completed, he waved at the bottle. This was his painkiller, he explained, but he was willing to share. "Sit down. Have a drink." The doctors in Dawson City later told Dad they couldn't have done much more with the medical supplies they had on hand. The tea bags worked and the old timer returned to his dog and cabin.

I was visiting Dad in the hospital, shortly before he died in 1977, and had just left his room when a nurse stopped me in the hall. "What type of blood do you have?" she demanded. "I don't know. Never had it checked," I answered. "Do you mind if we test you?" she asked even as she pulled me into a room and started rolling up my sleeve. I was a match for whatever they were looking for. A woman had been severely mauled by a grizzly bear, they told me. She needed blood quickly but the hospital had a shortage so they were grabbing everyone they could. They eventually medivaced the woman to Vancouver, BC. In a strange twist of events, twenty-two years later, I met the nurse who checked her into Vancouver General Hospital in 1977 and found out the woman had survived. There's satisfaction in helping to save a life, even if there's a certain lack of high drama in lying on a table with a needle stuck in your arm. I occasionally find myself thinking about her, wondering what that small part of me is doing. Am I a mother yet?

☙❧

That's not a question that bothers me this morning. We are paddling in a fog so thick I can barely see the water beside the canoe. Every once in a while, the grey silhouette of an island or a high rock bluff looms up unexpectedly out of the whiteness. It is impossible to make sense of the river map because I can't find any landmark with which to orient myself. I feel stranded in a cloud, completely detached from everything I can touch or know.

I know we probably won't collide with anything. The Venturi Effect will take care of that for us. That's when you are approaching an island and aren't sure which side to take to catch the best current. You paddle straight at the island and the greater volume of water will make the decision for you. When I feel the canoe being pulled in any direction in the fog, I don't fight it. What the hell, I figure: what you can't see can't hurt you.

Both John and I are exhausted. I slept poorly and little during our last stop. He didn't sleep at all. It is in this opaque pre-dawn hour, as I drift between waking and dreaming, that I most sense the history we are chasing. In the early morning mists I expect to see hulks of other boats rise up suddenly just off our bow. I occasionally stop paddling to listen for the sound of other oars or voices, but there is only the heavy, muffled silence of a cloud that has no edge and hangs motionless just above the water. Finally, the sun rises directly in front of us, glowing pale gold through the cool, thick mist with the consistency of a jar of marmalade. As it burns away the fog above us I can see clear blue sky and already the temperature is starting to climb. This last day into Dawson will be much like the first day from Dyea—long and hot.

Dawson City, NWT
6 September 1898

My Dearest Delia,
This is the idol to which we have committed our all.

There is a sacredness here. Attainable only by and through our dedication and determination to achieve. A person could worship here. Give myself over to a higher power and find awe, comfort, and solace in its embrace. Absorbed into some otherworldly pattern in which we find reasonable, inevitable purpose. There should be at least one thing in every life for which one will sacrifice everything else. It gives life an inner vitality that defies mortality.

Many maintain there are many ways or roads leading to a place prepared for us. The river was our road. The sun, as it settled below the Earth each evening, was a crimson and gold guide to keep us on the way: Not a way. Not some way. But on THE WAY. It has been five days since we arrived. I had such a feeling of euphoria as we angled for a spot on the riverfront that it was not until yesterday that I realized we had arrived on my birthday! It was as if we could leave this

*Dawson waterfront 1898*

PHOTO COURTESY OF: FIRTH FAMILY

river of harsh reality and venture, at long last, into a realm of golden fantasy where wealth must lie on the earth just waiting for us to step ashore and pick it up. Dawson City was why we were here and it was ours at last!

There was the most amazing painting of waters as we rowed towards the bank. After so long travelling on the grey and brown waters of the great river, I was astounded to see the water turn—suddenly and without warning—a clear, sparkling deep-ocean blue. We learned later that this is the influence of the Klondike River. Its water spills out into the main river, creating a wide swath of blue water that runs down the shore for quite a distance before being absorbed into the greater current.

There was barely enough room to beach behind another boat still in the process of being pulled from the water. Beyond us they were tied up three abreast. We barely secured the boat so it wouldn't drift away and took a few hesitant steps into our destination. The streets teem with raucous life. Irishmen. Swedes. Frenchmen. Italians. Americans. Men who panned for gold in California in '49. The dispossessed walk elbow to elbow with Dandy Jacks—with their threepenny cigars and walking sticks. Some Jacks appear to have earned their sporting role if one is to judge by the gold-nugget chains slung across the front of their tailored vests. A never ceasing procession aimlessly prowling the streets. Sitting motionless in doorways. Or enthroned on boxes watching new arrivals jostle for space along the water's edge. They complain of the hardness of the times and the difficulty of getting anything to do. Elsewhere, one might believe them to be too lazy to take on profitable and honest employment, but here they are merely biding their time.

Every few days, one fellow said, the streets empty as stories of a new strike circulate. Then they fill up again as the stampeders trickle sheepishly back empty-handed to await the next rumour. I know well that feeling.

Wagons, drawn by teams of scrawny horses, are stacked high with boxes and bags of every size and description. A crowd gathered spellbound around a fellow standing on a makeshift stage, reading a newspaper aloud. They hung on every word of current events—which are now only two or three months old.

The street is lined with buildings, many still in the process of being built. Stores. Restaurants. Hotels. Even a dress shop for ladies. A large space is devoted to physical pleasure and amusements. Saloons. Dance Halls. From these perfidious establishments of vice, one hears the ungentlemanly sin of swearing, which generally goes hand in hand with the misuse of strong drink. Every saloon has its ragtime piano—with no two of them pounding out the same melody at the same time.

In the midst of bedlam, a scruffy fellow dozed under warm sunshine in a wooden handcart, with two dogs curled up on the ground below him. When Robert jolted the end of the cart, the fellow raised his head, looked about, then promptly fell back asleep. The dogs watched us lazily for a moment longer, then they, too, dropped back to the dirt.

I am proud to be among this number. The men and women here

are among the finest and bravest I've known. The hardships we have shared are enough to make you weep. Some carry all their worldly wealth on board their boats. God knows how many of us have died, like Paul, along the way. It is amazing how much you can understand how other people feel. We all experience hope and fear . . . hunger sometimes . . . exhilaration. But mostly the sense of being so far from anything familiar. It is both frightening and uplifting to know such extraordinary individuals.

We have spent most of our days transferring cargo to land and asking questions of those who arrived before. They directed us to the mining recorder's office where we had to take turns waiting in a line-up that extended almost a city block. As we suspected, all of the best land has already been claimed. The city vibrates with stories of gold found in unlikely places—on hillsides where there should be none. On claims where previous owners had come up empty and sold for a pittance of the wealth the new owner uncovered. And of men broken by failure. Our success, should we achieve it, will probably come by accident rather than by design. Go south. Over the big hill, they told us, at the end of the creeks. Across Solomon's Dome there are apparently not so many miners, and ground as yet unstaked. So that is where we are bound.

I must break off here, for my companions have been patient as I write these words, and there is still a great deal to do before we can depart.

Sweet rosebud fragrant flower of love
The dearest bud in bloom
Whose perfumed leafy heart of power
Casts out love's doubt and gloom,
I've longed to know thy wondrous power
That seems to never die
That speaks of love's devotion
And with cupid's arrow fly
Sweet rosebud, fragrant flower
Teach me of thy wondrous power
That tells two hearts sweet love lurks near
And bids fond lips to "murmur" dear
Tommy

# CHAPTER TWENTY-THREE

## Dawson City
Wednesday, 25 June

Fame and fortune awaits the first team into Dawson City.

Fame. Television and print media news stories across Canada and the United States. Features in *Canoe & Kayak* and *Kanoemagazine* (Germany). Fortune. The first place teams claimed five thousand dollars in Klondike gold.

Respect. That's a little harder to come by.

When Dan Solie arrived, the first thing he needed to do was use an outhouse. Being pushed over the final day by the team of Tom Feil and Jeff Mettler, he hadn't stopped paddling, not even to pee. After the media finished interviewing him at the finish line, Dan hiked out in search of a restroom. He found one in the Northwest Territories Tourism Information Centre. Upon leaving the washroom, Dan was confronted by the centre's manager. "You one of the winners of the river race?" she demanded. Before he could respond she kept talking: "You've been on the river for four days." Handing him a bottle of bathroom cleanser and a rag, she directed him, "Go back in there and clean up the seat."

In 1997 the finish line isn't on the riverbank. It's at the office of the Klondike Centennials Commission (KCC), two blocks away. After hopping out of the canoes, competitors set up two claim posts and then stagger down the street to the office where we "file our claims" with race officials. At that point, Jeff Brady claps them on the back and shouts, "Welcome to Dawson City! You're now an official finisher of the Dyea-to-Dawson Race!" This process appears to be working fine until one team arrives in the middle of the night and stumbles to the office to find the door locked—and Jeff doesn't have a key.

"We paddled lots and slept none," is Jim Lokken's summation of the strategy that enables him and Art Ward to hang on for a two hour and four minute triumph over Todd Boonstra and Adam Varrier. He elaborates:

> You've got to know how fast to go for a week without hitting a wall—without crashing. You need to know what to eat and when

*The Palace Grand Theatre*
PHOTO COURTESY OF: JOHN FIRTH

to eat. You've got to drink all the time. You're basically just trying to keep the fuel tank full. If you go too hard you get an upset stomach and you can't eat any more, then you're out of it. It's a fine line. We thought people would stop more than they did. They were just going, going, going, to the point of being dead in the water. They would go too hard and then bonk. They were either throwing up, sick, or delirious.

The two complete the 610-mile trip from Dyea in an official time of four days, eight hours, forty-nine minutes and sixteen seconds.

Even with their one hour penalty for the use of illegal paddles on Bennett Lake, Boonstra and Verrier still manage to edge out Steve Reifenstuhl and Mark Gorman for second place. "We knew all about the Olympic skiers [Boonstra and Verrier]. We considered them to be the main competition," says Lokken; "But Phil [Moritz] and John [McConnochie] really impressed us. We never expected them to open up such a big lead."

"Three months ago, Jeff and I thought it would probably take ten to eleven days [for the winners to finish]," Buckwheat says as he rubs his eyes, which are puffy and red from lack of sleep. "About a month ago we thought, maybe it'll be seven or eight days. Then after the first couple of legs were completed we realized the total elapsed time was probably going to come in about five days or less. We were trying to keep ahead of these guys the whole time. It was a struggle."

"Buckwheat was trying to keep ahead of them until I joined him [in Whitehorse]," mumbles Jeff Brady. "And I still never caught up to them"— the leaders—"until now. I don't think I've had as much sleep as they have."

Even though the gold has been claimed and most of the teams have opted for the camaraderie rather than the competitiveness, there are still races inside the race. Thane Phillips triumphs over his brother Ross. Thane and Joe Bishop are in fourth place. Ross and Greg Fekete are in eleventh. "It's unbelievable how far you can push the body," says Thane; "I never thought I could go that long with that little sleep and paddle that hard. You reach a state where you're neutral. It hurts so much that you can't hurt anymore, and you're so tired it really doesn't matter any more."

"We didn't expect to win," Bishop adds. "We took turns sleeping in the boat, a half-hour at a time. We were making up ground on the leaders, but the pressure was pretty ridiculous."

"Once we got out of Whitehorse they got across Lake Laberge. There was no way we could catch them," says Ross, "so after that I figured this would happen. Greg and I were hoping that something would happen—like one of them would get sick, break a leg, break an arm, or someone would ram them. Snap a paddle. Some of those minor details. Fate wasn't kind. It didn't work out."

Derek Peterson and Dirk Miller play tortoise and hare with Ed Williams and Jason Rogers. Ed and Jason drift lazily down the river and earn themselves the nickname of "The Float Boys." Derek and Dirk paddle hard but stop for extended rest periods on the shore. "We made it our goal to beat these tortoises to Dawson," says Dirk. It is during one of those rest periods, just a short distance out of Dawson, that The Float Boys pass them for the last time. "Sssshhh," cautioned Jason, putting a finger to his lips, "don't wake them." When Derek and Dirk arrive in Dawson, their strategy has failed by just over forty minutes, though they have completed the race two days faster than originally anticipated. "There are so many fun people in the race and we got to know some of them very well," Derek says. "Dirk and I are much better friends now. And that's the best thing to come out of this race."

Sandy Sippola and Marjorie Logue travel with Jacques Chicoine and Gerard Cruchon. They decide there is no need to race any more and plan to arrive together. Stopping for a short nap on the riverbank, the two men fall asleep. Sandy and Marjorie look at each other: "Let's go," whispers Sandy, and they sneak ahead to the finish line. "My plan," claims Gerard, "was to let them win. Even if we have to stop the canoe and just drift. I love women. I respect them. So I cannot . . . I will let them win."

Bill Stewart and Stephen Jull are so emotionally and physically spent they have no sense of urgency. Then a canoe appears on the bend behind them. "We were getting really bagged out there. We figured they [Henry and Jeb Timm] couldn't catch us. Then about a mile from Dawson they show up and they've got a faster boat. We didn't know exactly how far we had to go to Dawson but they were gaining on us. If you're at all competitive, it just calls forth some primitive drive to survive, and it's almost like your survival is at stake. We just started to boot it: there was no way those guys were going to catch us." Bill and Stephen hit the shore first, plant their claim posts, and start stumbling up the street with the Timms just a minute behind. "Stephen and I were in full gallop to do all this stuff, and the Timms were also in full gallop. But we were able to get there first. It was a wonderful end to the race."

The closest finish belongs to Dwight Lambkin and Russ Bamford, who reach the KCC office just four seconds ahead of Chris Olson and Don Fairbanks.

A group of recreational paddlers are camped for the night on an island just upstream from Dawson. Suddenly, into the light cast by their huge roaring campfire, three canoes appear, one after another, their occupants paddling like mad. Then they are gone, leaving the campers to wonder if it was but a fleeting mirage. Separated only by minutes, the three are driving hard for the finish line. All they want to do is get this ordeal over with. Seth Plunkett and Ken Graham lead the trio, followed by Wendy Cairns and Chris Guenther, then Steve Cash and Geo Ljljenskjold.

As they approach Dawson the next morning, Wendy and Chris decide to finish in style. Modesty takes a back seat as both change from paddling clothes into cancan outfits. "As we were coming in," says Chris, "we were getting into costume again. There we are trying to get our false eyelashes on as we were coming past Sunnydale. We were yelling and hollering and singing and throwing our clothes all over the place. We looked just horrible. We set off a bear banger. We did almost everything you can do in a canoe . . . except use it as a bathroom. We found out later what some people used their gold pans for." At the finish line, they are the first women's team to arrive. The second one, Sandy and Marjorie, is still a day away from finishing. "We did the best we could," says Wendy, "we did everything we could to get to Dawson as quickly as we could. If you analyze it, I guess there were short cuts we could have taken, or things we maybe could have done better. There were strategy problems that we could have planned for better, but we didn't realize it was going to be so competitive. It was just really different from anything we expected."

"I discovered something about myself in this race," Wendy adds thoughtfully. "I discovered I'm terribly competitive. I never knew that about myself before."

The first mixed team to arrive is Jason Tinsley and Holly Edelson, but they can finish no higher than second in their category. The mixed team just behind them, Cynde Adams and Larry Gullingsrud, get five hours knocked off their time to account for their rescue of Jim Smith and Ken Brewer in Windy Arm.

Roger Hanberg is so happy to see Dawson he plants a big kiss on Jeff Brady's cheek. Kate Moylan and Michael Yee decide that each of the scrapes on the bottom of their canoe represents a memory. "This must be from when the bear was chasing you," Micheal points at one long scar. Kate responds with a gouge of her own: "That was when you fell asleep and I couldn't wake you up."

The Chilkoot Pass seems far in the past for most of us, but for Yvonne Harris it is the image that remains with her at the finish line. "In my book, there'll be someone like me. Struggling over the pass. Then some nice young man," she glances at Kevin McKague, who grins back, "comes and takes my pack from me. Cause it was so painful."

Fred O'Brien doesn't want the race to end. "Such a river . . . the Yukon River. Such people. Waking up by the river. Watching the sunrise and the sunset. The long days. I didn't even need sleep after a while. I could do this forever."

"The sunlight was a big highlight. The beautiful scenery was a big highlight. The whole thing was just one highlight after the next," exudes Steve Jaklitsch. "The Yukon is a pretty magical place to be."

For the teams arriving in the middle of the night, as Fred and I did in 1998, there is often no one awake—except the fish. As we paddled across the mouth of the Klondike River, the grayling were rising all around us, creating shimmering circular ripples on the surface of the water. Both of us swear we heard them hitting the bottom of the canoe and felt them strike the paddle blades. "I thought they were going to jump right in the canoe," said Fred; "I might have thought I was dreaming except another team said the same thing."

It was several minutes before a very bleary-eyed Buckwheat realized we had arrived at the finish line. "You're supposed to pan some gold," he told us, "but it's the middle of the night and I'm too tired. We'll just say you did. Welcome to Dawson."

There is even a race of sorts for last place. To see who can out-procrastinate whom. Ian Agnew–Gerry Gardiner join up with the Rosemary Matt–Paul Sergeant duo at Lake Lindeman and travel together. The officials call them the "red lantern phantoms." Everyone knows they were out there somewhere, but no one knows where. "We got more attention than most of the others because they were looking for us," says Gerry.

"It was a fantastic experience," says Ian, "I will do it again. By Lindeman I had already written in my journal that it didn't matter if I was forty-ninth or fiftieth in an event where I was already so victorious. How can I lose?"

Gerry agrees that she would paddle the river again, but balks at the Chilkoot Pass. "I wouldn't do the summit again. We were in it for the same reasons. Not to win it, but just to do the race."

The garbage bin down by the finish line is a primary beneficiary of the race rules. We carried a bunch of nails, a cast iron fry pan, a gold pan, and a hammer from start to finish. But once in Dawson the need for such items ends, and we are more than happy to dispose of them. As far as I am concerned, I would be delighted to hurl my fry pan into the river so it can rust away with all the other unloved junk on the bottom. "It was just like a hundred years ago," says Jeff Brady: "anything they didn't need, they would just throw aside." In the 1990s, we are more environmentally aware than they were in the 1890s. The garbage can gets very full.

Early one morning, lying in the motorhome being used as the checkpoint, Jeff overhears two men out for an early morning walk along the waterfront. "Hey look," says one voice, "that's a fry pan. And there's a gold pan."

"There's another one, and a hammer," adds the second voice. "Jeezzz. This whole can is full of them."

Jeff doesn't open the curtains to watch but he can hear pans and hammers being lifted out of the bin and piled on the ground beside it. "Why would anyone throw away a perfectly good gold pan?" queries voice number one as the two scurry away with their booty.

"I guess for people down south that sounds pretty funny," says Jeff, "but up here you have to wonder."

The motorhome also draws an unexpected reaction from American tourists. A banner for one of the sponsors—The Bank of Alaska—hangs on the side, and people stop by to try to cash their travellers cheques. "We only take deposits," responds one of the volunteers, "preferably in cash or gold."

CLO

Solomon Carriere and Steve Landick were at a loss when they arrived in Dawson in 1998. They shaved almost seven hours off the 1997 winning time and held a three-hour lead over their closest competitor. But the ceremonial finishing activity had them stumped. Instead of planting claim posts and filing their claim as we did in 1997, finishers had to "find colour" in a gold pan at the river's edge. "I can do the rest of this stuff," laughed the easy-going Solomon, "but pan for gold? No way."

When they did master some of the rudiments of gold panning, it ended the most grueling event that either marathon canoe racing veteran had ever been involved in. "That was the toughest. This breaks you. This wears you down," said Solomon. "We should get fifteen times that much gold for the amount of work we put in. What's tough about racing like this is you don't know what's going to happen to your body. You just get so tired, you want to nod off. But I'd do it again in a second."

Jim Lokken and Audun Endestad hung on for second place, but just barely. Robert Kazik and Stanislav Hajsky were twelve minutes behind, followed by John McConnochie and Phil Moritz twenty minutes later. Yvonne Harris and Donna Dunn were the top women's team, with Slovakia's Martin Misik and Lucia Misikova leading the way for mixed teams.

"Every day was a challenge," said Dom O'Brien as he sipped on his Guinness—a finish-line reward he had dreamed of since the race began. "There was something new every day. It wasn't your normal holiday where you could relax every day."

Ross Phillips suffered "total body meltdown" in 1998. He was lifted out of the canoe at the finish line and went through a period of physical and mental depression for several days following the race.

Dan Morrison filed his final story for *Outside Online*: "My feet are so

*Panning for gold on the Dawson waterfront*
PHOTO COURTESY OF: SKAGWAY CENTENNIAL COMMITTEE

swollen I can't put my shoes on, and my hands are covered with blisters and cuts and bruises," he wrote. "The parts of my body that aren't suffering immersion rot are bright red from sunburn. I have slept a total of seven hours in the last five days. I feel great."

"Before you ask someone whether or not they would do it again," said physician Danusia Kanachowski, "wait until the amnesia sets in. It's like the amnesia that affects women who give birth. While they're in labour and actually giving birth they wonder if they could ever endure this kind of pain again. Later . . . much later . . . they don't remember just how much it really hurt."

The panning for gold in 1998 went well until the arrival of Deana Darnell and Kim Staeck. The gravel in the pan was "salted" with a fairly large real gold nugget, borrowed by Buckwheat from a friend. The two women swirled the water around in the pan, reached into the muddy water, and handed the nugget to Beriah Brown. "There you go," they said. Beriah was a little confused. It was a nugget, but it wasn't the right nugget. Before he could say anything, one of the women threw the gravel into the river. "What are you doing!?" shouted Beriah. "It's OK," was the response, "we salted the pan with some fake gold." With a sinking heart, Beriah dropped the fake nugget and started pawing through the mud on the riverbank.

"Then you just threw the real one into the river," he wailed. The organizers sifted the dirt for two days but never did find it.

Later I spotted one of the canoeists wandering along the riverbank peering intently into the water. "It was around here they threw the gold nugget into the river wasn't it?" he asked. "Yeh," I responded, watching him turn rocks and dirt with the toe of his boot, "somewhere along there."

The casual gazing at the ground and the turning of rocks and dirt is a common feature amongst visitors and new arrivals to Dawson City. It was something that T. A. Firth saw in the men wandering the riverbank when he arrived here on 1 September 1898, his thirty-first birthday. By then, the best claims had already been staked. It was slim pickings for most of the forty thousand men and women who arrived in '97 and '98. Some had skills, such as reading and writing, that were in demand. Others took jobs on the creeks, working for wages. Many prowled the streets, prodding the ground with their toes, peering with interest under sidewalks—all in the hope of finding a nugget or some gold dust that might have fallen there.

A fortune is found where you seek it. People offered their janitorial services to saloons or dance halls for free. All they asked was to be allowed to pan the sawdust on the floors at the end of each night's business before they started their work. It was enough to provide them with a decent living. "Lots of gold in the sawdust," said "Sawdust Mike" Wineage, a tall Yugoslavian who arrived late for the gold rush but found a way to mine the saloon floors. "You might get fifty or a hundred nuggets depending on how big the pile [of sawdust] was." In the 1950s and 60s, white channel gravel was used to provide surfacing for the streets in the city. The yellowish material was put through dredges, which churned up the earth for miles around Dawson City, washing it clean and exposing the quartz—a crystalline mineral usually found in conjunction with gold. When the sun shone on the streets of Dawson City, the pebbles tinged like Jerusalem Stone and the quartz crystals acted as prisms, giving off a rainbow sheen. After being told of how the stampeders believed the streets were paved with gold, tourists stood on the roads and saw the sunlight's reflection. "Oh my God!" they murmured in hushed tones, overwhelmed by the truth of what they had heard. And stuck their toes into the ground in hopes of turning up a nugget.

Named after George Dawson, Director of the Geological and Natural History Survey of Canada from 1895 to 1901, it was originally a moose pasture that was transformed in a matter of months into the second largest city west of the Mississippi River (San Francisco being the largest). Dance halls, an opera house, restaurants, hotels, breweries, saw mills, moneylenders, barbershops, brothels, stores, and government offices: all were packed together in a central core surrounded on all sides by a city of tents and sod-roofed cabins. It was the most exciting place to be on earth—even for those who never struck it rich—because it defied convention.

The only acceptable currency was unrefined gold. Paper currency had little meaning, other than being somewhat more convenient to carry around. Every store, every saloon, every dance hall had a small set of scales upon which they weighed out the amount of gold required to settle a bill. There were all sorts of scams by which bar tenders and storekeepers made sure that more gold was left on the scales than was needed. The miners didn't care. Money was a cheap commodity because it could be dug out of the ground whenever it was needed.

It was a skewed world in which individuals became lifelong friends and acquaintances of people who, under other circumstances, they might never have mingled with. The most dramatic example of all was "Big Alex" MacDonald. Socially unpolished, he was often called the "Big Moose from Antigonish" because of his ungainly manner and rough verbal skills. Despite being handicapped by the very things despised by upper-class society, he had an instinctive gift for trading, leasing, and bartering gold claims that soon made "The King of the Klondike" the wealthiest man in the city and welcome in the parlours of the finest families. T. A. Firth was hired to read and write cheques for him because he couldn't do it himself.

The experience of reaching this distant, isolated place challenged the soul-felt beliefs of many who came. Elizabeth Mills was a respectable girl with a strong puritanical upbringing. Having fled to Canada from the potato famine in Ireland, she met John Warne—a Dawson City businessman—in Vancouver in 1899. Elizabeth married John and headed north. Upon arrival in Dawson City, John went in search of shelter, leaving her on the beach to guard their outfit. Left alone after defying an environment that tested her stamina to the utmost, she perched on a wooden crate, protected by only a shawl; soaked through by the rain and homesick, Elizabeth broke down and wept. Then she heard a female voice, soft and southern: "Would y'all like a hot cup of Tea, huney?" Raised among "respectable and moral" white Christian men and women, her world revolved around the social perception of good and evil that dominated nineteenth-century religious teachings. That moment, when she blinked away her tears and gratefully accepted the steaming cup from an African American practitioner of the world's oldest profession, her world ended and her life began.

In every direction, the rivers and creeks' valleys had been torn apart by the gold miners, and the hills denuded of trees to fuel the construction boom. The waterfront was dominated not by riverboats or the docks that were still being built, but by massive rafts of logs that had been floated down river to be sold to the sawmills. The First Nations people up the Pelly River assembled rafts that held one hundred cords of wood or more, set up a couple of tents and wood stoves in the centre of each raft, and then floated past Fort Selkirk to Dawson City. Sweepers at either end of the unwieldy vessel gave them limited mobility, so other river traffic gave them wide berth. The last of the great wood rafts came down river in 1959.

Dawson City virtually emptied overnight when gold was discovered in Nome and Fairbanks, both in Alaska, in 1901. There was still plenty left in the Klondike, but the truth about stampeders is that it's not the gold that gives contentment, it's the stampeding. They stuck it out for one or two winters, but they itched to move on almost from the moment they arrived. They couldn't go back. Some had no homes to return to. Others feared returning empty handed. So, when another strike was found, off they went.

A few, T. A. Firth among them, decided to stay and build a future. He opened an employment centre and then, in 1906, hung out his shingle as a stockbroker and insurance agent. The insurance business exists to this day, the last of the original, family-owned businesses in the Yukon. Unlike most gold rush towns, the people who stayed enabled Dawson City to live beyond the moment—and even managed to avoid the Great Depression.

One evening in 1937, my parents found two men on their doorstep. One of them, Mike Telep, explained how he and his partner heard there was work in the North so they took the boat to Skagway, a train to Whitehorse, and walked the rest of the way to Dawson. When they arrived, footsore, penniless, and hungry, they were directed to this house as a good place to go. Mom fed them and gave them a place to sleep, then put them to work painting the house. Mike's children still live in the Yukon.

The gold consortiums, financed by families like the Guggenheims, the Rothschilds, and US President Herbert Hoover, pulled gold from the creeks with massive floating dredges until the 1950s. When the dredges stopped operating, and the capital moved in 1953 to Whitehorse, Dawson finally seemed destined for the garbage heap of forgotten gold rush towns.

By 1960, all that remained was fading glory. The gaudy paints peeled away, the wood weathered grey on the buildings—many of which still stood with their false fronts, bay windows, fluted pillars, and scrolled cornices. The Occidental Hotel. The Royal Alexandra, with its famous portrait of a nude woman (the painting was packed over the Chilkoot Pass). The Flora Dora. The Monte Carlo. The Oddfellows Hall, used as a storage building for much of the furniture and artifacts of hotels that no longer stand. The Carnegie Library. The Post Office. The Commissioner's residence. The former administration building for the Yukon Government, which contained the original Territorial Legislative chambers.

The moose pasture started to reclaim its home. The Third Avenue Blacksmith Shop, most recently used as a bicycle repair shop, had waist-high grass and reeds growing up between the tables and equipment, and willows hanging out of the windows. Buggies, wagons, and entire train engines parked near the old administration building were barely visible through the brush that grew around them.

The permafrost twisted building foundations until they had a kinked look to them. One of them, the old Gun and Ammo Shop, leaned so far out over the street that it needed wooden beams and metal supports to hold it up. Its unnatural tilt made it the most photographed building in the city. When staying in the Downtown Hotel, one could lie in bed and watch the feet and ankles of people walking in the hallway. The building kept shifting, and the owners cut approximately six inches off the bottom of each door so that they wouldn't snag on the warps as they moved back and forth over the floor. Wooden sidewalks took on the appearance of a rolling sea.

∽

In 1952, the citizens of Dawson, recognizing the need to develop a tourism industry, formed the Klondike Visitors Association (KVA) with the mandate to revive the glamour of the gold rush era. Ten years later, with the help of Tom Patterson, founder of Ontario's Stratford Shakespeare Festival, the KVA hosted the Dawson City Festival—an event that aimed to highlight the restoration of some of the city's older structures—as part of their overall tourism marketing strategy.

The first structure rebuilt was the Palace Grand Theatre, originally opened on 4 July 1899 by Arizona Charlie Meadows, and reopened on 1 July

*Winners Jim Lokken and Art Ward at the finish line.*

1962. The first performance was a way-off-Broadway production of *Foxy*, starring Bert Lahr, the cowardly lion from the movie *The Wizard of Oz*. Later, they pulled the SS *Keno* out of the river, turned it into a dance hall, and finally a steamship museum.

Then the Arctic Brotherhood Hall was renovated into Diamond Tooth Gerties, the first legalized gambling house in all of Canada. Half of Jack London's cabin, discovered on the Stewart River in the 1980s, made it to Dawson. The other half ended up in Jack London Square in San Francisco. All of Robert Service's cabin was turned into a shrine where professional performers read the bard's poetry.

The festival lost money that first year, but successfully launched a program that, over the past thirty-six years, has drawn millions from around the world to see the Yukon's pride and past—the City of Gold.

*Ruby's place*

PHOTO COURTESY OF: JOHN FIRTH

# CHAPTER TWENTY-FOUR

## Dawson City

Our arrival is anti-climatic. There is no great whooping and hollering. No jumping around waving arms in the air. Jeff and Buckwheat are there to give us hugs and handshakes. "Welcome to Dawson!" shouts Jeff, backed up by Buckwheat's howl. Brendan and Anne have the camera in our face and the microphone boom hovering overhead. A couple of tourists stand back and watch, not really understanding exactly what is going on. I feel like a balloon that has been deflated. No immediate aura of accomplishment or satisfaction, just an overwhelming desire for sleep.

We get a hotel room, but I find myself getting claustrophobic indoors. Even with the windows wide open the air is dank and heavy. Sleeping under a single sheet is too hot, the walls too confining. For the past eight days the wind has been my air conditioner. The sun my heater. The sky and stars my ceiling. The forest my walls. The river my running water. The canoe my home. It is more comfortable to walk than it is to sleep. So that's what I do.

In the dusky solitude of the almost empty streets—even a small city doesn't sleep at night—I think of all that has passed before. The history of this place has all the wildness of romance. I imagine the people of the past peer at me from shadowed doorways as I prowl the streets. They are familiar ghosts. I grew up here. Dawson City and the Klondike Gold Rush was my backyard. Do others come here and feel their presence?

When they pass Diamond Tooth Gerties, casino, do they see it as the Arctic Brotherhood Hall—fraternal home for men who chased golden dreams at the turn of the century? This building was the heart of the cultural community, hosting live musical concerts and dances.

"You've got to realize," said my mother, "there was no contact with the outside world. This was your social life." She continued:

> The churches had the big suppers. The AB Hall would have your dances . . . Mother Firth loved the dances. When Howard and I were getting married she sent down the message, "Make sure Nancy is married in a floor-length dress so she can have a formal

gown for the dances." Any excuse to have a dance. Armistice Day. April Fools Day. Longest Day. Shortest Day. First Tourist Dance, when the first boat arrived in the spring. I don't think we ever went without someone who could play the piano. There were bankers, doctors, or teachers. They were all excellent musicians. We all could dance. We had wonderful dances.

At the tail end of *Me and Sam McGee*, a 1973 film documentary on the Yukon River, there is a brief glimpse of my father in his tuxedo and my mother in a formal black evening gown as they whirl around the dance floor in the Palace Grand Theatre. Once again alive to the music, their feet glide elegantly with the familiarity of forty years of sharing each other's embrace. It was the last time they would ever dance together.

The first silent moving pictures were shown in the AB Hall. T. A. had my dad read the film's sub-titles aloud to show how well he learned his letters. His first job was in the box office selling tickets.

Newly restored by Parks Canada, the post office is one of the largest structures in the city, and everyone goes there because it's novel to mail a letter from an old post office in a gold rush city. Almost unnoticed at the west end of the building is a small addition. A plaque identifies it as the old telegraph office. The same office from which T. A. sent a cable to his son, who was working in Fernie, BC, for the Bank of Commerce in 1937. "Resign from bank," it read; "Marry Nancy. Come home." The plaque doesn't mention that the second floor contained the offices of T. A. Firth Insurance, the same offices T. A. entered to start his business day on 13 June 1941. The seventy-three-year-old hung his jacket up, removed his bowler hat, and brushed some dust off the display cabinets holding his collection of minerals from every mine in the Yukon and Alaska. He sat down to prepare for his first meeting. His customer found him there; he thought at first that T. A. had dozed off as older people are prone to do, then realized he was dead. A failing heart had finally caught up to him.

Tourists stop to read the fading sign in front of St. Andrew's Anglican Church. It is silent today but what God-fearing Christian could sleep through the pipe organ when it was still in use? When the organist started playing prior to the Sunday morning service, every dog in town started howling in harmony.

What do they see in their imagination as they pass Ruby's Place? Women

*Dawson City, 1899*

PHOTO COURTESY OF: FIRTH FAMILY

of liberty hanging from the windows in tawdry dress, luring the innocent into a luxurious palace of pleasures? Ruby Scott ran the last "legal" brothel in Canada. According to my father, medical authorities persuaded the police to turn a blind eye to her activities. That way, they figured, if the girls kept track of their customers they could control the transmission of sexually transmitted diseases. One doctor considered planting newspaper ads asking people to refrain from sex in December to prevent pregnancies from interfering with his September moose hunt. The men, he probably thought, could satisfy their needs at Ruby's—another reason for keeping it around. He had no suggestions for the women. The newspaper's editor persuaded him it wouldn't work.

According to Bill Hakonson, who lived across the street from Ruby's Place, Ruby had scruples—for a madame. She didn't abide with married men having sport with her girls. Single men, only, were permitted upstairs into rooms that held not much more than the bare essentials of the trade—a coat rack, a wash stand, a bed. Married men gathered in the lounge downstairs to play cards and drink. Bill recalls a night when he sat at home reading and his phone rang. "Do you know where Howard is?" my mother demanded. "No Mrs. Firth"—he always called her Mrs. Firth—"I don't," lied Bill, who had earlier driven Dad to Ruby's Place in his taxi.

"Have you seen him at all?" A second chance to tell or even hint at the truth.

"No, I haven't."

A few minutes later the phone rang again. It was from one of our neighbours. "Bill," he said, "Nancy Firth is heading down Seventh Avenue on a bicycle and she's on her way to Ruby's."

Bill charged across the street. "Howie. You'd better get out of here. Your wife just called me looking for you." Dad barely managed to get out of the building before Mom arrived to find him—slightly inebriated and obviously guilty—on the street in front.

"I really liked and respected your mother," Bill told me one afternoon. "But after that night she never talked to me again. She knew I had lied to her and never forgave me. But I always liked her."

The brothel's days were numbered. In the early 1950s a newly arrived Anglican minister, unfamiliar with the reasons for tolerance, wrote a letter of protest to the Canadian Government. A few weeks later Ruby and her girls were gone. A few weeks later, the minister was gone too.

The march of time is not always a pretty sight, and it leaves a great deal of destruction in its path. Sometimes the best part of a dream is lost in its plundering. While buildings hold their spectres, vacant lots also contain ghosts not apparent to the naked eye.

There are no markers to identify where the "Bucket of Blood" once stood, and no evidence to indicate that the inn got its nickname from anything more than an urban legend. The story goes that a man discovered his wife sharing a bed with a hotel guest and took an axe to them. There was so much blood it seeped through the floorboards, and dripped on the heads of the patrons in the bar below. The "Bucket of Blood" was torn down years ago and the space turned into a parking lot for the Penguin Hotel, now renamed the Midnight Sun.

Another parking lot sits adjacent to the Palace Grand Theatre. It was where the Pearl Harbor Hotel stood. One had to know how to sleep on an incline to stay in the hotel because it had a permanent kink in it. Stained glass chandeliers hung from the coffered ceiling. Mahogany wainscoting trimmed the top of the lavishly papered walls. The check-in counter was ornately designed with scrolls and flutes, with a model wooden gold dredge parked on one end of it. A sofa, with massive steer horns forming the back and arms, provided seating. The hotel tavern was where all the locals met to have a drink and shoot the breeze. A few of the patrons were prone to drinking a little too much at times. Every now and then one of my dad's friends had to be pushed home in a wheelbarrow by his wife. On one occasion two men, one of them a pilot, apparently started disputing exactly how the bombing of Pearl Harbor was carried out in 1941. To make his point, the pilot dragged his friend out to the plane, along with a case of toilet paper. They flew back and forth over the hotel, throwing rolls of toilet paper onto the roof in what they probably believed was an exact replication of the Japanese tactics. In the end, it wasn't bombs but a chimney fire that sank the Pearl Harbor.

The old Fire Hall stood on the waterfront, near the Bank of Commerce building, in what is now a picnic area. My parents donated all of T. A. and Delia's papers to the Dawson City Museum. The museum, not having enough storage space, asked them to leave the boxes in the Fire Hall until such a time as they could pick them up. "We knew how important those papers were. We packed up all the minutes, ledgers, and records of the founding of the Arctic Brotherhood into big trunks. Then Howard carried them upstairs to the second floor," recalls my mother.

Two years later the Fire Hall burned to the ground. The museum hadn't gotten around to picking up the trunks.

How many times do people encounter this past and not recognize it? A film production company once decided not to use Dawson City in the making of a movie about the Klondike Gold Rush. Pointing to the overhead electrical wires, they suggested their presence detracted from the authenticity of the setting. Gold rush towns in the 1890s didn't have overhead electrical wiring, they insisted, and off they went to find a more realistic Dawson. They should have read their history books. Dawson was the first city in Western Canada to have electric lights—in 1898. The overhead power lines were more authentic than the movie was.

It always amazes me how some believe the present is the only time that matters. That today's world is compelling and new, with no place for days gone by. They prefer to overlook that everything and everyone has a past. We are a new generation—doing exactly what our ancestors did and convincing ourselves we are the first to do it.

I respect the ghosts with whom we have raced. They call to us from their

*Brendan Hennigan and Andrew Simpson—gold pans for everyone at the finish line*

PHOTO COURTESY OF: SKAGWAY CENTENNIAL COMMITTEE

memories to remind us of our past. For those who came before us, some were fueled by dreams of gold. Others desired a rite of passage to enter into adulthood. And some, like T. A. Firth, wanted one more fling at adventure. What they got was an experience from which they shaped the rest of their lives.

But what about us? What do we get from all of this? There are some common threads with the past: pride in being part of a small group of people who made the journey, a shared sense of accomplishment and camaraderie, memories of a once-in-a-lifetime experience that will in some way bond those who were a part of it.

"The river means different things to different people," wrote Mark Kelsey in an article for *Canoe and Kayak Magazine* (Dec. 1997), "but for a few days in June, for 92 people, it meant, most of all, a chance to relive history. . . . All who came to be part of the race—from ultramarathoners and former Olympians to recreational paddlers—were destined to make their own history."

Cynde Adams just shakes her head in amazement: "Traveling six hundred miles by your own means. It's amazing to think they endured it. 'Cause we certainly all feel like we've endured and we had it easy compared to them."

"I'm glad I did it for this one reason," says Steve Cash. "Now I understand the whole flow of it and why people took the river. Once you're on it you realize the connection. Even though you can look at maps and see it all. . . . Until you do it, you don't really understand it."

"The feeling I had on that journey was something I didn't really expect," Brendan Hennigan mutters over a beer in The Snake Pit. "Once I started to realize how important the Yukon River was . . . or still is. I would say that anyone who wants to call themselves a Yukoner, young or old—it doesn't matter what age—part of your responsibility is to go down the Yukon River."

Jeff Brady's love affair with the river matured over the years, growing from an irresistible longing to experience romance and adventure to contemplating the sense of place. "I've always been drawn to it in the same way I'm drawn to the Chilkoot. It's not really a wilderness river because you run into people all the time, but I like the idea of travelling through history."

Joe Jack was quietly satisfied when he reached Dawson City. "The river is important to me. Mostly spiritually. When I have a need to balance my inner self—sometimes you need a certain kind of energy. You can go to certain sacred sites in the mountains. Sometimes you need the water. What water does is mellow you out. It makes you feel lucid. Calm. Quiet. Every once in a while I need that. The river is also stories. Stories of before white people came to the Yukon. The river is familiar places. Places I've been before."

For Solomon Carriere, the proud professional who believed his sport was progressing to extinction, it was the future finding a way to catch up with us. "In professional races we use a racing canoe. Some people call them racing shells. What that has done is create a shrinking, elite class of competitive canoeists using high tech equipment. It has basically discouraged the recreational canoeist from taking part and every year there are fewer and fewer competitors taking part. The use of real canoes will regenerate interest in the professional canoeing circuit and attract people who otherwise would not get involved. Returning to the roots of the sport will result in it having a future." He illustrated his point by naming several of the competitors in the Dyea-to-Dawson races. "Jim. Audun. John. Phil. It was exciting. We had never raced against any of these guys before. We had never raced this kind of distance before. And it had been a long time since we raced in a real canoe."

⌘

The race is a means of re-evaluating my real world. It means letting go of my comfort level. Testing the limits of my body and mind, then reaching past them towards a greater potential, much as I imagine T. A. Firth had to do. I travelled this river seeking a current that could sweep me momentarily into the past. T. A. came, not necessarily looking for anything at all. He found something up here that made him stay, that cured the wanderlust that had affected him since his formative years. He found a home where he no longer needed to try to fit in. That's why, when new discoveries lured the bulk of the stampeders further north, he remained. In Dawson he became a married man, a father, a pillar of the community, a God-fearing man, although, unlike his father, he was a Mason, not a Baptist. At the drop of a hat he would stand up and make a speech. Toast the bride. Deliver a eulogy. Preach a sermon. Any occasion that needed an oration he could be relied upon to deliver one. His ability provided him with social status, along with his knowledge of legal and administrative affairs concerning the business of gold mining.

He may have been good at selling stocks, but he wasn't much good at buying them. We could wallpaper . . . we have wallpapered a room . . . with stock certificates purchased by him. My favourite: "Highland Surprise Gold Mines." That lived up to its name when it disappeared from the trading floor without a trace. I tried to trace the share certificate to find out if it had any residual value. It proved to be a gold mine of amusement.

At one point he owned a six hundred-acre ranch—something he acquired in payment for some job he did. In 1985 I actually camped on one end of it while canoeing the Stewart River, although I had no knowledge of it at the time. He either traded it away or forgot about it. In 1998, the land was still registered in his name, although it had long before reverted back to the crown for nonpayment of back taxes.

享

If you believe the theory that time is nothing more than an infinite series of multiple universes existing simultaneously, side-by-side, then you must also accept that there is no place where you are truly alone. That there are some places—call them crossroads in time when spirits escape the tomb. Call them what you will, they can make the past feel more real. There are some times, usually the middle of the night, that make those places more potent.

享

For a moment, as I walk, I think he might fall into step beside me. But it isn't until I sit on a bench, high on the dyke that now denies the town visual connection with the river, that he makes his appearance. I'm not exactly sure how long he is there before I become aware of him. It's just the vaguest of movements that alerts me. Leaning towards me, holding out his pipe, he is obviously asking for a match. I'm not a smoker, but like any camper I carry some in my pocket. I strike one and hold the flame out. He sucks on his pipe. The tobacco sizzles and smoke billows from the corners of his mouth. My match apparently does the trick, although the flame never once wavers.

After hallucinating occasionally over the past few days, I don't find his presence at all unusual. All I can think about is the contrast in our garb. He sitting there in his Prince Albert suit, his gold fob watch chain dangling across the top of his stomach, bowler hat perched on top of his head, contentedly puffing away on his pipe. Me, six inches taller, in my Gore-Tex windbreaker, a digital watch velcroed to my wrist, wearing a fleece vest and dumbly holding a burning match until it scorches my fingers. The smoke drifts towards me and I can smell the seasoning. Ground tobacco packed into the stump of a poplar tree, soaked through with a bottle of good Jamaican Rum, and sealed up to cure for a month or so.

We sit there in contemplative quietness. I want to say something. Anything. Something profound. Poetic maybe. What do you say to someone whose most recent experience in life was dying fifty-seven years ago. He seems quite content just to share the same space without words. In death, he has found peace. Watching in spectral silence as his city struggles to resist the ravages of time and preserve itself in the image of his era.

I see the twilight emanating from the swirling surface of the river. A canoe, one of the other competitors, is straining to cross the current to the finish line a hundred yards or so downstream from where we are. T. A. glances at me, then he too turns his attention to the canoe. Together we watch, silently cheering on the exhausted paddlers. Both of us have been there, in a vessel on the river, pulling hard to make landfall on this very same riverbank.

I know he is gone even before I turn back to where he was sitting. For eight days I pursued a ghost. He no longer seems so distant, so ethereal.

৩৩

In 1898, columnist Ambrose Pierce wrote about the '98er in the *San Francisco Examiner*. "Nothing will come of him," he said. "He is a word in the wind, a brother to the fog. At the scene of his activity no memory of him will remain. . . ."

The reminders of our physical mortality may one day be lost. Each year that passes it gets more difficult to clear the willows and grass from his resting place in the Masonic graveyard on the hillside above Dawson. One day, people will stop trying. Delia died in Vancouver, BC, six months after T. A. passed away, and was buried there. Her grave has already been lost.

The Yukon River is the living thread that binds the ends of the century together. A six-hundred-mile-long museum populated by ghosts. The dead, though freed from their earthly existence, have chosen to remain. Spirits whispering half sentences of their memories of life in another place and another time. Maintaining substance and experience vicariously through the living. Jan and Jerry Couture. Faye Chamberlain. Gus Karpes. Joe Jack. Wendy Cairns. Fred O'Brien. Solomon Carriere. Jeff Brady. Buckwheat O'Donohue. Fred Farkvam. John Small. Me.

All of us embody some part of their purpose in continuing to exist. These are all journeys, in life and on the water, that were planned—but probably not by us.

Dawson City, Yukon Territory
20 January 1905

My dearest Delia,

I embrace our future as I long to embrace you. Our future—a place of hope. Of love. Intoxicating to imagine. How infinitely wise and beautiful are the arrangements of our Great Creator. With a rising sun, what can be more in harmony with the sunshine and blue skies than our betrothal.

"And I shall betroth thee unto me forever: yea, I will betroth thee unto me in righteousness, and in judgement, and in loving kindness and in mercies."

This ring has been molded from the last of the gold we mined from Little Blanche Creek. Although it has been five years since we abandoned our claims and took up residence in the city, I have hoarded this small supply towards the day when you place it on your finger.

I have decided to once again hang my shingle as a stock promoter. In this land of gold and gold miners, it is still the opportunity I

*Delia*

PHOTO COURTESY OF: FIRTH FAMILY

believed it to be almost eight years ago. Has it truly been that long!?

And as a broker of insurance. Do not express shock. When I informed Franklin of the insurance he raised his eyebrows in that indomitable manner he has. "A vile and tawdry profession," he said, "but one that has long been needed in this country."

The licence alone will cost me fifty dollars! So this is a decision not taken lightly.

Franklin, also, has not received word of Robert's well-being. It has now been in excess of a year since we last heard from him. Pray this is the natural end of a friendship terminated by time and distance and not the result of some unknown tragedy. It is necessary for me to remember his qualities of character—kindness, generosity, loyalty. A restless soul in search of a sturdy home. Have faith he found one.

What astounds me is that it has taken me till now to realize this is probably what I should have been doing since the beginning. All of these years and all of these false occupations. Keeper of the Hounds. Doing legal and notary work on behalf of the miners. Finding them honest employment. Writing letters for those far from home. Agent for the Cunard Line. Accounting and corresponding for gold men and companies. What things men will do in pursuit of money.

It was Alex MacDonald who first suggested I consider this. Whatever educational failings he may have had, he always did display an astounding perception of character. "Trade your pick for a pen," he once said; "Horse trading and writing are what you are best at." What made those words stick in my mind was not the truth of them, but the hearty, bone-shattering slap he gave me on my back that sent me reeling even as he spoke.

But back then we had the hope and promise of Little Blanche Creek, and that blinded me to the validity of his wisdom at the time. I have been negotiating with a property and casualty company from Wawanesa, Manitoba, to become their first representative west of the Rockie Mountains. It will be then, when I am at last established in my new business, that I shall come to bring you home. That day shall not come soon enough for me.

I understand the fear you must feel in the consideration of departing your home to venture into a place you know only through my words. But there is no need for apprehension. I shall be with you always, and it shall not be long before you, also, will understand what it is about this place that denies me the desire to return to the world that you know so well and I have left so far behind.

This country becomes your breath and life. It is the host of darkest fears. The cradle of mysteries always intriguing. It is sunlight and green hills, cool waters, and the golden warmth of sunrises. It is as ruthless and uncompromising as the deepest winter. It yields nothing to any man. Yet offers an integrity, a pulse of life, that no "outsider" can experience.

When a man tires of this country, he tires of life itself. For there is here all that life can afford. I know of no place that I love better. I know of no people I respect more. I must make haste to post this for my pledge to you must be delayed no longer. I delight that at least I will see you once again before very long. I thank God for blessing me with you.

TO MY SWEETHEART
DELIA

This little token I send to thee.
It speaks of truest constancy;
Keep it and wear it, for life, dear one,
It seals the vow from the heart you've won.
Think of the sender ere you can,
He's not much, but still always a man.
Who'll love but one and that one is thee.
Wear this ring always and think of me.
Devotedly yours
Tommy

(T. A. Firth and Delia married on 6 April 1909 in Pennsylvania. Nine months to the day, their only child, Howard Wesley Firth, was born. Delia made several trips out of the Yukon following my father's birth, but T. A. never left the Yukon again. His 1897–98 travelling companion, Franklin, who also died in 1941, is buried beside him in the Masonic Cemetery in Dawson City.)

*Marathon paddlers on the Yukon River*

PHOTO COURTESY OF: JOHN FIRTH

## APPENDIX A

### 1997 Dyea-to-Dawson Centennial Race

**Sunday, 15 June—Pre-race preperation**

Noon–3:00 PM—Inspection/loading of ALL CANOES and gear for train at WP & YR flatcar spur (just north of 15th & Broadway past where pavement ends; look for canoes on flatcars) Canoes go into Bennett on Monday morning train.

3:00–4:00 PM—Teams pick up Chilkoot Trail permits & special race passports during dedication of Trail Centre, 2nd & Broadway.

4:00–6:00 PM—Pre-race orientation meeting with US National Parks Service and Parks Canada at National Park Service Visitor Centre, 2nd & Broadway. All participants, race staff, and members of the Chilkoot media pool are required to attend this meeting.

6:30–8:30 PM—Pre-race carbo-loading banquet and media briefing at the Westmark Inn Skagway, 3rd and Spring.

**Monday, 16 June—Race starts—Dyea to Sheep Camp**

Important: Teams must carry enough food in their backpacks to get them to the first resupply point at Carcross. Always allow at least an extra day's food.

7:00 AM—Shuttle to Dyea. Frontier Excursion buses will pick up racers, pool media, and their packs at WP & YR parking lot (2nd and Spring). Everyone needs to be at pick-up point at 7:00 AM.

8:00–9:30 AM—Pack weigh-in and inspection at Dyea.

10:00–11:32 AM—Staggered starts every two minutes at Chilkoot Trailhead in Dyea.

Arrival at Sheep Camp—Teams will be timed into Sheep Camp by race officials based on the crossing of the second team member. Teams will be pointed to a campsite upon their arrival. As there is only limited space in the designated cooking shelters, team members should eat dinner immediately after they set up camp. Media will camp at Pleasant Camp.

Evening—National Park Service will present a Chilkoot Trail program.

**Tuesday, 17 June**

Checkpoint #1—Sheep Camp/Chilkoot Pass Summit/Historic Photo Shoot and Check-in

7:00–9:00 AM—Teams will begin to leave Sheep Camp in reverse order of how they arrived. They will hike to The Scales, where they will line up for a photo reenacting the line going up the "Golden Stairs" at 9 AM.

267

9:00–11:00 AM—Historic photo shoot of the initial climb up the pass. Teams will line up in order of their times into Sheep Camp for the photo shoot. Following this they will proceed to the top. At the Summit Chute they will be checked in by members of the RCMP and Canada Customs to make sure they have the required gear and proceed through the chute to the re-start.

11:00 AM–1:00 PM—Summit re-start. Teams will be re-started at the summit at two minute intervals, in the order of their times into Sheep Camp. From this point teams have the option of camping in designated sites at Happy Camp, Deep Lake, Lindeman City, Bare Loon Lake, and Lake Bennett. Teams may hike all night if they wish. The race is on!

Checkpoint #2—Bennett Lake, British Columbia

Canoes and river gear will be transported to Lake Bennett via White Pass and Yukon Route railway. WP & YR will run a special train on Monday from Skagway to Bennett for this race. In Bennett, race officials will unload the gear for secure storage southeast of the depot on railroad property. No food will be allowed in the boats. Canoes and gear will be watched by race officials until participants arrive. Boats will be loaded with required river gear for the beginning of their water journey from a designated launching spot near the station. An additional outhouse and drinking water will be provided.

Checkpoint # 3—Carcross, Yukon Territory

Canoes will be checked at the beach just before reaching the footbridge, then journey under the railroad bridge and into Nares, Tagish and Nares lakes. After Marsh, teams are advised to portage around the locks. They will enter the Yukon River at this point and journey through Miles Canyon before stopping at Whitehorse.

Checkpoint # 4—Whitehorse (12 hour layover)

After the lakes, teams and boats will stop at the Whitehorse/Schwatka Lake checkpoint (first float plane dock on left) and boats will be transported by race volunteers to Robert Service Campground. Teams will camp here for a mandatory 12-hour layover. Gear will be watched by race officials at the campground. Re-start for each team will occur at the campground boat landing 12 hours after arrival. Storytelling festival will be going on at Rotary Park, so wave at the spectators as you go by.

Checkpoint # 5—Carmacks & Five Finger Rapids

After Whitehorse, teams and boats will proceed through Lake Laberge (safety boat stationed at halfway), the Thirty Mile section, past Hootalinqua (confluence of Teslin) to historic Big Salmon (YTG observation post) and Little

Salmon villages (optional cultural stops), and on to Carmacks. Checkpoint in Carmacks will be just past bridge at the pullout on the left bank, adjacent to the campground. After Carmacks, canoes enter Five Finger Rapids (class II at worst). Middle channel is dangerous, stay in the right channel!

Checkpoint # 6—Fort Selkirk

After Five Finger Rapids and Rink Rapids (also stay right) canoes proceed to Minto (last road access until Dawson) and Yukon Crossing. Teams will stop at historic Fort Selkirk for a mandatory 8-hour layover. This site is managed by the Selkirk First Nation and Yukon Tourism/Heritage Branch, who will assist race officials at the layover checkpoint. After Selkirk, canoes will proceed to White River confluence and past Stewart Island about seventy miles from Dawson. Teams will know they are approaching Dawson when they see the telltale moosehide scar on the mountain above. Stay on the right-hand side of the river once the scar is in sight for easy access to the Klondike City checkpoint and Dawson City finish.

Checkpoint #7—Dawson City Finish (teams must stake and register "claims" to finish the race)

Upon your arrival at the Dawson boat landing, a race official will issue stakes and direct teams to the staking area. After staking "claims" the team members must run three blocks to register their claim at the finish line at the Klondyke Centennial Society building, just off King Street on Third. Canoes will be transferred to the Parks Canada compound for secure storage.

## 1 July 1997—Dawson City, Yukon-Post-Race Festivities

5:00 PM—Post-race barbeque and Awards Ceremony begins in the Fort Herchemer area behind the restored Commissioner's residence off Front Street. After the awards presentations, all racers will be invited to "do the Dawson" as guests of honour at the historic Diamond Tooth Gerties gambling hall, 4th and Queen.

Important: The event officially ends at 5:00 PM 1 July, but race officials will be on hand for two more days to keep times for late teams. Race officials will not be held responsible for any teams on the river after 5:00 PM on 3 July 1997.

Required Gold Rush & Safety Gear

Trail Backpacks along the Chilkoot Trail from Dyea to Lake Bennett/ Carcross

Minimum 50-lb. pack per person: no skis or snowshoes; racers must hike and carry enough food to get them to Carcross; no food caches will be allowed with the canoes at Bennett due to potential bear activity. Support crews can resupply racers only at checkpoints 3, 4, and 6. No other support is allowed at any other point during this race, except in an emergency situation.

### Recreational Canoes from Lake Bennett to Dawson City

Recreational touring/wilderness trip-class or cruiser-class canoes that meet these specs: 15–18' in length; 32–37' width at midship; 13–16' depth at midship. NO EXCEPTIONS. All canoes will be measured and photographed prior to being loaded on the train in Skagway and will be checked against the photo at checkpoints and observation posts. No kayaks, no sails [and in 1998, no umbrellas], no kites, no motors. Single blade canoe paddles only (no kayak paddles, no oar rings for rowing; teams should carry at least one extra paddle. Spray skirts are advisable for the lakes.

Backpacks and Canoes must carry the following from Dyea to Dawson:

During the Klondike Gold Rush, the North West Mounted Police required each person entering Canada to carry a year's supply of provisions. In the spirit of that time, we will require each team to carry certain items from that list.

Items 1–5 must go the entire journey from Dyea to Dawson; items 6–10 may be consumed after the Chilkoot Trail is completed:

One 12" gold pan
One 10" cast iron frying pan
One hatchet
One shovel, 8" diameter or larger
One 17 oz. hammer & 5 lbs. of nails
One 5 lb. sack of beans
One 5 lb. sack of flour
One 1 lb. sack of coffee
One 1 lb. sack of sugar
One 5 lb. sack of dried fruit

In addition, these PERSONAL SAFETY ITEMS are also required per person: Wool or polarfleece-style blanket, box of kitchen safety matches, compass, team medical kit.

The following WATER SAFETY GEAR is required per canoe from Bennett to Dawson: Two coast-guard approved PFD life jackets with pealess-type whistles attached; and three red aerial flares.

# APPENDIX B

On 18 November 1898, the North West Mounted Police issued an order barring any persons who had less than two months of provisions and $500 in cash, or six months of provisions and $200 in cash, from entering the Yukon. The goal was to prevent a repeat of the starvation winter of 1897 when Dawson City ran out of grub with which to feed the hoards of stampeders who were arriving daily.

Outfitters in cities like Victoria, BC, Seattle, WA, or Portland, OR, had published lists of supplies that people would need to survive in the North. Many, like T. A. Firth, had personal shopping lists similar to the following, and carried more than a ton of goods over the Chilkoot Pass.

400 pounds of flour, 50 pounds of cornmeal, 50 pounds of oatmeal, 25 pounds of rice, 100 pounds of beans, 100 pounds of granulated sugar, 150 pounds of bacon, 8 pounds of baking soda, 40 pounds of candles, 15 pounds of salt, 25 pounds of dried peaches, 25 pounds of dried apples, 10 pounds of pitted plums, 50 pounds of dried onions, 50 pounds of dried potatoes, 24 pounds of coffee, 5 pounds of tea, four dozen cans of milk, 25 cans of butter, 16 pounds of nails, 1 gallon vinegar, hatchet, stove, gold pan, shovel, pick, box of candles, fry pan, hand saw, axe, medicine chest, coffee pot, rope, pitch and oakum, 35 pounds of yeast, box of soap, whetstone, packboard. Sufficient changes of clothes to accommodate temperatures from minus fifty to plus one hundred.

The cost of an outfit could reach as high as $500.

## APPENDIX C

## Results of the Dyea to Dawson Race               1997

days:hours:minutes:seconds

1. Jim Lokken–Art Ward (Alaska, $5,000)            4:08:49:16
2. Todd Boonstra–Adam Verrier (Alaska, $1,500)     4:10:53:16
3. Steve Reifenstuhl–Mark Gorman (Alaska, $300)    4:11:35:10
4. Joe Bishop–Thane Phillips (Yukon)               4:13:01:38
5. Terry Jacobsen–Paul Wheeler (Alaska)            4:18:52:03
6. Richard Gillings–Karl Skomp (Alaska)            4:21:06:09
7. Stephen Jull–Bill Stewart (Yukon)               5:00:06:28
8. Henry Timm–Jeb Timm (Alaska)                    5:00:06:28
9. Roman Dial–Vern Tejas (Alaska)                  5:01:32:31
10. Branden Bennett–Brenton Kelsey (Yukon)         5:03:06:50
11. Greg Fekete–Ross Phillips (Yukon)              5:03:46:53
12. Ron Theunissen–Eric Carmichael (Yukon)         5:07:12:20
13. Cynde Adams–Larry Gullingsrud (Alaska, 1st mixed, $300)   5:13:18:12
14. James Hayes–Robert Ameen (Alaska)              5:13:54:08
15. Larry Seethaler–Harry Johnson (Alaska)         5:14:40:50
16. Jason Tinsley–Holly Edelson (Alaska)           5:16:09:31
17. Joe Lishman–Geoff Rushant (Yukon)              5:23:53:10
18. Ken Russo–Doug Sanvick (Alaska)                6:06:13:25
19. Dwight Lambkin–Russ Bamford (Yukon)            6:07:08:10
20. Chris Olson–Don Fairbanks (Alaska)             6:07:08:14
21. Gerard Parsons–Suzanne Crocker (Yukon)         6:08:54:21
22. Malke Weller–Sebastien Jones (Yukon)           6:12:04:47
23. Seth Plunkett–Ken Graham (Alaska)              6:20:53:51
24. Wendy Cairns–Chris Guenther (Yukon, 1st women, $300)   6:21:29:15
25. Steve Cash–Geo Ljljenskjold (Yukon)            6:21:36:20
26. Steve Jaklitsch–Jeremy Schader (Alaska)        7:10:27:36
27. Roger Hanberg–Jeremy Lancaster (Yukon)         7:12:46:18
28. Kevin McKague–Yvonne Harris (Yukon)            7:19:24:41
29. Sandy Sippola–Marjorie Logue (Yukon)           7:22:04:07
30. Gerard Cruchon–Jacques Chicoine (Yukon)        7:23:23:58
31. Michael Yee–Kate Moylan (Alaska–Yukon)         7:23:58:10
32. John Small–John Firth (Yukon)                  8:06:03:22

| | |
|---|---|
| 33. Ed Williams–Jason Rogers (Alaska) | 8:13:57:46 |
| 34. Derek Peterson–Dirk Miller (Alaska) | 8:14:38:50 |
| 35. Billy Still–Dirk Miller (Alaska) | 8:14:39:26 |
| 36. Fred O'Brien–Karl Dittmar (Yukon) | 10:12:19:35 |
| 37. Michelle Ramsey–Jim Heckler (Alaska) | 12:19:40:48 |
| 38. Rosemary Matt–Paul Sargent (Alaska, tied for last) | 14:20:00:00 |
| 38. Geraldine Gardiner–Ian Agnew (Yukon, tied for last) | 14:20:00:00 |

**Unofficial Teams that completed race**

| | |
|---|---|
| Bruce Schindler–Klas Stolpe (Alaska) | 6:21:09:04 |

(team formed after respective partners scratched in Whitehorse)

| | |
|---|---|
| Brendan Hennigan–Anne Lynagh | 8:06:08:23 |

(CBC television crew used motor on their canoe)

**Scratched**

Three teams withdrew prior to race start

| | |
|---|---|
| Eric Lindskoog–Scott Otterbacher (Alaska) | Carcross |
| Ken Brewer–Jimmy Smith (Alaska) | Carcross |
| Dan Turgeon–Klas Stolpe (Alaska) | Whitehorse |
| Thomas Tetz–Hans Gatt (Yukon) | Whitehorse |
| Bruce Schindler–Fred Wilson (Alaska) | Whitehorse |
| John McConnochie–Phil Moritz (Alaska) | Carmacks |
| Mark Kelsey–Karen Lester (Alaska) | Carmacks |

## Results of the Dyea to Dawson Race    1998

days:hours:minutes

| | |
|---|---|
| 1. Solomon Carriere–Steve Landick (SK–Michigan,$5,000) | 4:01:52 |
| 2. Jim Lokken–Audun Endestad (Alaska, $1,500) | 4:04:50 |
| 3. Robert Kazik–Stanislav Hajsky (Czech Republic, $600) | 4:05:02 |
| 4. John McConnochie–Phil Moritz (Alaska) | 4:05:34 |
| 5. Randy Olson–Chris Cupp (Washington) | 4:09:04 |
| 6. Matthias Jakob–Markus Kellerhals (Germany–BC) | 4:13:12 |
| 7. Stephen Jull–Kevin McKague (Yukon) | 4:14:19 |
| 8. Carlos Settle–Tom Zidek (Alberta) | 4:16:00 |
| 8. Greg Fekete–Ross Phillips (Yukon) | 4:16:00 |
| 9. Terry Jacobsen–Phil Wheeler (Alaska) | 4:16:58 |
| 10. Steve Reifenstuhl–Mike Gaede (Alaska) | 4:17:20 |
| 11. David Albisser–Benoit Labelle (Yukon) | 4:19:00 |

12. John Cobb–Andrew Cobb (Oregon)      4:19:52

13. Hank Timm–Jeb Timm (Alaska)      4:22:24

14. Bruce Todd–Rod Leighton (Yukon–British Columbia)      4:22:51

15. Steve Varieur–Mike Varieur (Ontario–Alberta)      5:03:13

16. Ken Brewer–Gene Whiting (Alaska)      5:05:41

17. Martin Misik–Lucia Misikova (Slovakia, 1st mixed, $600)      5:08:08

18. Torry Moore–Jim Jager (Minnesota–Alaska)      5:15:33

19. Russ Bamford–Bob Staples (Yukon–Alberta)      5:16:34

20. Troy Suzuki–Brent MacDonald (Yukon)      5:19:15

21. Frank Timmermans–Mary Louise Timmermans (Yukon)      5:21:38

22. Larry Seethaler–Brenda Forsythe (Alaska)      6:00:49

23. Rip Heminway–Liz Carr (Washington)      6:01:50

24. Alex McLain–Kristin McLain (New Hampshire)      6:12:43

25. Tony Arcand–Ron Lutz (Yukon)      6:12:57

26. Corey Rousell–Rex Brown (Yukon)      6:14:12

27. Greg Broten–John Costa (Saskatchewan)      6:18:23

28. Joe Jack–Mike Winstanley (Yukon)      6:23:11

29. Dennis Bousson–Ken Russo (Alaska)      7:00:32

30. Glen Martin–Mike Garrett (Washington)      7:00:46

31. Yvonne Harris–Donna Dunn (Yukon, 1st women, $600)      7:01:36

32. Jerry Dixon–Charlie Crangle (Alaska)      7:09:58

33. John Soderstrom–Todd McKibben (Illinois)      7:10:13

34. Kim Staeck–Deana Darnell (Alaska)      7:10:41

35. Dan Morrison–Cathy Tibbetts (Texas–New Mexico)      7:12:23

36. Michelle Ramsey–James Slocum (Alaska)      7:14:08

37. Robert Zimmerman–Sally MacDonald (Yukon)      7:15:33

38. John Firth–Fred Farkvam (Yukon)      7:19:23

39. Reinald Nohal–Hanne Raab (Germany–Austria)      7:23:01

40. Dominic O'Brien–Fred O'Brien (Ireland–Yukon)      7:23:10

41. Andrew Simpson–Brendan Hennigan (England–Yukon)      7:23:17

42. Jan Fermont–Erna Theunissen (Holland)      8:23:08

43. Karl Hartwick–Michael Harwick (Ontario)      11:04:38

44. Bob Davis–Alex Stewart (Ontario–Maine)      11:06:27

45. Hugh Stewart–Ian McClatchy (Quebec)      11:06:28

46. Jon Koons–Anthony Reid (California–Oregon)      11:11:03

### Scratched

| | |
|---|---|
| Mark Bayard–Harry James (British Columbia) | Carcross |
| Morris Blake–Clarence Robert (Northwest Territories) | Carcross |
| Joe Bishop–Jody Schick (Yukon) | Lake Laberge |
| Charlie Robb–Chris Norbury (England) | Whitehorse |
| Richard Muse–Stu Smith (Washington) | Whitehorse |
| Dan Solie–Matthew Sturm (Alaska) | Carmacks |

### Unofficial Finishers

Charlie Robb in a solo kayak.

Dan Solie recruited substitute paddler in Carmacks

Richard Muse–Stu Smith caught ride to Carmacks, resumed paddling

# SELECTED BIBLIOGRAPHY

Pierre Berton, *Klondike*, McClelland & Stewart, Toronto, Ontario, 1958

Hugh Bostock, *Pack Horse Tracks*, Geological Survey of Canada, 1990

Ken Coates and Bill Morrison, *The Sinking of the Princess Sophia*, University of Alaska Press, Fairbanks, Alaska, 1991

R. Coutts, *Yukon Places & Names*, Greys R. Publishing Ltd., Sydney, BC, 1980

Walter Curtin, *Yukon Voyage*, Caxton Printers, Caldwell, Idaho, 1938

R. N. De Armond, *'Stroller' White, Tales of a Klondike Newsman*, Mitchell Press United, Vancouver, BC

W. S. Dill, *The Long Day*, Graphic Publishers, Ottawa, Ontario, 1926

Allan Duncan, *Medicine, Madams and Mounties*, Raincoast Books, Vancouver, BC, 1989

Brian Fagan, *The Great Journey*, Thames and Hudson, New York, New York, 1987

Douglas Fetherling, *The Gold Crusades*, University of Toronto Press, Toronto, Ontario, 1997

Michael Gates, *Gold at Forty Mile Creek*, UBC Press, Vancouver, BC, 1994

A. C. Harris, *The Klondike Gold Fields*, 1897

William Haskell, *Two Years in the Klondike & Alaskan Gold Fields*, University of Alaska Press, Fairbanks, Alaska, 1998

James Albert Johnson, *Carmacks of the Klondike*, Epicentre Press, Seattle, Washington, 1990

Arthur Knutson, *Sternwheelers on the Yukon*, Knutson Enterprises, Kirkland, Washington, 1979

John Leonard, *Gold Fields of the Klondike*, A. N. Marquis & Company, Chicago, Illinois, 1897

Murray Lundberg, *Fractured Veins & Broken Dreams*, Pathfinder Publications, Whitehorse, Yukon, 1996

Jeremiah Lynch, *Three Years in the Klondike*, Lakeside Press, Chicago, Illinois, 1967

Ella Lung Martinsen, *Black Sand & Gold*, Metropolitan Press, Portland, Oregon, 1956

Richard Mathews, *The Yukon*, Rivers of America, 1968

W. D. McBride, *Yukon River Boats All My Rivers Flowed West*, Beringian Books, Whitehorse, Yukon, 1991

Joaquin Miller, *Alaska & the Yukon*, Stanford University Press, Stanford, California, 1997

Roy Minter, *The White Pass*, McClelland & Stewart, Toronto, Ontario, 1987

David Neufeld and Frank Norris, *Chilkoot Trail*, Lost Moose Publishing, Whitehorse, Yukon, 1996

William Ogilvie, *Early Days on the Yukon*, Bell & Cockburn, Toronto, Ontario, 1898

W. H. T. Olive, *The Olive Diary*, Timberholme Books, Surrey, BC, 1998

Gerald Pennington, *Klondike Stampeders Register*, 1997

Jim Robb, *Colourful Five Per Cent Illustrated*, Colourful Five Per Cent Incorporated, Whitehorse, Yukon

Archie Satterfield, *Chilkoot Pass*, Alaska Northwest Publishing, Anchorage, Alaska, 1973

William Sharpe, *Faith of Fools*, Washington State University Press, Pullman, Washington, 1998

Charles Sheldon, *The Wilderness of the Upper Yukon*, Charles Scribner & Sons, New York, New York, 1911

Emma Smythe, *Yukon Lady*, Hancock House, Vancouver, BC, 1985

Keith Tryck, *Yukon Passage*, Times Books, New York, New York, 1980

William White, *Writing Home*, T. D. Sanders, West Hill, Ottery St. Mary, England, 1990

Allan Wright, *Prelude to Bonanza*, Gray's Publishing, Surrey, BC, 1976

Joyce Yardley, *Yukon Riverboat Days*, Hancock House, Surrey, BC, 1996

## Selected Publications and Newspapers

*Yukoner Magazine, Yukon News, Whitehorse Star, National Geographic, Alaska Magazine, Canadian Geographic, Carcross Chronicle, Canoe & Kayak, Ottawa Citizen, Skagway News, Juneau Empire, Dawson City Insider, The Klondike Sun, Skagway Alaskan, Up Here Magazine, Seward Phoenix, Dawson Weekly News, Dawson Daily News, Seattle Times, Fairbanks NewsMiner, Toronto Globe & Mail, The Weekly Star, Dawson Nugget, Paddler Magazine, Warren Evening Times, Guide to the Goldfields, Klondike Gold Rush, Bennett Sun, Seattle Post-Intelligencer*

## Unpublished Manuscripts

C. D. Taylor memoirs; notebooks of Alan Innes Taylor; River Trip Journal of Robyn Mexted; Memoirs of C. W. Craig; River Trip Journal of C. W. Craig, H. W. Firth and T. P. Firth; Log of the TA-ON kept by John Hoyt, Lorraine Hoyt, George Dawson.

Letters written by T. A. Firth during his journey into the Klondike and in the years preceding his marriage to Delia were destroyed by the same fire that burned the records of the founding of the Arctic Brotherhood. Only business letters written by him in his later years have survived. The letters written here are composites that reflect his writing style, the events he would have been witness to, the places to which he went, and how he may have reacted to them. All of the names in the letters represent real people, and all of the relationships and professions refered to actually existed, with the exception of the fourth companion, Robert. All we know for sure is that there was a fourth companion.

Only T. A.'s poetry has survived. It is written here as it was published.

Written under the pseudonym of Paul Reddington: *Gems of Poesy*, Dehaye Publishing Company, 1904.

Published under his own name: *Sweet Rosebud*, National Manuscript Bureau, New York, New York, 1931.

The final poem in this book, *To My Sweetheart, Delia*, has not been published before now. It is the only poem written in T. A. Firth's own hand that is still in existence. The engagement ring it refers to was mailed to Delia wrapped in the poem.

# ACKNOWLEDGEMENTS

An incredible number of people contributed to this book and supported its writing. It's always good for a writer to get phone calls or be stopped on the street and asked, "How's the book going? Do you need anything more?"

To all of the following individuals, and to any others I may have overlooked, a thank you just doesn't seem like enough.

**For support on the river:** Dawn Dimond, Sharon Denton, Norma Farkvam, Nancy and Dave Huston, Gail Chester, Peter Deer, the late Eiko Stenzig, Tom and Bea Firth, Aubyn Coad, MaryMae Dimond, T. A. Firth Insurance, Chilkoot Breweries, Sorel Boots, George Arcand and Softball Yukon, Deb Chambers, the late Ben Sheardown, Penny Lou Sheardown, Gerard Cruchon, Hans-Joachim Schwarz (Austria), Maria Van Bibber, Mark Mather, Reinald Nohal, Jeff Brady, Buckwheat O'Donohue, Erin Briemon, Keiran and Logan Small, and the woman with the driveway in Carcross in 1997.

**For support in the research:** Roger Hanberg, Steve Cash, John Small, Dawn Dimond, Tom and Bea Firth, Norma and Fred Farkvam, Howard Firth, Nancy Huston, Sheila Firth, Richard Griffiths, John Dines, Buckwheat O'Donohue, CBC Radio, CBC Television, Fred O'Brien, Steve Landick, Sandy Sippola, Maggie's Museum, Jan Couture, Faye Chamberlain, Bill Drury Sr., John Storer, Gerard Cruchon, Gord Mitchell, Rob Toohey, Kevin and Maryanne Schackell, Wendy Cairns, Christine Guenther, Catherine Small, Cal and Norma Waddington, Yukon Archives, Jeff Brady, Ruth Goddard, Anne Nayern, Solomon Carriere, Cor Guimond, Betty Taylor, Tom Randall and Elsie Wain, Tim Gerberding, Yvonne Burian, Maria Van Bibber, Bruce Barrett, Yvonne Harris, Wyckham Porteous, Joe Jack, Steve Morison and Charlotte Mougeot, Thomas Tetz, Greg Kent, Ken Brewer, Ida Calmagane, Reinald Nohal, Mark Kelsey, Rosemary Matt, Clary Craig, Goldi Productions, Jacqueline Brown, Beriah Brown, Peter Carr, Charlie Roots, Barb Dawson, Craig Moddle, Cynde Adams, Christine Hedgcock, Ron Chambers, Jerry Dixon, John Hoyt, Charlie Crangle, Paul Sargent, Bill Stewart, Bill Hakonsen, Gus Karpes, Barry Enders, Flo Whyard, *Whitehorse Star, Yukon News,* Yukon Archives, Skagway Centennial Committee. At NeWest Press, Don Kerr and Ruth Linka.

Patsy Henderson's story is told with the permission of his daughter, Edi Bohmer.

A special thank you to the Yukon Foundation for its support.

JOHN FIRTH was born in Edmonton, Alberta and adopted into the Yukon Territory. He grew up in Dawson City and Whitehorse where he worked as a journalist, prospector, public relations director, theatre owner, and, currently, as a financial advisor. He makes his home in Whitehorse, Yukon Territory, where he is the Chairperson of the Yukon Foundation. He has received the Commissioners Award for Public Service for his work in preserving Yukon history and culture. An avid outdoorsman, he has been a marathon runner for 35 years and was the founding President of the Yukon River Marathon Paddling Association. This is his second book. Firth and his nephew were featured in a documentary of the Dyea to Dawson Race that aired in the winter of 1997 on CBC television. They also appeared in a second TV documentary on the race that is still occasionally shown on Life Channel.